John Benjamin Wisely

**Studies in the Science of English grammar**

John Benjamin Wisely

**Studies in the Science of English grammar**

ISBN/EAN: 9783742897046

Manufactured in Europe, USA, Canada, Australia, Japa

Cover: Foto ©Thomas Meinert / pixelio.de

Manufactured and distributed by brebook publishing software
(www.brebook.com)

John Benjamin Wisely

**Studies in the Science of English grammar**

# STUDIES

# Science of English Grammar

BY

J. B. WISELY, A. M.

*Department of Grammar and Composition,*
*Indiana State Normal School.*

*Every existing form of human speech is a body of arbitrary and conventional signs for thought, handed down by tradition from one generation to another * * * the instrument ever adapting itself to the uses which it is to subserve.—Whitney.*

TERRE HAUTE, IND.:
THE INLAND PUBLISHING COMPANY.
1896.

# PREFACE.

This book was first prepared for the use of the author's own classes in grammar. . It is intended to be a protest against the formal manner in which technical grammar is usually studied, and, judging by the manner in which the first three editions have been received by teachers and friends of education, the author is led to believe there is a place for it.

It is believed that the study of the science phase of language need not be entirely a memory study—a mere committing of rules and statements, and an unqualified acceptance of the same by the student, upon authority, but that the student may be led, by means of a careful examination of sentences, to think out and state for himself most of the laws and principles which underlie correct sentence construction.

With the thought just stated, in mind, it has been the purpose of the author to present suitable sentences and to ask such questions upon them as will lead the student to construct the science of grammar for himself. To this end, *all definitions and statements of facts of whatever kind have been studiously avoided, as depriving the student of so much mental activity as would be required in thinking them out for himself.*

In former times, when the student wanted to master anatomy and physiology, he was given texts upon the subject and he spent his time in reading *about* the brain, the heart, the eye. Now the scalpel and the microscope have subjugated the text, so that it has become a means of assisting the student to study the real brain, heart, and eye, by the aid of the knife and the glass. Agassiz was about the first to ask his students to " Study the fish." The example was contagious and the laboratory is now considered a necessity in all science teaching.

We are somewhat slower in learning that there is a *fish* in literature, a *fish* in rhetoric, and a *fish* in grammar, and that the student should follow Agassiz's dictum in these subjects as well as in the sciences.

The sentence is composed of three parts : subject, predicate, and copula. A phrase is a group of words not having a subject, predicate, or copula, and used in the sentence with the value of a single word.

There are two ways of learning these and all other facts of grammar. The teacher may send the child to Whitney's grammar to commit the statements to memory, or he may have the child study sentence and see them in the sentence for himself. It is evident that the last way exercises the faculties of the mind, while the first way fails to afford this mental exercise, and when we consider, that the mind is developed in proportion to the degree in which all its faculties are kept stretched to their highest tension, it is readily seen that the last way gives the student more power than the first, and in this point does its superiority consist.

It must not be thought, however, that there is no place for the text. It is very valuable as a means or aid in studying the *real unit* of the subject. By reference to it, the student can better formulate and express that which he has discovered

for himself. The text will help him to correct his con-
clusions often, and send him back to observe the real thing
more carefully. References have been given throughout this
work, not only to grammars, but to psychologies, logics, rhet-
orics, etc. These have been given especially for the benefit
of the teacher, with a view of freeing her mind from the text-
book and making her view broader than any one text; for
the text-book is often mistaken for the subject of grammar
and studied accordingly.

There is no need of committing any law or principle of
grammar from a text-book. The laws and principles which
underlie the construction of sentences, are all embodied in
sentences, and the student may study them directly, *first hand*,
just as he studies the flower in botany or the rock in geology,
and if he forgets the rule, he has only to examine a few sentences and restate it for himself.

There is no need to tell the student that the flower has
petals and stamens, or to send him to a book to read it, says
the botanist; he can discover it for himself. Can he not also
discover the uses of the substantive clause? If he is able to
see that the plant has root, stem, and leaves, why can he not
see for himself that the noun has person, gender, number,
and case?

There is a close resemblance between the method of pro-
cedure here in the language studies and that followed in the
study of natural sciences. True, no special apartment, fitted
up with tables, cases of instruments, or vials of various con-
coctions, as in the sciences, is necessary; the real unit of the
subject is the materials upon which we work; the instruments
are the minds of the pupils, being constantly at hand, still not
in the way. The superiority of this way of working in the
language studies over its recognized value in the natural

sciences, will at once appear, for the work can be carried on conveniently without so many appliances, and without the disagreeable associations which sometimes enter into such operations in the scientific laboratory.

The following work is based upon the thought that there is a *fish* in grammar, that it is the *sentence as it is determined by the thought which it expresses*, and that the method which should be pursued in studying it, might appropriately be called the *laboratory* method.

TERRE HAUTE, Ind., March, 6, 1896.

# INTRODUCTION.

English grammar is that language study which has for its subject-matter the sentence. It is both a science and an art. As a science, it deals with the fundamentals of sentence structure. It makes known to the student the laws and principles which underlie correct sentence construction. As an art, it aims to enable the student to acquire a skillful use of the sentence as an instrument in expressing his thought. These two phases are not inseparable. One may understand the science of grammar and not be able to use good English in conversation, and one may be very skillful in the use of language and at the same time know little or nothing about the laws and principles which govern correct sentence construction.

As a mastery of the art side of grammar is an accomplishment which comes only through long and careful practice, it is essential that the teacher devote much time to this side of the child's education in English. His language will need the careful supervision of all his teachers in all his work, and he, himself, must keep a constant watch over his language in order to become proficient and skillful in its use. It follows that the greater part of the work in technical grammar can be devoted to the mastery of the science of grammar, and it is thought that in this way the student may become tolerably proficient in this phase.

It is not here claimed that the art phase of grammar is unimportant, but that in addition to it, the scientific knowledge,
on the part of the teacher, is necessary, and that on account
of the nature of the art phase, it can only be mastered by
careful and attentive experience in expressing thought in connection with all other subjects as well as that of grammar.
The art is necessary for the teacher, not only because she is
rated in the educational market of the world largely by the
language she uses, but because children imitate the language
of the teacher. But it may be clearly shown that no rational
teaching of the subject of grammar can be done without a
conscious mastery of the science, on the part of the teacher.
The truth of the preceding statement may be made to appear by a discussion of the science of grammar.

There is a body of facts which we call grammar. What is
it to know these facts scientifically? This group of facts is
related to other groups of facts. Grammar is related to the
word studies of the language group. It is also a near relative
of reading, composition and rhetoric, and literature—those
language studies which have discourse for their subject-matter.
Grammar is the handmaid of logic. All its forms are determined by and adapted to the thought they express. The
relations which are found in the subject are logical relations
and the true study of these facts is the study of the logic of
the English sentence. Dr. C. C. Everett, of Harvard University, in his "Science of Thought," says: "*Certainly while
logic derives such help from grammar, the reverse should be done,
and our grammars placed upon a direct logical footing.*"

When the student studies grammar in the light of the relations set forth above, when he sees it as based upon and
growing out of logic, as a practical illustration of psychology,
as being conditioned by the word studies, and preparing for

and aiding in a mastery of the discourse studies, he is studying the subject "constructively," as Dr. W. T. Harris says. Heretofore, he has learned a great many of the facts of orthography, orthoepy, grammar, reading, composition, rhetoric, and literature, but these are somewhat fused together in his mind and mixed, to some extent, with the facts of history, geography, and all other subjects which he has studied. Now he sees the language group clearly set off from all other studies, he sees the place of each study in this group, and he sees all of them in the light of these higher studies; the word studies and grammar in the light of psychology and logic, and the discourse studies in the light of psychology, logic, ethics, and aesthetics. He thus fixes the place of grammar among the language studies, sees its relations to all other subjects of study, and realizes to some extent its true purpose and "educational value in developing the minds and enlarging the information of the pupils of the public schools."

But while the student is coming into a complete comprehension of the relations stated above, he learns that the facts of grammar have certain relations to one another and to the subject as a whole. In the consideration of such a common object as the table, he has noticed that it is made up of parts, each one holding a certain relation to every other one, and all together forming the whole. Without any one of these parts, the whole would not be complete. In this case, he sees a common idea, the idea of design or purpose, embodied in every part of the table and binding all the parts together into the whole. The table is to write upon and at the same time is to be ornamental, and every part and attribute of it, legs, sides, top, color, etc., embodies the central idea of the table. Why was the table not painted red? Why are the legs all the same length? Why is this bit of carving on the side? Why is it made of hard wood? To answer any of these questions is to refer it to the central idea in the table.

It will be readily seen, that the student might take another view of the table. He might see it as a number of isolated parts, existing in space—a mere heap of material. What is the difference between this view and the first one? The parts are all in the second view. The legs, top, sides, etc., every bit of carving, all the attributes of the parts, color, form, etc., all materials are present. But the view of the table is not the same as the first, because these parts are not seen in their relations. They are not bound into a whole by a unifying idea.

It will be seen from the foregoing discussion that there were two phases or sides in this first view of the table; viz., the part phase or fact phase, and the relation phase or unifying idea.

It is claimed, that the relations existing among the facts of grammar are similar to the relations existing among the parts of the table with one exception. The relations existing among the parts of the table are mechanical relations, and the whole is a mechanical whole, while the relations existing among the facts of grammar are vital, and the subject may be shown to be a vital unity.

Grammar then may be viewed from these two points of view: (1). The student may consider the fact side, sentences in their great variety of form and many different shades of meaning, together with the words which compose these sentences in their various uses in the sentences. These form the subject-matter of grammar upon which the mind of the student is to be exercised. (2). The student may consider the relation phase of the subject. This is the central idea, which is found in some measure embodied in all the facts of the subject, and which binds them all together. The two points just stated are not two different subjects. They are the same thing viewed from two points of view; it takes both to form the science of grammar; and any knowledge which leaves out either phase of the subject could not be said to be a scientific knowledge of grammar.

Science, it has often been said, is organized knowledge or facts reduced to a system. To know a thing scientifically is to know it in its relations. To know any subject scientifically, is to know the relations which exist among the facts of that subject; to see the relation of each fact to the other and to the whole through or by means of the fundamental idea in the subject; and to see the relations of the subject as a whole to other subjects of study. To answer directly the question asked at the beginning of this discussion, the facts of grammar to be scientifically known, must be seen under the relations set forth above. In short, the subject of grammar must be viewed from the two points of view stated above in "(1)" and "(2)": the facts and the central or relating idea. When the student sees the subject in this way, he may be said to have an organized knowledge of grammar. He sees the subject of grammar as Paul saw the Church when he said: "So we being many are one body in Christ, and every one members one of another."

The sentence cannot say to the subject, "I have no need of thee;" nor the adverb to the verb, "I have no need of you;" nor can grammar say to the most insignificant fact in it, "I have no need of you." For this body of facts which belong to grammar, being many, are at the same time one, by reason of a common idea which is found in all of them, and every one members one of another.

It is a matter of observation, both in this Normal School and others, that the students who enter them, having done most of their grammar work in the grades below the high school, have dealt mainly with the fact phase of grammar, and have not been made conscious of the relation phase. It may be held that the work in the grades ought to do more for the students in this line than it now does, but however true this may be, it does not concern us here. The fact still remains, that the students come to the Normal School in the condition stated above. The knowledge they possess, as a rule, is not a teaching knowledge of the subject of grammar, and it is held to be the duty of the Normal School to help its students to discover this higher and scientific phase of the subject, leaving it in their minds an organized and consistent whole.

It has been said, that sentences in their manifold variety of form and many shades of meaning, together with the multitude of facts concerning them, which the student must know in order to understand how thoughts are expressed in sentences, form the subject-matter of grammar. The student is to think this vast array of facts into an organized whole by means of what has been called "the relation phase" or "unifying idea." This unifying idea or central principle of the subject of grammar must be a general truth, because every fact in the subject must partake of its nature. It must be a primary truth, because every fact in the subject is to be built into it and connected with it. It must be a determining idea or relating truth, because by means of it, all the facts of grammar are to be logically arranged or organized.

Since the subject-matter of grammar is the sentence, this determining idea or unifying idea or universal attribute, into which all sentences are organized, will be found in the nature of the sentence itself.

The only use of a sentence is to express a thought. How does the sentence express thought? The mowing machine expresses thought. By observing its parts and how they all cooperate to do the work of the machine, one can see design in it and adaptation of means to end. He becomes aware of the fact, that all this existed in the mind of the inventor before it was put into this form. The mowing machine is simply the thought of the designer objectified, and the machine expresses his thought. In the same way, every object in the universe expresses thought.

The sentence does not express thought in the way indicated above. A judgment or thought is the decision by the mind that a certain relation exists between ideas; or a judgment or thought is a mental product in which the mind affirms a relation between ideas. There are three elements in every such judgment: (1). The idea about which the mind thinks something, which may be called the thought subject. (2). The idea which the mind thinks with the first idea and which it affirms or denies of it. This may be called the thought predicate. (3). The relation which the mind sees between these ideas, which is always one of agreement or disagreement and which may be termed the thought relation. I have in mind the idea, *sun-dog*, and the idea, *bright*, but these do not form a judgment. I must see a relation between the two. My mind must think the two ideas into a unity in which I see *bright* as belonging to or forming one of the attributes of *sun-dog*. In this way, my mind forms the judgment or thought expressed by the sentence, "The sun-dog is bright." It is this triple unity which the sentence expresses, and in order to express it, the sentence must take on the triple form of the thought.

A sentence is the expression of a judgment or thought in

words. Why is it necessary that the sentence should have the triple form of the thought? (1). A subject, expressing the thought subject of the judgment. (2). A predicate, expressing the thought predicate of the judgment. (3). A copula, expressing the thought relation of the judgment. A picture expresses thought but it does not express thought as the sentence does. There are no three parts to the picture. It expresses thought by resemblance. Its form is determined by the form of the object which it represents. But there is no resemblance between a thought and the sentence which expresses it, such as exists in the picture. The thought is spiritual, subjective; the sentence is physical, objective. The sentence is adapted to the thought for the purpose of expressing it, and is determined by the thought. Since the thought is not like the sentence and cannot be like it in any other particular, except in the number of its elements, the sentence, in order to express the thought, must take on the triple form of the thought. The thought imposes its form upon the sentence.

It might be said here, that grammarians while recognizing the fact that the sentence has three * parts, have not considered it of enough importance to make the distinction, at all times, between predicate and copula. Since the thought predicate and thought relation are so frequently expressed by the same word, they have fallen into the inaccuracy of dividing sentences into two parts, a subject and a predicate.

---

*See Reed and Kellogg's Grammar, beginning of Lesson 29.

Whitney's Essentials of English Grammar, p. 158, par. 353.

"Our Language," p. 84.

Lee & Hadley, pp. 53–55.

The greatest linguist * in this country says: "The verb *be*, in all its various forms, has come to stand as a mere connective of assertion between a subject and some word or words describing that subject, and so to have no meaning of its own except that of signifying the assertion." And he adds, "Indeed, every verb admits of being taken apart, or analyzed, into some form of this copula *be*, which expresses the act of assertion, and a predicate noun or adjective (especially the verbal adjective, the present participle), expressing the condition or quality or action predicated. Thus, *I stand* is nearly *I am erect*, or, still more nearly, *I am standing;* again, *They beg.* is equivalent to *They are beggars*, or *They are begging.*"

In the above examples, each sentence has three parts. For example, in "They are begging," the word, "They," is the subject of the sentence and expresses the thought subject of the judgment; the word, "begging," is the predicate of the sentence and expresses the thought predicate of the judgment; and the word, "are," is the copula of the sentence and expresses the relation which the mind sees between the thought subject and thought predicate, or the thought relation of the judgment.

Since every sentence must contain a verb, it follows, that, if the above statement of Dr. Whitney is correct, every sentence may not only be separated into three parts, but must contain three parts, and no group of words can be a sentence or can possibly express a thought if it lacks either a subject or predicate or copula.

In addition to the foregoing discussion, which seems to the

---

* The late Dr. William Dwight Whitney, Professor of Sanskrit and Comparative Philology, and instructor in modern languages in Yale College; author of "Language and the Study of Language," "Life and Growth of Language," etc., etc.

writer to set forth the reason in the case, it might be said, that psychologists and logicians in all times and almost without exception, have insisted, that the sentence must have three parts corresponding to the three elements of the judgment. The inaccuracy, on the part of grammarians, has come about, as Dr. C. C. Everett, of Harvard University, points out, because they have divorced grammar from logic, which is sure to lead to error, since the sentence is only an instrument in expressing the thought, and grammar is directly dependent upon logic at every point. If one word contains two parts of the sentence in which it occurs, that is all the more reason why the analysis of the student should be subtle enough to discover that fact and to identify each part of the sentence with the element of the thought which it expresses. To express two elements of the thought in one part of the sentence would be confusing, to say the least.

This fundamental attribute in the nature of the sentence, as it is determined by the nature of the thought, is the most universal truth in the subject of grammar. To put it in other words, the most general truth, or central, or determining, or relating idea in the subject of grammar may be stated as follows: *The three elements of the thought as they are accurately expressed in the three parts of the sentence.* The student must see the sentence as the expression of the thought. This it does in common with a great many other things; the picture, the piece of music, the statue, etc., all express thought; but the sentence is arbitrary, expressing thought in a particular way, by means of its triple form, and the student must see this. This states the end and purpose of all the study of the science of grammar. Why does the student study the simple sentence or the declarative sentence? To see how the three elements of the thought are expressed in those language-forms. He wants to know how the sentence form, which we call complex, is adapted to express the thought. Why does he study noun or adverb? To see what part they play in the expression of the three elements of the thought in the sentence. To see how these language forms are adapted to the expressions of the thought and how they are determined by the thought.

How do we know that the principle just stated is the most general, and, therefore, the governing truth in the subject of grammar? "By their fruits ye shall know them." This is the truth which organizes the subject. It touches every fact in the subject and states the essential attribute of every such fact. It is the truth to which every question concerning the subject of grammar must be referred for its answer, just as every question concerning the table can be answered only by referring it to the central idea in the table. This central truth of the subject of grammar is the most general truth in the subject, because every other fact of the subject depends upon it.

The value of this view of the subject to the teacher may be made clear by pointing out what the governing or central idea of any subject will indicate to the teacher concerning that subject. The organizing truth of a subject will determine the following points with regard to the subject: (1). It will set off the subject-matter of the study from the subject-matter of all other studies. (2). It will indicate the logical order in the subject. (3). It will determine the order of acquisition or presentation of the subject. (4). It will indicate the important and unimportant facts. (5). It will indicate the important and unimportant elements in each fact of the subject. (6). It will test the definitions of the subject. (7). It will indicate the mental steps which the student must take

G—2

to master the subject, and the materials which the teacher should put before the student in order to induce his mind to take these steps.

There must be some reason why mathematicians have grouped a certain number of facts and call that group arithmetic. It is not mere chance that scientists include just the facts they do include in the subject of geography and exclude all other facts. There is certainly some method by which grammarians have been able to decide what facts constitute the science of grammar. It is the central idea in the subject which sets off the facts of that subject from all other facts. The central idea or organizing truth of the subject contains the most universal attribute of the subject. Any fact possessing this attribute is a fact of the subject. Any fact which has to do with the accurate expression of the three elements of the thought in the sentence form is a fact of grammar.

This organizing truth of the subject is the most general or universal truth in the subject. Every fact in the subject is related to it. Some facts in the subject are more closely related to it than others. The fact of the subject which stands most closely related to the organizing truth, is first in the subject; one equally near in its relation to the central truth is coordinate to it, one containing a less degree of the general truth is subordinate to both, and so on with all the facts of the subject. When each fact is given its place in the subject, according to the relation which it bears to the central idea, the subject is organized. This means that the order of dependence among the facts of the subject has been discovered; the relative importance of the facts and of the elements in each fact is seen; and the teacher sees the order in which the facts of the subject should be presented and why they should be presented in that order.

The organizing truth tests the definitions of the subject. Every fact in the subject contains a certain degree of the general truth or universal attribute of the subject. To define any fact of the subject is to show its* relation to the central idea of the subject. A definition of the noun which does not show its relation to the organizing truth of grammar, which does not show how it helps to express the three elements of the thought in the three parts of the sentence, is faulty.

When the student sees the central idea of the subject of grammar and all it indicates with regard to the subject, as set forth in the preceding discussion, he may be said to have an organized or scientific knowledge of the subject.

He is free from text-books, except as he uses them as a means, and he sees the subject in the light of reason and in all its relations.

Can the teacher be satisfied, or do intelligent work in the schoolroom, with a less comprehensive view?

The most severe criticism which could be pronounced upon grammarians and teachers of grammar is that made by Dr. C. C. Everett, of Harvard, when he says, they have divorced grammar from logic. And any one who has carefully examined our text-books in grammar, or observed thoughtfully much of the work done in our schools in this subject, will be compelled to admit that there is more truth than poetry in this charge. The study of grammar has become largely a study of dry form; a mere classification of words; a kind of jugglery with symbols. What wonder that most boys and girls, with normal minds, hate it!

But if, as Dr. Harris says,* " Grammar defines and fixes

---

* See Report of Board of Public Schools, St. Louis, bound volume of 1872-73.

speech; by its mastery man obtains the first mastery over his
mind as an instrument. * * * * * It is the key to all
that is spiritual. * * * * * Grammar as Etymology
and Syntax initiates the pupil into the general forms of
thought itself.   Thus there branch out Logic, Psychology,
and Metaphysics, as well as the various phases of Philosophy.
Has it not been said, indeed, that the father of Logic discovered its forms through grammar?   Under a thin veil the
pupil deals with pure thought when he studies Syntax"—if
this be true, then there is no lack of opportunity for thinking
in the study of grammar.

The sentence is only the " veil"; it is composed of mere
words; but this form has a content, the thought, and to understand the sentence, the student must be able to separate,
in thought, this form from its content.   The student must
constantly hold these two elements in mind while dealing
with the sentence.   When he considers the sentence, *Glass
is brittle*, he views it as the expression of a thought composed
of three elements: (1).   A thought subject, the idea, *glass*.
(2).   A thought predicate, the idea, *brittle*.  (3).   A thought
relation of agreement between the two.   In the expression
itself, he sees parts corresponding to the elements of the
thought:  (1).   A subject, the word, "glass," expressing the
thought subject. (2).   A predicate, the word, "brittle," expressing the thought predicate. (3).   A copula or relational
element, the word, "is," expressing the thought relation.
When he considers the word, "sour," in the sentence, *The
sour apple ripened rapidly*, he sees two elements; first, the *form*
or *word* and second its *content*.   The word, "sour," expresses
an attribute which belongs to the idea expressed by the word,
" apple."   So in dealing with the word, " rapidly," he sees
that it expresses an attribute of the attribute expressed by the

word, "ripened." In each case the student is required first, to distinguish between the *form* and its *content*, and second, to think the two together again to see how the form organizes itself around the thought and is determined by it.

This seeing of *form* and *content* and the relations between the two cannot be too strongly emphasized. The failure on the part of the grammarians and teachers to keep it in mind has given to the study of grammar its formal and lifeless nature. The study of the sentence from this point of view is no simple mental activity. It requires the most careful attention and very close and accurate thinking on the part of the student. He is first conscious of the sentence form, a group of words, and having obtained the thought which it expresses, he proceeds to analyze that thought into its elements. He finds that there are three principal elements in every thought, a thought subject, a thought predicate, and a thought relation, each of which may be composed of several elements. Finally, he associates each element of the thought with some part of the sentence, thus making the parts of the sentence, the relations existing among them, and their relation to the thought to appear clearly. It will be seen that this is a complex activity, the student being required to hold several points in mind, while he thinks his way carefully through the sentence. These two processes of separating form and content from each other, and each one into its elements, *analysis*, and thinking form and content back again into a vital unity, in order to see how the thought determines the form, *synthesis*, are the two fundamental processes in the mastery of grammar.

The principles already discussed would indicate, that in thinking the almost infinite variety of sentences into the unity of a single principle, and in gaining the mastery over the sentence as an instrument for communicating thought, it is necessary for the student to deal with the subject-matter in the following ways:

### Part I.    The Study of Sentences as Wholes.

1. The study of the class whole.    In this phase of the work, only those attributes or characteristics of the sentence which are universal are noticed.    The student has as many different kinds of sentences as can be obtained placed before him, and in all this variety, he is asked to see the resemblances, the universal attribute which makes them all sentences.    He finds that some of these individual examples are long and some short: some declarative and some interrogative; some simple and some complex; some inverted order and some natural order; but one characteristic is found in each of them.    Not every sentence is imperative; not every one has a compound subject; but they all have, either explicit or implicit in them, the triple form expressing the thought.    This fact enables him to unify this great variety of sentence forms, and to see the unity in the thought of each sentence.    It is not an easy matter for the student to grasp the unity of thought in a long and involved sentence; to see the thought subject and thought predicate, which the mind unites by an act of thinking into the triple unity — the thought, and which the sentence expresses.    But this is what he must do, if he ever masters the sentence, either as an instrument in expressing his own thought, or as a medium in obtaining the thought of others.

At the close of this phase of his study in grammar, the student should be able to take any sentence, distinguish between its form and content, analyze its content into its three essential elements, see the triple organic form of the sentence as determined by the thought, the relation of each element of the thought to its corresponding part of the sentence, and should be able to express the result of his thinking in *some* concise form, such as the following: *The large book is certainly very cheap.* This is a sentence, because it is the expression of a thought in words. The subject of the sentence is the words, "The large book," because they express the thought subject. The predicate of the sentence is the words, "very cheap," because they express the thought predicate. The copula or relational element of the sentence is the words, "is certainly," because they express the thought relation, or unifying act of the mind.

It is not intended that the above form shall always be used by the student in expressing the result of his thinking. The chief thing is to have his mind perform the two mental processes of analysis and synthesis as indicated above, and any set form of expressing the result is rather to be avoided, as having a tendency to make the student mechanical and formal.

Throughout this entire first circle of the work, the student's attention is directed to but one thing—the universal sentence form as determined by the thought. He is not permitted to say that the idea expressed by the word, "book," in the above sentence, is the thought subject, or that the word, "book," is the subject of the sentence; but he must see each element of the thought and each part of the sentence as a unit. The idea expressed by the words, "The large book," for that is one idea, though a complex one, is the thought subject, and all those words form the subject of the sentence. When the student is able to see in any sentence each one of the three elements of the thought, which is expressed, and see it as a unit, no matter how complex it may be, and when he sees each of the three essential parts of the sentence in the same way, and has thought the whole into an organic unity, in which he sees the sentence as standing for or expressing the thought, he is ready to pass from the first circle of the grammar work. It will usually take, with the students in the Normal School, from two to three weeks of hard work to accomplish this, but it is well worth the time, for the student who has done it thoroughly is forever free from mechanical or formal work in the subject, and is a long stride on his way in the mastery of grammar as based upon logic.

2.    In the second circle of the work, the student still deals with sentences as wholes, but he finds there are likenesses and differences among them which enable him to classify them. He notices that one kind expresses a phase of thought which appeals to the intellect. It communicates some information. Another kind also expresses a phase of thought which appeals to the intellect, but it inquires for information, asks for some element of the thought which is unknown and sought for. Still another kind expresses a phase of thought which awakens the emotions. Some information may be communicated, but it is to the end of awakening feeling. Lastly, he notices that some sentences express thought which is intended to produce an act of will. So, on basis of meaning, or phase of mental activity which is prominent, or power of mind addressed, he divides sentences into the classes: Declarative, Interrogative, Exclamatory, Imperative. Some thoughts are simple; some are complex; some are compound. The student sees also that sentences must be of these kinds, since they express the thought. He, therefore, classifies sentences on basis of form, as determined by the form of the thought expressed, into: Simple, Complex, and Compound. When the student is able to view sentences, as determined by the thought, in the ways just indicated, he is ready to pass from the second circle of the grammar work.

## Part 2.  Study of Sentences in Parts.

1.   In the third circle of the work, the study of the organic parts of the sentence is taken up.   Subjects of sentences are not all of the same kind.   Some are simple, consisting of but one word; others are long and complex.   This requires a combination of words, for, however long the subject of the sentence may be, it must be a unity.   This means that the pupil must deal with the words, composing the subject of the sentence, expressing the unified thought subject, just as he has dealt with the sentence, which expresses the unity called the thought.   He must separate form from content; the extent and content of ideas present themselves to him; and he sees the whole subject of modifiers growing out of this distinction. He discusses the thought material, out of which thought subjects, thought predicates, and thought relations are made, and he sees how the words composing the subjects, predicates, and relational elements of sentences may be unified, because of the ideas they express.   All the different forms which subjects, predicates, and copulas of sentences may have, are seen to be adapted to the expression of thought subjects, thought predicates, and thought relations, and determined by them.

2.   In the last circle of the grammar work, the student finishes the work for which he has laid the foundation in the circle immediately preceding, so that, the last circle is to the third, what the second was to the first.   In the third circle, he became familiar with the different kinds of ideas expressed by words: objects of thought, attributes, and ideas of relation. On that basis, he classified words into: substantive, attributive, and relation words.   Two other kinds, he learned, were sometimes used without much meaning, merely to fill out the form of the sentence; form words and feeling words.

Now, in the fourth circle, by observing likenesses and differences, he subdivides these classes of words, and thus arrives at "Parts of Speech." When the student sees the parts of speech, with all their properties, in the same light in which he has seen all the other parts of the sentence, as indicated in the previous discussion, he has finished the fourth circle of the grammar work, and may be said to have fairly mastered the science of the subject.

The word, "circle," is an appropriate word to name these phases of the grammar work, as, in each case, the student starts with the sentence, and, after considering parts, refers them all back to the sentence again; or he starts with a whole, and, having reduced it to parts, recombines it again into a whole—analysis and synthesis. The process is a passing from unity, through great variety, back to the unity of thought, as expressed in the universal sentence form.

It might be said in closing this introduction, that the discussion is meager and inadequate. Many reasons for the order, indicated above, both from the point of view of principles of subject and principles of mind, have been omitted on account of space. The same might be said of other parts of the discussion. The purpose is not to give a complete exposition of grammar in all its details, but to give the basis for the work which follows, and to show that there is a science of the subject; that it may be known scientifically; that there are certain principles which should govern the teaching of it; that the student who would master the subject must see all language forms as adapted to and determined by the thought they express; that in addition to all the analyzing which he does, the student is to synthesize the entire subject into an organized whole, by means of a central or relating idea.

The difference between grammar studied in this way, and

technical grammar as it is too often taught, is the difference
between life and death to the student; it is the difference
between an intelligent, healthful, life-giving, mental gym-
nastic, and a mechanical, deadening, verbal memory grind.
The one process leaves him with the arbitrary technic of the
subject, a mere crust, which he loathes; the other makes him
feel, as Dr. C. C. Everett* says, that, "There is hardly anything more interesting than to see how the laws of grammar,
which seem at first sight so hard and arbitrary, are simply the
laws of the expression of logical relations in concrete form."

---

* See his "Science of Thought," a book which no student of grammar should fail to consult, page 82.

THE SPIRIT only can teach. Not any sensual, not any liar, not any slave can teach, but only he can give who has; he only can create, who is. The man on whom the soul descends, through whom the soul speaks, alone can teach. Courage, purity, love, wisdom, can teach; and every man can open his door to these angels, and they shall bring him the gift of tongues. But the man who aims to speak as books enable, as synods use, as the fashion guides, and as interest commands, babbles. Let him hush.—*Emerson*.

# GRAMMAR.

Give the literal meaning of the word, definition.

See Century Dictionary.

State the marks of a good definition. Illustrate by any common definition.

See Elements of Psychology, Davis, p. 61. *5 0*

To what group of subjects does grammar belong? Name the other subjects of the group. How do you distinguish grammar from the others?

See Introduction, p. 8.

Define grammar. Show that your definition conforms to the requirements of a true definition.

See Introduction, p. 7.

With what does grammar deal or what is its subject-matter?

See Introduction, p. 12.

(Make an outline of language subjects, showing the place of grammar among them.)

See Introduction, pp. 8 and 9.

## The Sentence as a Whole.

What is a sentence?

See Introduction, pp. 13 and 14.

What is thought or judgment?

See Introduction, p. 13.

What are the necessary elements of a thought or judgment?

See Introduction, p. 13.

See the following references:

Jevons's Lessons in Logic, p. 60.  *6 0*
Dewey's Psychology, p. 213.
Sully's Psychology, p. 391. *1 5 0 . 7 0*
Schuyler's Psychology, p. 299. *1 5 0*
Brook's Mental Science, p. 228.
Elements of Psychology, Davis, p. 78. *1 5 0*
Everett's Science of Thought, p. 93. *1 6 0*
Hamilton's Logic, Day, p. 104.
Elements of Logic, Day, p. 70. *1 6 0*
The Modalist, Hamilton, pp. 6 and 79. *1 6*
Human Psychology, Janes, p. 172.

In the following sentences, point out the three elements of each thought expressed:

1. The house is large.
2. The trees are maples.
3. The school studies.

NOTE.—Other examples may be found in Part II.

Name and define each of the elements of a thought or judgment.    Illustrate.

Name the parts of the sentence.   To what elements of the thought do they correspond?

See Introduction, p. 14.

In the following sentences, point out the principal elements of each thought expressed, and the corresponding parts of the sentences:

1. Science is organized knowledge.
2. Flowers are plants.
3. Knowledge is power.

4. Planning saves time.

5. The human heart refuses to believe in a universe without a purpose.

6. Each is bound to all.

7. Artists are nearest God.

8. Do to-day thy nearest duty.

9. Could we rest, we must become smaller in soul.

10. Take sentences on p. 45, Whitney's Grammar; lessons 85 and 109, sentences at the close of the lessons, Reed & Kellogg's Grammar.

Indiana Grammar, p. 79.

Note.—Teacher may find other sentences in Part II.

Define each of the parts of the sentence. Give literal meaning of each term.

See Century Dictionary.

Read the following references:

Everett's Science of Thought, p. 94. / 6

Jevon's Lessons in Logic, pp. 61 and 88. / 6 6

Porter's Elements of Intellectual Science, p. 361.

Sully's Psychology, p. 392. / 5 0. 7 0

Schuyler's Psychology, p. 299. / 5 0

Human Psychology, Janes, p. 173.

Brooks' Mental Science, p. 230.

System of Logic, Mill, p. 49.

The Modalist, Hamilton, p. 79. / .6 6

Elements of Logic, Day, p. 44. / 6 6

Reed & Kellogg's Grammar, lesson 29.

Our Language, p. 184.

Lee & Hadley's Grammar, pp. 53–55.

Whitney's Grammar, p. 158.

Indiana Grammar, p. 105.

Complete Rhetoric, Welsh, p. 6.

Art of Composition, Day, p. 70.

Make an outline of the principal elements of the thought and the principal parts of the sentence.

**Relations Existing Between Thought Subjects and Thought Predicates.**

In the thoughts expressed in the following sentences, state which contains more attributes, the thought subject or the thought predicate:

1. The rose is red.
2. The flowers are violets.
3. The tree is an oak.
4. He is a king, every inch of him.
5. The cranium is the skull.
6. Superstition is the spleen of the soul.
7. The coin that is most current among mankind is flattery.
8. Time works wonders.
9. The Creator's power is seen everywhere.
10. Those that think govern those that toil.

Porter's Elements of Intellectual Science, p. 361.

In the following sentences, state which idea is applicable to more objects of thought, the thought subject or the thought predicate:

1. The poem is Longfellow's.
2. The fox is an animal.
3. New York is the metropolis of the United States.
4. Columbus was a native of Genoa.
5. To see it is to believe it.
6. Dickens was our greatest novelist.
7. Charles I. was King of England.
8. The Mississippi is the father of waters.
9. Truth is a mighty weapon.
10. Fire is a good servant, but it is a bad master.

In the following sentences, state the relation existing between the thought subject and thought predicate:

1. Feathers are not heavy.
2. Iron is not valuable.
3. Gold is not plentiful.
4. The book is not interesting.
5. James is not studying.
6. The Lord will not suffer the soul of the righteous to famish.
7. Blessings are not upon the wicked.
8. Wisdom is not found in the life of him that hath not understanding.
9. When I return, I shall not say anything.
10. "Try not the pass," the old man said.

NOTE.—In each of these cases, more sentences may be found in Part II.

Give the literal meaning of the words, content, intent, and extent.   Define and illustrate content and extent.

See the Century Dictionary.

Read the following references:
Jevons's Lessons in Logic, p. 37.   *I 6 8*
Elements of Logic, Day, p. 88.   *I 6 8*
System of Logic, Mill, p. 16.
The Modalist, Hamilton, p. 37. *I 6 C*
The Science of Rhetoric, D. J. Hill, p. 96.
Dewey's Psychology, p. 209.
Human Psychology, Janes, p. 239.
Elements of Psychology, Davis, p. 219.

### Classes of Sentences.

*State the effect which each of the following sentences produces on the mind. Point out the principal elements of each thought expressed:

1. The sun is shining brightly.
2. Is the sun shining brightly?
3. Oh, how brightly the sun is shining!
4. John, look out the window and see if the sun is shining brightly.
5. Constant dropping wears away stones.
6. Tom rowed with untired vigor, and with a different speed from poor Maggie's.
7. Mercy, sir, how the folks will talk of it!
8. Men's evil manners live in brass, their virtues we write in water.
9. Come, Rollo, let us take a walk.
10. "Think you, able," said Paul at last, "that the storm drove thither?"
11. Why was the French Revolution so bloody and destructive?
12. Praise ye the Lord.
13. Honey from out the quarreled hive I'll bring.
14. Lead us to some far-off sunny isle.
15. Where are you going, my pretty maid?

---

*Note.—These questions and suggestions should be simplified and expanded by the teacher to suit the grade of mind with which she is working. They are intended to be suggestive, and any explanation the teacher can make in assigning the lesson, to make it more definite, will be helpful; e. g., What is the meaning of each of the following sentences? What does each one make you think? Suppose you used each one yourself, what purpose would you have? etc., etc.

16. The teacher asked, " What are you doing?"
17. The Lord said to Cain, " Where is thy brother?"
18. Cain said, " Am I my brother's keeper?"
19. Judge not, that ye be not judged.
20. The way was long, the wind was cold,
    The minstrel was infirm and old.

How many different kinds of sentences do you find in the preceding list? Define and illustrate each. On what basis is the division made?

Read Whitney's Essentials of English Grammar, paragraphs 463-481 inclusive.
Maxwell's Grammar, pp. 6 and 231.
Indiana Grammar, p. 103.
Metcalf's Grammar, p. 14.

State concerning the following sentences, (whether they simply express a thought) or express a thought some element of which is unknown and sought for. If the latter, state what element of the thought is unknown and sought for. State what word or words denote the unknown element of thought, or what it is tells you there is an unknown element of thought. Also point out sentences which do neither of the above and state their use.

1. I am a poor man.
2. Who will help me?
3. Every man's task is his life-preserver.
4. Whose book have you?
5. What will you take?
6. Of whom do you speak?
7. When shall it be morn in the grave?
8. The devil can catch a lazy man with a bare hook.
9. Am I required to go?
10. Can'st thou number the stars?

11. Send the letter in the first mail. *imperative*

12. Hath the rain a father? *Declarative, same as 7 & 10.*

13. How frightful is the grave! *exclamatory*

14. Can'st thou stop the winds in their course? *Same as 12*

15. Will you bring me the book? *polite imperative*

16. Bring me the book. *imperative*

17. How beautiful upon the mountains are the feet of him that bringeth glad tidings! *arrang — interrog, exclam*

18. Children, obey your parents.

19. Go in peace and sin no more.

20. How far yon candle throws its little beam! *same as 17*

21. There is no place like home. *Decler, interrog*

22. Great is Diana of the Ephesians. *interrog*

23. "If it feed nothing else," said Shylock, "it will feed my revenge.

24. How wonderful is sleep! *infer*

25. Be ye perfect, even as your Father in Heaven is perfect. *arrang interrog*

26. How completely his passion has blinded him!

27. Consider my servant Job.

28. Thou shalt not steal. *arrang Declara*

29. I wish to know how far it is to Xenia. *interrog Declar*

30. The truth, itself, is not believed,
From one who often has deceived.

31. My poor mother was worried all day.

32. The poor child is dead.

33. That you have wronged me doth appear in this.

34. Charity begins at home.

35. The Romans, having conquered the world, were unable to conquer themselves.

Observe the position of the words in the preceding sen-

*36 Tell me your name*
*interrogative arrang imperative.*

tences and state the arrangement of the different classes of
sentences.

See Reed & Kellogg's Grammar, lessons 51 to 56 inclusive.
Indiana Grammar, pp. 105 and 144.
English composition, Welsh, p. 14.

What do we mean by arrangement? What kinds have
we? Define and illustrate each. Write a sentence with the
subject of thought unknown and sought for; the predicate
of thought or a part of it; the thought relation. What distinguishes an exclamatory sentence from a declarative sentence which expresses feeling? Illustrate. What do we
mean by a sentence interrogative in form and declarative
in meaning; declarative in form but imperative in meaning; interrogative in form and imperative in meaning?
Illustrate each.

Punctuate the following sentences, giving reasons.

1. Oh, what a fall was there my countrymen
2. Oh, for a lodge in some vast wilderness
3. Oh, how happy I am
4. Oh that I had the wings of a dove
5. Alas that thou shouldst die
6. Oh that this too too solid flesh would melt
7. Oh that those lips had language
8. Oh, it hurts me.
9. Oh father listen to me.
10. Oh wretched state
11. Oh, where shall rest be found
12. Fie on him
13. Oh, that I could find him
14. O bosom black as death
15. O for a kindling touch from that pure flame
16. O what a rapturous cry.

17. Strike, oh Muse, in a measure bold ,

18. O what a fair and ministering angel!

19. A horse a horse my kingdom for a horse !

20. What a piece of work is man how noble in reason how infinite in faculties in form and moving how express and admirable in action how like an an angel in apprehension how like a god the beauty of the world the paragon of animals /

State the punctuation of the Declarative, Interrogative, Exclamatory, and Imperative sentences.

See Southworth and Goddard's Elements of Composition and Grammar, p. 3.

Welsh-Greenwood, p. 207.

Indiana Grammar, p. 102.

Composition and Rhetoric, Hart, pp. 47 and 173.

When do we spell the word *o-h* and when *O?*

Metcalf's Grammar, p. 77.

See Reed & Kellogg's Grammar, lesson 21.

See Dictionary.

Welsh-Greenwood, p. 21.

Composition and Rhetoric, Hart, p. 48.

Make an outline of sentences on bases of effect produced upon the mind, or use, or meaning, including the following points:

1. Definition.

2. Classes.

3. Arrangement.

4. Punctuation.

### Classes of Sentences.

Examine the following sentences and be able to state the principal elements in the thought expressed by each.   How do the sentences differ? How many kinds are there on basis of the fundamental difference?

1. Washington, the father of his country, was our first president.

2. Washington, who was the father of his country, was our first president.

3. Washington was the father of his country, and he was our first president.

Name, give literal meaning of terms, and define the classes of sentences just illustrated. Upon what basis is this division made? Classify the following sentences on that basis and state the principal elements of each thought expressed:

1. William Cullen Bryant was born at Cummington, Massachusetts, November 3, 1794.

2. *The Embargo* was published in Boston in 1809, and was written when Bryant was but thirteen years old.

3. The Catskill Mountains have always been a region full of fable.

4. He used to tell his story to every stranger that arrived at Mr. Doolittle's hotel.

5. Rip's story was soon told, for the whole twenty years had been to him but as one night.

6. There is a Power whose care
    Teaches thy way along that pathless coast.

7. Vainly the fowler's eye
    Might mark thy distant flight to do thee wrong.

8. All that breathe
    Will share thy destiny.

9. I have heard that nothing gives an author so great pleasure as to have his works respectfully quoted by other learned authors.

10. This pleasure I have seldom enjoyed.

11. Silently, one by one, in the infinite meadows of heaven, blossomed the lovely stars.

12. Example appeals not to our understanding alone, but to our passions likewise.

13. If thou didst ever thy dear father love, revenge his foul and most uncommon murder.

14. There is no flock, however watched and tended,
    But one dead lamb is there!
    There is no fireside, howsoe'er defended,
    But has one vacant chair!

15. Thou lingering star, with lessening ray,
    That lov'st to greet the early morn,
    Again thou usherest in the day
    My Mary from my soul was torn.

16. Lightly and brightly breaks away
    The morning from her mantle gray.

17. The strength he gains is from the embrace he gives.

18. Softly sweet in Lydian measures,
    Soon he soothed his soul to pleasures;
    War, he sung, is toil and trouble;
    Honor but an empty bubble.

19. If you blow your neighbor's fire, don't complain if the sparks fly in your face.

20. Do not measure other people in your half bushel.

21. 'Tis an old maxim in the schools,
    That flattery's the food of fools;
    Yet now and then young men of wit
    Will condescend to take a bit.

22. 'Tis with our judgments as our watches: none
    Are just alike, yet each believes his own.

23. Love is the ladder on which we climb
   To a likeness with God.

24. *Heaven from all creatures hides the book of fate,
   All but the page prescribed, their present state.

25. Faith builds a bridge across the gulf of death.

**Take sentences on pp. 235 and 236, Whitney's Essentials of English Grammar. Indiana Grammar, p. 158. Sentences in Reed & Kellogg's Grammar, lesson 130.**
Other good sentences may be found in Part II.

Read the following:

Southworth & Goddard, pp. 197 and 120.
Welsh-Greenwood, pp. 30 and 31.
Meiklejohn, pp. 87, 93 and 94.
Indiana Grammar, p. 103.
Metcalf's English Grammar, p. 179.

----

## Thought Material and Classes of Words.

Classify the ideas expressed by the words in the following sentences. State how they are alike and how they differ. Classify the words in the sentences and state their uses:

1. Lincoln, the martyr to the cause of freedom, was a good president.

2. The boy's friend ran home to send a telegram to his anxious mother.

3. He, himself, sent his boy to me.

4. It is I; be not afraid.

5. The people watched them in silence.

6. I will go with you.

7. He of the rueful countenance answered without delay.

8. Bread and milk is very good food.

9. The flag is red, white, and blue.

10. The tall boy is doubtless exceedingly helpful to his mother.

11. The well is just thirty feet deep.

12. The president administers the government very well for the people.

13. You should have come an hour sooner.

14. The child read an hour.

15. The man is doubtless honest.

16. The house stands just across the river.

17. The blue and yellow badge belongs to Michigan University.

18. The man gave money to the poor.

19. Minneapolis is a beautiful city.

20. Truth, crushed to earth, will rise again.

21. Goodness is commendable.

22. He left yesterday.

23. The stove is hot.

24. The smooth glass is transparent.

25. Dry leaves are brittle.

26. The soft fur is warm.

27. The sour cider was made to-day.

28. The red sky is beautiful.

29. The running stream murmurs sweetly.

30. The rushing storm is frightful.

31. Thisbe met a roaring lion.

32. The soul is that which thinks, feels, and wills.

33. Who knoweth the spirit of man that goeth upward or the spirit of the beast which goeth downward?

34. The Mississippi is the longest river in the world.

35. There were giants in those days.

36. Pshaw! I do not care a fig.

37. Now Barrabas was a robber.

38. Well, what did he say?

39. Now then, I will proceed.

How To Parse, Abbott, p. 105.

40. Man, like the child, accepts the proffered boon,
And clasps the bauble, where he asked the moon.

41. In the shipwreck of the state, trifles float and are preserved; while everything solid and valuable sinks to the bottom, and is lost forever.

42. In peace, children bury their parents; in war parents bury their children.

43. If you wish to enrich a person, study not to increase his stores, but to diminish his desires.

44. Words are the counters of wise men, and the money of fools.

45. A juggler is a wit in things, and a wit a juggler in words.

46. Charity creates much of the misery it relieves, but does not relieve all the misery it creates.

47. Worth makes the man, the want of it the fellow.

48. Know then this truth, enough for man to know,
Virtue alone is happiness below.

49. A soft answer turneth away wrath.

50. The poor and the rich, the weak and the strong, the young and the old have one common Father.

Name and define the classes of ideas you have found expressed in the preceding sentences. Name and define the classes of words used in expressing them. What is the basis of your division? Give the literal meaning of *object, concrete, abstract, attribute, attributive, substantive.*

See Century Dictionary.

Make a complete outline of thought material or ideas, and words.

---

### Modifiers.

Explain the use of each italicized expression in the following:

1. James, the *mason*, is ill.

How to parse, Abbott, p. 97.

2. *Mary's* book is soiled.
3. The *great* plains are *good grazing* districts.
4. The *white* snow hurts *my eyes*.
5. He sold *Henry* a book.

How To Parse, Abbott, pp. 88, 92.
Lee and Hadley, pp. 188, 189.
New English Grammar, H. Sweet, p. 95.

6. The work was *neatly* done.
7. The child was good *in school*.
8. The boy was tardy *yesterday*.
9. He comes *because he is entertained*.
10. The man is charitable *in his way*.
11. The apple is *very* sweet.
12. The girl is *often* tardy.
13. The stranger is charitable, *that he may receive praise*.
14. The teacher is strict *with his pupils*.
15. The boy went *along with his mother*.
16. The judge is generous *except with his enemies*.
17. The minister had lately come *from the East*.
18. The cistern had been filled *from the spout*.
19. The girl is not good, *even if she is entertained*.
20. The garden was prepared *with the spade*.
21. It is *probably* true.

22. The story is *certainly* interesting and *perhaps* true.
23. He traded *with an Indian.*
24. He built the house *with his own money.*
25. The demonstration is *necessarily* true.
26. The ground is *not* wet.
27. Cleveland is *at this time* president.
28. *When the shadows of evening fall,* the sunbeams fly away.
29. We stood *upon the ragged rocks*
    *When the long day was nearly done.*
30. Make hay *while the sun shines.*
31. Some must watch *while others weep.*
32. The buttercup comes *early in the spring.*
33. The party walked *home.*

How To Parse, Abbott, pp. 260 and 93.
Composition and Grammar, Bain, p. 132.
See Whitney, par. 390.
New English Grammar, H. Sweet, p. 91.

34. The river is a *mile* broad.
35. You should have come *an hour* sooner.
36. The bird built her nest *six inches* above the door.

Classify, name, and define the expressions considered in the preceding sentences. What is the basis of your division? Make a complete outline of modifiers.

Read Southward and Goddard, pp 220-241.
Indiana Grammar, pp. 11 and 117.
Maxwell's Grammar, pp. 16, 35-39.
Metcalf's Grammar, pp. 52, 57-60, 43, 118.

---

### Predicates.

State the use of each italicized expression in the following:

1. *Corwin* was *an excellent advocate.*

*He was president si*

2. The stranger *listened* eagerly to the story.

3. *The Normal School* is *a school for teachers.*

4. The boys were *handsome and manly.*

5. Languages have long, almost always indeed, been *a subject of study.* .

6. But one may be *an accomplished linguist,* reading and speaking many tongues, without being *an adept* in the science of language.

7. Professor Max Müller, of the University of Oxford, and Professor William Dwight Whitney, of Yale, are *the great authorities* on the science of language.

8. Is the pen *mightier* than the sword?

9. A rolling stone *gathers* no moss.

10. It *takes* two to quarrel.

What differences have you noticed in the predicates of the preceding sentences? Name and define the classes. Upon what basis have you divided them?

Metcalf's Grammar, pp. 15, 45, 54, 181.
Maxwell's Grammar, pp. 8, 223, 224.
Welsh-Greenwood, pp. 16, 23, 165.

**The Simple Sentence.**

State the uses of the italicized words in the following sentences. Classify the sentences and the italicized words:

1. *Washington,* the first *president* of the *United States,* was a great *statesman.*

2. The *child's anxious teacher* sent the *boy home* to *his mother.*

3. *Gad,* a *troop* shall overtake *him.*

4. *He, himself,* wrote *me* the *note.*

5. *It* is *I.*
6. The teacher saw *them* studying.
7. Without *me,* ye can do *nothing.*
8. I *along* am left to tell the story.
9. *Yellow* and *blue* makes a pretty badge.
10. The flower is *red and white.*
11. *I, myself,* will assist *you.*
12. A righteous *man* needs no *monument.*
13. *God* does not expect us *to have charity for sin.*
14. Dyed *whiskers* are like hypocrisy.
15. *They* deceive only one *person.*

State all the uses of the Noun and Pronoun in the simple sentence and state all the modifiers which may belong to them.

Classify and state the use of each italicized word in the following sentences. Classify the sentences:

1. The *large* horse is *doubtless exceedingly useful* to his *owner.*
2. The house stands *just* across the river.
3. The river is a *mile* broad.
4. The *honest* boy *very promptly gave the man his money.*
5. The lesson should have been prepared *an hour* sooner.
6. The river fell *six inches.*

Read Whitney's Grammar, par. 390 to 393 inclusive.

State all the uses and modifiers which attributive words may have in the simple sentence. Illustrate each by one example.

State the use of each italicized expression in the following sentences and classify the sentences:

1. You *are doubtless* right.
2. The bird built her nest *just above* the door.
3. The boy *is* devoted *to* his mother.

4. The poet *and* scholar *is* dead.

State all the uses and modifiers of relation words in the simple sentence. Give one example of each.

State the use of the italicized words in the following and classify the sentences:

1. *Pooh!* I do not believe it.
2. *Alas!* what mortal terror we are in!
3. *Well,* did you vote?
4. *Now,* I do not believe a word of it.
5. *There* is a pleasure in the pathless wood.
6. *There* have always been people who loved to tell bad news.

State the use of each italicized expression in the following. Classify the expressions on as many different bases as you are able to discover by noting important differences among the expressions. Name and define each class of expressions:

1. The State University *of Minnesota* is located *in the city of Minneapolis.*
2. He has learned *to love and obey his teacher.*
3. The boy, *to be chosen,* must be intelligent *to be useful.*
4. He lives *to assist his friends.*
5. *To lie willingly* is base.
6. *Walking the race* was tiresome to the man *wearing the blue coat.*
7. We could not cross, *being unable to ford the river.*
8. *Being a member of the regiment,* he passed unchallenged.
9. The city *of large dimensions* sends the most goods *to foreign countries.*
10. *Out of sight* is out of mind.
11. Cæsar *might have been* king.

See Whitney's Grammar, par. 280.

State whether or not the conjunction, in the following sentences, expresses the relation between coordinate thoughts, or between coordinate parts of the same thought:

1. Mary learns easily but she forgets soon.
2. The cow and calf are together.
3. Pinks and roses are fragrant.
4. That is a red and a white flower.
5. Birds chirp and sing.
6. Five and four are nine.
7. You and I are going.
8. The great statesman and orator is dead.
9. The moon and stars are shining.
10. The scholar and poet was also a christian and patriot.

State the difference between sentences having different uses of the conjunction. Define each kind of sentence illustrated in the preceding sentences. Make an outline of the simple sentence.

Classify the following sentences, and point out the uses of the words in them:

1. Night, sable goddess, from her ebon throne,
   In rayless majesty, now stretches forth
   Her leaden scepter, o'er a slumbering world.
2. What kind of people first inhabited England?
3. Forbid it, Almighty God!
4. The ship left at sunrise.
5. Sweet is the breath of morn.
6. There can be no natural desire of artificial good.
7. Why do you weave around you this thread of occupation?
8. How oft the sight of means to do ill deeds makes ill deeds done!

G—4

9. After to-morrow is the bane of many a life.
10. Old John of Gaunt is grievous sick, my lord.
11. The meeting points the sacred hairs dissever,
From her fair head forever and forever.
12. To Thee we bow, Friend, Father, King of Kings!
13. Break, break, break,
On thy cold, gray stones, O Sea!
14. Oh soul! be changed into small water-drops.
15. Pride goeth before destruction.

NOTE.—For other sentences, see Part II.

---

### The Compound Sentence.

In the following sentences, state the uses of each italicized expression. Divide the expressions into classes by noting their differences. Make definitions.

1. *The river is deep* but *we can ford it.*
2. The person *who knows when he should stop* is wise.
3. The person *who has access to good books* is fortunate.
4. The boy *who is diligent and who obeys his superiors* will be respected.
5. *When spring returns,* the flowers will bloom.
6. Galileo believed *that the earth is round.*

Point out the clauses and conjunctions in the following, and try to state the kind of relation expressed by each conjunction:

1. I awoke and I got up at once.
2. The sun was up but it was hidden behind the clouds.
3. The bird was shot or some one had struck it.
4. It is my duty, therefore I must do it.
5. A king must win or he must forfeit his crown forever.

6. A fool speaks all his mind, but a wise man reserves something until hereafter.

7. It is not snowing, nor is it raining.

8. Some are born great; some achieve greatness; and others have greatness thrust upon them.

9. The man dies but his memory lives.

10. The man pays his debts promptly, therefore he is honest.

11. Be temperate in youth or you will have to be abstinent in old age.

12. Of thy unspoken word thou art master; thy spoken word is master of thee.

13. A soft answer turneth away wrath, but grievous words stir up strife.

14. There was a gay maiden lived down by the mill—
    Ferry me over the ferry—
    Her hair was as bright as the waves of a rill,
    When the sun on the brink of his setting stands still,
    Her lips were as full as a cherry.

15. This world is all a fleeting show,
    For man's illusion given;
    The smiles of joy, the tears of woe,
    Deceitful shine, deceitful flow—
    There's nothing true but heaven!

16. The splendor falls on castle walls
    And snowy summits old in story;
    The long light shakes across the lakes,
    And the wild cataract leaps in glory.

17. And now there came both mist and snow,
    And it grew wondrous cold,
    And ice mast-high came floating by,
    As green as emerald.

18. The day is done; and slowly from the scene
    The stooping sun upgathers his spent shafts,
    And puts them back into his golden quiver.

19. Night dropped her sable curtain down, and pinned it with a star.

20. A blind man is a poor man, and blind a poor man is; for the former seeth no man, and the latter no man sees.

What is meant by the members of compound sentences? Define and illustrate the different kinds of relations which may exist between the thoughts expressed by the members of compound sentences.

See Conklin's English Grammar and Composition, p. 34.
Indiana Grammar, pp. 99 and 100.
Essentials of English, Welsh, p. 139.

State the members of the following compound sentences; the kinds of relation existing between the thoughts expressed by the members; the conjunction expressing the relation; and note and explain the punctuation.

1. Places near the sea are not extremely cold in winter, nor are they extremely warm in summer.

2. The man takes plenty of exercise; he is well.

3. We must conquer our passions or they will conquer us.

4. People in the streets are carrying umbrellas; hence it must be raining.

5. Neither James nor John had his lesson.

6. Solomon was both learned and wise.

7. Though it is deep, yet it is clear.

8. I care not whether it rains or snows.

9. Unto us was the gospel preached as well as unto them.

10. The house was built upon a rock; it did not fall.

11. The prodigal robs his heirs; the miser robs himself.

12. Mirth should be the embroidery of conversation, but it should not be the web.

13. I was told to go else I should remain.

14. Be industrious, otherwise you will come to grief.

15. Margaret Fuller, whom the waves buried, accomplished much good ; but she was taken away in the midst of her usefulness.

16. Ignorance is the curse of God, knowledge the wing wherewith we fly to Heaven.

17. The conscious water saw its Lord and blushed.

18. The aspen heard them and she trembled.

19. O dark and cruel deep, reveal
The secret that thy waves conceal!
And ye wild sea-birds hither wheel
And tell it me.

20. He cast off his friends as a huntsman his pack,
For he knew when he wished he could whistle them
back.

21. There is much that is deciduous in books, but all that gives them a title to rank as literature in the highest sense is perennial.

22. I do not like to say it, but he has sometimes smothered the child-like simplicity of Chaucer under feather-beds of verbiage.

23. Zeal and duty are not slow,
But on occasion's forelock watchful wait.

24. Earth felt the wound; and nature from her seat
Sighing, through all her works gave signs of woe.

25. In peace, thou art the gale of spring; in war, the mountain storm.

State the typical conjunction used to express each kind of relation. Give the literal meaning of each. Write lists of conjunctions used to express the different kinds of relations existing between the thoughts expressed by the members of compound sentences.   Be able to use each conjunction in sentences.   (See Whitney's Grammar, par. 329 to 331 inclusive.)   State the punctuation of the compound sentence, mentioning all the modifying influences.   Punctuate the following sentences, giving reasons; state the kind of relation existing between the thoughts expressed by the members; and separate each member into its principal parts:

1.  No one ought to wound the feelings of another or to insult him

2.  A wise man seeks to shine in himself a fool to outshine others

3.  Men are not to be judged by their looks habits and appearances but by their lives

4.  Stones grow plants grow animals grow feel and live

5.  Avoid affectation it is a contemptible weakness

6.  Harbor no malice in thy heart it will be a viper in the bosom

7.  Crafty men contemn studies simple men admire them and wise men use them

8.  The wise man considers what he wants the fool what he abounds in.

9.  The noblest prophets have been children lisping the speech laughing the laugh of childhood

10.  The mountains rise and circling oceans flow

11.  He suffered but his pangs are o'er
     Enjoyed but his delights are fled
     Had friends his friends are now no more
     And foes his foes are dead

12. Swift to the breach his comrades fly
Make way for liberty they cry
And through the Austrian phalanx dart
As rushed the spears through Arnold's heart

13. Leaves have their time to fall
And flowers to wither at the north wind's breath
And stars to set but all
Thou hast all seasons for thine own O Death

14. Themistocles was cautious and he was also valiant
but the wisdom of the serpent and the courage of the lion
could not prevail against destiny

15. Turn gentle hermit of the vale
And guide thy lonely way
To where yon taper cheers the dale
With hospitable ray

Define and illustrate a regular compound sentence; an
abridged compound sentence; a simple sentence with a
compound element; and a compound-complex sentence. Be
ready to expand your abridged compound sentences into
regular compound sentences, and show that your simple
sentences with compound elements cannot be expanded.

State the following facts of the following sentences:

1. Classify the sentence.

2. Read the members.

3. Name the conjunction and state the kind of relation
expressed by it.

4. Verify the punctuation.

5. Analyze each member.

    a. Give entire subject.

    b. Give entire predicate.

    c. Give entire relational element.

d. Give principal word of the subject and the modifiers of it.

e. Same of other parts.

1. Apply yourselves to study; it will redound to your honor.

2. Every man desires to live long but no man would be old.

3. Few and short were the prayers we said,
   And we spake not a word of sorrow;
   But we silently gazed on the face of the dead,
   And we bitterly thought of the morrow.

4. So Heaven decrees; with Heaven who can contend?

5. Faithful are the wounds of a friend, but the kisses of an enemy are deceitful.

6. May I govern my passions with absolute sway,
   And grow wiser and better as life wears away.

7. Full many a flower is born to blush unseen,
   And waste its sweetness on the desert air.

8. Upon her breast a sparkling cross she wore,
   Which Jews might kiss and infidels adore;
   Her lively looks a sprightly mind disclose —
   Quick as her eyes, and as unfixed as those;
   Favors to none, to all she smiles extends;
   Oft she rejects, but never once offends.

9. The vine still clings to the mouldering wall,
   But at every gust the dead leaves fall.

10. And as a hare, when hounds and horns pursue,
    Pants to the place from whence at first he flew,
    I still had hopes, my long vexations past,
    Here to return, and die at home at last.

11. Take her up tenderly,
    Lift her with care,
    Fashioned so slenderly,
    Young and so fair.

12. Come as the winds come, when
    Forests are rended;
    Come as the wind comes, when
    Navies are stranded.

13. Alas, 'tis true I have gone here and there,
    And made myself a motley to the view,
    Gored mine own thoughts, sold cheap what is most
      dear.

14. Fond fool! six feet of earth is all thy store,
    And he that seeks for all shall have no more.

15. This is the state of man: to-day he puts forth
    The tender leaves of hope; to-morrow blossoms,
    And bears his blushing honors thick upon him;
    The third day comes a frost, a killing frost.

16. A professed Catholic, he imprisoned the Pope; a pretended patriot, he impoverished the country.

17. There are but few voices in the world but many echoes.

18. He is a freeman whom the truth makes free,
    And all are slaves beside.

19. And neither the angels in heaven above,
    Nor the demons down under the sea,
    Can ever dissever my soul from the soul
    Of the beautiful Annabel Lee.

20. Night's candles are burnt out, and jocund Day
    Stands tiptoe on the mountain tops.

21. Any nobleness begins at once to refine a man's features,—any meanness or sensuality to imbrute them.

22. This should have been a noble creature; he
    Hath all the energy which would have made
    A goodly frame of glorious elements,
    Had they been wisely mingled.
23. But look, the morn in russet mantle clad
    Walks o'er the dew of yon high, eastern hill.
24. See how the morning opes her golden gates,
    And takes her farewell of the glorious sun!
25. I saw from the beach when the morning was shining,
    A bark o'er the waters move gloriously on;
    I came, when the sun o'er that beach was declining—
    The bark was still there, but the waters were gone.

NOTE.—More sentences may be found on p. 203, Whitney's Grammar, and in lesson 77, Reed & Kellogg.

Indiana Grammar, p. 117.

For other good sentences, see Part II.

Make an outline of the compound sentence.

---

### The Complex Sentence.

State the use of each italicized expression in the following sentences. Substitute a clause for each expression, making the sentences complex:

1. *Weakness* is your excuse.
2. The result was *the signing of the treaty.*
3. They asked *his presence.*
4. This fact, *the rotundity of the earth,* is believed by all.
5. There is some dispute about *the real discoverer of America.*
6. We are desirous of *your success.*

7. They insisted *on your remaining.*

State the use of the clause you have substituted in each case in the preceding sentences.

In the following sentences, read the principal clause and then the subordinate. State the use of each subordinate clause. Note and explain the punctuation.

1. What you say is of little consequence.
2. My home is wherever I am happy.
3. I know not where they have laid him.
4. The fact, that it was done by him, is apparent.
5. He traded with what capital he had.
6. When letters were first used, is not certainly known.
7. A peculiarity of English is that it has so many borrowed words.
8. The fact, that mold is a plant, is wonderful.
9. That stars are suns, is the belief of astronomers.
10. Astronomers believe that stars are suns.
11. The belief of astronomers is that stars are suns.
12. The belief, that stars are suns, is held by astronomers.
13. That the caterpillar turns to a butterfly, is a curious fact.
14. The thought, that we are spinning around the sun some twenty miles a second, almost makes one dizzy.
15. We are quite sorry that it is so.
16. He was afraid lest he should fall.
17. We are not certain that an open sea surrounds the pole.

Read carefully paragraphs 147, 422, 423, and 424 to 436 inclusive, Whitney's Grammar.

18. They gave the goods to whoever wanted them.
19. The old lady put the question to whomever she met.
20. The missionaries preached to what people remained.

State all the uses of the substantive clause, usual form, in the complex sentence. Write one original example of each use.

State the principal clause and the subordinate clause in each of the following sentences. State the use of the subordinate clause. Note and explain the punctuation. How do the clauses differ from those in the preceding list?

1. "Mental power can never be gained from senseless fiction," says a certain writer.

2. The peacock struts about, saying, "What a fine tail I have!"

3. Socrates's greatest saying was, "Know thyself."

4. Shakespeare's metaphor, "Night's candles are burned out," is one of the finest in literature.

5. The shortest verse in the Bible is this: "Jesus wept."

6. "What have I done?" is asked by the knave and the thief.

7. Hamlet's exclamation was, "What a piece of work is man!"

8. Cries of, "Long live the king!" rent the air.

9. The traveler said that he was weary.

10. The speaker said that Protection was a failure.

11. "You will," he said, "be well satisfied with the change."

12. A writer says, "I have heard more than one person say, 'I am thankful.'"

13. I will ask you, "What can you do?"

14. The message ran thus: "England expects every man to do his duty."

15. Charles Lamb, reading the epitaphs in a churchyard, inquired, "Where be all the bad people buried?"

16. In studying grammar through the English language,

we must purge our minds of the wooden notion, that it is an inherent quality of a word to be this or that part of speech.

17. The whole force of conversation depends on how much you can take for granted.

18. Nathan Hale's only regret was, that he had but one life to give to his country.

19. Byron, seeing Moore eating an under-done beefsteak, asked if he were not afraid of committing murder after such a meal.

20. Lowell has long been certain that the greatest vice of American writing and speaking is a studied want of simplicity.

Explain the difference between a direct and an indirect quotation; between a substantive clause and a direct quotation; between a substantive clause and an indirect quotation. State the punctuation of the direct quotation. State all the uses of the direct quotation in the complex sentence. Write an original example of each use.

Punctuate and capitalize the following sentences, giving reasons:

1. This we know that our future depends upon our present

2. The story of Washington's hatchet it is now believed is untrue

3. Why me the stern usurper spared I knew not

4. The project it is certain will succeed

5. Whatever is is right

6. He said the maxim a fool and his money are soon parted is many times exemplified

7. In the New Testament are the following words Jesus answered the Jews is it not written in your law

8. The English said Voltaire gain two hours a day by clipping words

9. Gallop gasped Joris for Aix is in sight

10. The Queen said repeatedly with a firm voice into thy hands O Lord I commend my spirit

11. You lazy fellow cried Hercules how dare you send for me till you have tried to do without me

12. Fly Rebecca for no human aid can avail you said Ivanhoe

13. Said the school master when asked about Esau the pupil said Esau wrote a famous book of fables and sold the copyright for a bottle of potash

14. What teacher of rhetoric has not sympathized with the delighful Portia in the Merchant of Venice when she says with a sigh If to do were as easy as to know what were good to do chapels had been churches and poor men's cottages princes' palaces

15. Truth gets well says a certain writer even if she be run over by a locomotive

16. The Mohammedans say God gave two-thirds of all the beauty to Eve

17. We daily verify the saying man's extremity is God's opportunity

18. The principle involved in Resistance to tyrants is obedience to God was the seminal principle of the American Revolution

19 The Ram's Horn says a self-made man likes to boast of his job

20. One historian says if we track Queen Elizabeth through her tortuous mazes of lying and intrigue the sense of her greatness is almost lost in a sense of contempt

State all the rules for punctuating the substantive clause, both in its usual form and as a direct quotation.

See Elements of Composition and Grammar, Southworth & Godard, pp. 3–10 inclusive.

Butler's School English, p. 218.

Hart's Composition and Rhetoric, pp. 21–63.

· State the use of each italicized expression in the following sentences. State whether they narrow the meaning of the word modified or simply make prominent an attribute of an object of thought:

1. Mahomet, *the founder of the faith of Islam,* was born in Mecca.

2. *Sunderland's* crime was never forgiven by James.

3. A man *of good character* will win respect.

4. The prisoner, *stupefied with terror,* could not respond.

5. The army, *conquered at Waterloo,* was commanded by Napoleon.

6. Solomon, *the builder of the Temple,* was the son of David.

7. It was a sight *to gladden the heart.*

8. Rice, *largely consumed by the natives of Eastern Asia,* requires a damp soil.

9. Procrastination, *the thief of time,* is our worst enemy.

10. A selfish man, *the ugliest thing upon which the angels have to look,* is a disgrace to humanity.

Change each of the preceding sentences into a complex sentence. State the principal clause and the subordinate clause in each. State whether the subordinate clause is limiting or descriptive. Point out the connective word and state its uses.

Observe the above instructions with regard to the following sentences:

1. God rules the world, which he created.

2. A city that is set on a hill cannot be hid.

3. The man who conquers selfishness is brave.

4. The evil that men do lives after them.

5. I thrice presented him a kingly crown, which he did thrice refuse.

6. My father whom all loved, was fond of flowers.

7. The girl and the cat, that were in the room, were having a frolic.

8. The person who first ran to the sepulcher was a woman.

9. He purchased such books as were wanted.

10. To live in hearts we leave behind is not to die.

11. There is not a man here but knows it.

See Whitney, par. 187.

12. There is no fireside, but has one vacant chair.

13. As many as received him, to them gave he power.

14. Such as I have, give I unto thee.

15. To him who in the love of nature holds communion with her visible forms, she speaks a various language.

16. It was to me that he gave the book.

17. It was from him that I received the information.

18. The lever which moves the world's mind is the printing press.

19. The knights of the round table, who flourished in the reign of King Arthur, were brave.

20. Margaret Fuller, whom the waves buried, was a good woman.

State the use of each italicized expression in the following. Try to substitute one word for the entire italicized expression in each case. State all the uses of the word which you substitute:

1. *He who* wins may laugh.

2. *The thing which* is right is safe.
3. He wants *anything which* he sees.
4. *The person whom* falsehood pleases, truth offends.
5. Do *the thing which* is right.
6. The Lord chasteneth *any person whom* he loveth.
7. *Any person who* runs may read.
8. *The person who* keepeth the law is a wise son.
9. I speak as to wise men; judge ye *the thing which* I say.
10. *The person who* enters here should have a pure heart.

State all the uses of the italicized expressions in the following. Expand the words so as more clearly to show all their uses:

1. *Whoever* sees not the sun is blind.
2. He knows *whomever* he has once seen.
3. *Whoso* keepeth the law is a wise son.
4. *Whatever* he doeth shall prosper.
5. *Whosoever* sweareth by the gift that is on the altar is guilty.
6. *Whoever* child you have wronged shall be avenged.
7. *Whosesoever* sins ye forgive shall be forgiven.
8. I will be satisfied with *whomsoever* you may appoint.
9. You may have *whichever* you want.
10. *Whatsoever* ye shall ask, that will I do.
11. The child does *whatever* he pleases.
12. He will do *what* is right.
13. You may select *whichsoever* you desire.
14. *What* he says is true.
15. *Whosoever* shall smite you on the right cheek, turn to him the other also.
16. Into *whatsoever* city ye shall enter, inquire who is worthy.

17. *Whosoever* shall be ashamed of me, of him shall the son of man be ashamed.

18. *Whoever* studies will learn.

19. *Whoever* does no good does harm.

20. *Whoever* brings the treasure will receive the reward.

Make complete lists of the simple and compound relative pronouns. State the kind of object expressed by each. Show how the compound relatives are formed. When is the word *as* used as a relative? (See Whitney, par. 186.) Define relative pronoun; simple, compound. What is an antecedent? What determines the case form of the compound relative pronoun? State the punctuation of the adjective clause. (Read Whitney's Grammar, par. 181, on *what* as a relative.) Write a sentence in which the compound relative has a nominative use in the principal clause and an objective use in the subordinate clause; one in which the reverse is true.

Explain the use of the following italicized expressions, and the use of the clauses in which they occur. Substitute a single word for each italicized expression, and state the uses of the word thus substituted:

1. Youth is the time *at which* the seeds of character are sown.

2. I saw the city *in which* Longfellow lived.

3. The place *to which* she fled is unknown.

4. I know a bank *on which* the wild thyme grows.

5. You take the means *by which* I live.

6. This is the arrow *with which* he killed Cock Robin.

7. This is the house *from which* Arnold fled.

8. I know the place *of which* you speak.

9. I do not like the platform *on which* they stand.

10. The principal *on which* he acts is just.

In the following sentences, state the principal clause : the subordinate clause and the word it modifies; the connective word and all its uses :

1. We came unto the land whither thou sentest us.

2. I have shook off the regal thoughts wherewith I reigned.

3. The play's the thing wherein I'll catch the conscience of the king.

4. It was a time when men's hearts were tried.

5. The place where he fell is unknown.

6. He would give the duke no reasons why he followed a losing suit.

7. Mark those laws whereby the universe is conducted.

8. A depot is a place where stores are kept.

9. A verb is a word whereby the chief action of the mind is expressed.

10. The valley of Chamouni is a place where the traveler loves to linger for days and even for weeks.

What is a conjunctive adverb? Make an outline of the adjective clause, showing all the words which may be used in joining it to the principal clause.

Read Paragraphs 185, 186, 331, and 430, Whitney's Grammar.

Pp. 105-108, Lessons 65 to 69 inclusive, Reed & Kellogg.

Metcalf's English Grammar, pp. 203-205.

Explain the uses of the italicized expressions in the following sentences. Try to substitute a single word for each expression, and then state all the uses of the substituted word:

1. Improve your moments *during the time at which* you are in school.

2. Swiftly glide the hours *at the time at which* the heart is young.

3. Smooth runs the water *at the place at which* the brook is deep.

4. *At the time at which* he slept, she over him would spread his mantle.

5. He sleeps *at the place at which* night overtakes him.

6. The boy does *in the manner in which* he pleases.

7. He became humbler *in the degree in which* he grew wiser.

8. Truth is strange *in a degree in which* fiction is not strange.

9. *In the manner in which* the twig is bent, the tree is inclined.

10. *At the time at which* Raleigh was launching paper navies, Shakespeare was stretching his baby hands for the moon.

Make a definition of the class of words you have just been substituting. In the following sentences, state the principal clause; the subordinate clause, stating what word it modifies; the connective word and all its uses:

1. Gather dewdrops while they sparkle.

2. Peace rules the day when reason rules the hour.

3. Master, I will follow thee whithersoever thou goest.

4. Children of the Heavenly King,
   As we journey, let us sing.

5. When Greeks joined Greeks, then began the tug of war.

6. Where the bee sucks, there suck I.

7. Whither I go ye cannot come.

8. When the heart beats no more, then the life ends.

9. Mammon wins his way, where seraphs might despair.

10. Wheresoever the carcass is, there will the eagles be gathered together.

11. Hell trembled as he strode.

12. In Britain, the conquered race became as barbarous as the conquerers were.

13. Death itself is not so painful as is this sudden horror and surprise.

14. His misery was such that none of the bystanders could refrain from weeping.

15. He gazed so long, that both of his eyes were dazzled.

16. As heroes think, so thought the Bruce.

17. The earlier you rise, the better your nerves will bear study.

18. Pride may be pampered, while the flesh grows lean.

19. They are better than we had expected.

20. He was so weak, that he fell.

State the use of the italicized words in the following sentences:

1. I left *before* sunrise.

2. I left *before* the sun rose.

3. George Washington died *after* the accomplishment of his great work.

4. George Washington died *after* his great work was accomplished.

5. The Lord hath blessed thee *since* my coming.

6. The Lord hath blessed thee *since* I came.

7. You should drink from the fountain of knowledge *ere* your departure.

8. You should drink from the fountain of knowledge *ere* you depart.

9. You may wait *till* the arrival of the train.

10. You may wait *till* the train arrives.

11. He sat and talked *until* his death.

12. He sat and talked *until* he died.

State the principal and subordinate clauses in each of the following sentences, and explain the use of the connective:

1. He rushes to battle as if he were summoned to a banquet.
2. Our friends visited us as frequently as they could.
3. I will run as far as God has any ground.
4. Oft as the morning dawns should gratitude arise.
5. His head ached, so that he could scarcely study.
6. Since you insist upon it, I consent.
7. God was angry with the children of Israel, for he overthrew them in the wilderness.
8. Our fathers sought these shores in order that they might escape from persecution.
9. In case that we are beaten, we shall retreat.
10. How happy I could be with either,
    Were t'other dear charmer away.
11. Cursed be I, that I did so.
12. Though he slay me, yet will I trust him.
13. If the War of the Roses did not utterly destroy English freedom, it arrested its progress for a hundred years.
14. Obey the law of nature lest thou become unnatural.
15. Whereas the embargo act injured the commerce of America, it was repealed.
16. I will pay him so he will have no excuse for returning.
17. Except ye become as little children, ye can in no wise enter the Kingdom of Heaven.
18. Unless you are competent seek no promotion.
19. Ye know the heart of a stranger, seeing ye were strangers in a strange land.
20. That is strange, notwithstanding he is your neighbor.
21. I must go whether the train goes or not.

22. Although the wound soon healed again, yet, as he ran, he yelled for pain.

23. Milton almost requires a service to be played before you enter on him.

24. The waves of sound do not move so rapidly as the waves of light.

25. The more we know of ancient literature, the more we are struck with its modernness.

Make an outline of the adverbial clause, state the kinds of connective words which may be used to join the adverbial clause to the principal clause, define and make lists of each of these classes of connectives, and finish your outline of the complex sentence. State the punctuation of the adverbial clause.

Analyze the following sentences according to the following form:

1. Classify the sentence as a whole.

2. State the principal parts of it.

3. Give the principal word in each part, and all its modifiers.

### Sentences.

1. Where beams of warm imagination play,
   The memory's soft figures melt away.

2. He who knows only his own side of the case, knows little of that.

. 3. When we go forth in the morning, we lay a moulding hand upon our destiny.

4. Knowledge and timber should not be used much till they are seasoned.

5. Whoever seeks the good of others will himself be blessed.

6. That man has been from time immemorial a right-handed animal, is beyond dispute.

7. If I forget thee, O Jerusalem, let my right hand forget her cunning.

8.        Still the wonder grew,
That one small head could carry all he knew.

9. The man who grumbles much prays little.

10. The smallest dewdrop, that lies on the meadow at night, has a star sleeping in its bosom.

11. Not a soldier discharged his farewell shot,
O'er the grave where our hero was buried.

12. All seems infected that the infected spy,
As all looks yellow to the jaundiced eye.

13. All are but parts of one stupendous whole
Whose body nature is, and God the soul.

14. Much pleased was he to find,
That, though on pleasure she was bent,
She had a frugal mind.

15. Too many who have not learned to follow, want to lead.

16. Some people appear to think that whining is religion.

17. When an honest man stays away from the polls, the devil votes.

18. It generally takes a blockhead a good while to find out what ails him.

19. One of the greatest foes the devil has is a Christian mother.

20. If our faults were written on our faces, how quickly we would all hang our heads.

21. As the genuineness of a coin is made apparent by the touch of an acid, so are the qualities of manhood manifested by the test of trial.

22. The man who lives only for himself will not have many mourners at his funeral.

23. Read from some humbler poet
     Whose songs gushed from his heart,
     As showers from the clouds of summer
     Or tears from the eyelids start.

24. A man he was to all the country dear,
     And passing rich with forty pounds a year.

25. Oh, well for the fisherman's boy.
     That he shouts with his sister at play!
     Oh, well for the sailor lad
     That he sings in his boat on the bay!

26. You must wake and call me early, call me early,
         mother dear;
     To-morrow'll be the happiest time of all the glad
         New Year;
     Of all the glad New Year, mother, the maddest,
         merriest day;
     For I'm to be Queen o' the May, mother, I'm to be
         Queen o' the May.

27. Worth makes the man and want of it the fellow.

28. In one rude clash he struck the lyre, and swept with hurried hand the strings.

29. He listened to the song of the Sirens, yet he glided by without being seduced to their shore.

30. Joy comes, grief goes, we know not how;
     Everything is happy now,
     Everything is upward striving;
     'Tis as easy now for the heart to be true
     As for grass to be green or skies to be blue.—
     'Tis the natural way of living.

Define regular compound sentence, and abridged compound sentence. Review compound and complex sentences.

Other good sentences for analysis may be found in Reed & Kellogg's Higher Lessons in English, Lessons 78, 80, 81 and 84. Whitney's Essentials of English Grammar, par. 437.

Indiana Grammar, p. 225.

Part II. of this book.

Punctuate and capitalize the following, giving reasons:

1. It is mind after all which does the work of the world

2. His passions however prevented his seeing the danger

3. The affair passed off to your satisfaction no doubt

4. Nelson has at last got into the senate

5. He promised however to set about reform at once

6. However much he promised it was but little that he performed

7. Here all is peace and quietness there all is turmoil and strife

8. Why this is all wrong

9. Joseph who happened to be in the field at the time saw the carriage approach and in an ecstasy of delight hastened to meet it

10. If you would succeed in business be honest and industrious

11. The tree will not bear fruit in autumn unless it blossoms in the spring

12. Breathe into a man an earnest purpose and you awaken in him a new power

13. Give time to the study of nature whose laws are all deeply interesting

14. Those friends who in the native vigor of his powers preceived the dawn of Robertson's future eminence were at length amply rewarded

15. He preaches most eloquently who leads the most pious life

16. No thought can be just of which good sense is not the groundwork

17. There are men and women whose desire for knowledge is never satisfied

18. Modern engineering spans whole continents tunnels alike mountains and rivers and dykes out old ocean himself

19. Did God create for the poor a coarser earth a thinner air a paler sky

20. Aristotle Hamilton Wheatley and McCosh are high authorities in logic

21. The poor and the rich the weak and the strong the young and the old have one common Father

22. Himself the greatest of agitators Napoleon became the most oppressive of tyrants

23. Paul the apostle was a man of energy

24. The word *poet* meaning a maker a creator is derived from the the Greek

25. The greatest poet among the ancients Homer like the greatest among the moderns Milton was blind

26. At the request of the Rt Rev W H Hooker D D the vote was taken

27. I beg leave sir to present my friend Lord Hargrave

28. Show pity Lord O Lord forgive

29. Then came Jesus the doors being shut and stood in their midst

30. To obtain an education he was willing to make sacrifices

31. Awkward in person he was ill adapted to gain respect

32. Reading maketh a full man conference a ready man writing an exact man

33. Semiramis built Babylon Dido Carthage and Romulus Rome

34. Some one justly remarks it is a great loss to lose an affliction

35. Patrick Henry began his great speech by saying it is natural to man to indulge in the illusions of hope

36. As we perceived the shadow to have moved but did not perceive its moving so our advances in learning consisting of such minute steps are perceivable only by the distance

37. So sad and dark a story is scarcely to be found in any work of fiction and we are little disposed to envy the moralist who can read it without being softened

38. If we think of glory in the field of wisdom in the cabinet of the purest patriotism of the highest integrity public and private of morals without a stain of religious feeling without intolerance and without extravagance the august figure of Washington presents itself as the personation of all these

39. The temples are profaned the soldier's oath resounds in the house of God the marble pavement is trampled by iron hoofs horses neigh beside the altar      .

40. Greece has given us three great historians namely Herodotus Xenophon and Thucydides

41. Adjective Pronouns are divided into three classes Distributive Demonstrative and Indefinite

42. Speaking of party Pope makes this remark there never was any party faction sect or cabal whatsoever in which the most ignorant were not the most violent

43. Can these words add vigor to your hearts yes they can do it they have often done it

44. Yes my lords I am amazed at his lordship's speech

45. Shall a man obtain the favor of Heaven by impiety by murder by falsehood by theft

46. Oh what a fair and ministering angel

47. Ho trumpets sound a war note

48. Socrates said that he believed the soul to be immortal

49. Some one has said what an argument for prayer is contained in the words Our Father which art in Heaven

50. Trench says what a lesson the word diligence contains

51. There is but one object says Augustine greater than the soul and that is its Creator

52. Let me make the ballads of a nation said Fletcher and I care not who makes the laws

53. What do you think I'll shave you for nothing and give you a drink

54. To Greece we are indebted for the three principal orders of architecture the Doric the Ionic and the Corinthian

55. He who is his own lawyer is said to have a fool for a client

56. 'Tis not the whole of life to live
Nor all of death to die .

57. To honor God to benefit mankind
To serve with lofty gifts the lowly needs
Of the poor race for which the God-man died
And do it all for love oh this is great

58. A still small voice spake unto me
Thou art so full of misery
Were it not better not to be

59. The lilies behold how we
Preach without words of purity

60. And I will trust that He who heeds .
    The life that hides in mead and wold
    Who hangs yon alder's crimson beads
    And stains these mosses'green and gold
    Will still as He hath done incline
    His gracious ear to me and mine

Complete Rhetoric, Welsh, p. 127.
School English, Butler, p. 218.
Indiana Grammar, p. 102.
Elements of Composition and Grammar, Southworth and
    Goddard, p. 3.
Welsh-Greenwood, p. 207.
Essentials of English, Welsh, p. 158.

# PARTS OF SPEECH.

## Substantive Words.

In the following sentences, point out the words which express objects of thought, and state what kind of an object of thought each one expresses; notice how the word expresses the object of thought. Does it emphasize the common attributes of the object of thought or the peculiar attributes? Does it express the object of thought for the purpose of calling attention to that particular object of thought, or for the purpose of calling attention to its peculiarities?

1. The house is made of brick.
2. The cup and spoon were presents.
3. The horse is a useful animal.
4. The girl's cheeks are rosy.
5. The man placed his hand on the boy's head.
6. The boat turned on her side.
7. Flesh and blood cannot enter the Kingdom of Heaven.
8. Silver and gold have I none.
9. The articles are made of wood and iron.
10. The odor of the flower was pleasant.
11. Do you like the flavor of the fruit?
12. Thunder and lightning are frightful.
13. Then shall this body return to dust, and the soul to God, who gave it.
14. The man is six feet in height.
15. Truth is stranger than fiction.

16. The lad's goodness of heart atoned for his ugliness of feature.

17. His absence is more to be desired than his presence.

18. Cæsar's anger knew no bounds.

19. Which was greater, Martin Luther or Mohammed?

20. Oliver was on his way from Ludgate to Cornhill, when he met a group of boot-blacks.

21. A troop of children gamboled on the green.

22. The family became uneasy.

23. The school consisted of a dozen children.

24. Jupiter is larger than Venus.

25. Paul was the greatest missionary the church has ever had.

Name and define the class of words with which you have been dealing. Divide this class of words into sub-classes. State the bases of your divisions. Name and define each class.

See Whitney, par. 108, etc.
Lee & Hadley, p. 107.
Reed & Kellogg, Lesson 85.
Indiana Grammar, p. 13, etc.
System of Logic, John Stuart Mill, p. 22.
Everett's Science of Thought, Chap. Logic of Language.

In the following sentences, state the sex of the objects of thought expressed by the italicized words:

1. The *boy* learns rapidly.

2. The *girl* assists her *brother*.

3. The *child* was carried to its *mother*.

4. Willow *trees* grow rapidly.

5. The *eye* of *day* hath oped its *lid*.

Write the following words in two columns; in one column,,

write the masculine form of each word, and in the other, the feminine:

Bachelor, bride, sister, boy, cock, duck, earl, mother, gentleman, hart, female, man, Mr., sir, niece, son, aunt, Charles, Augustus, abbott, baron, hostess, actor, prior, benefactor, executor, murderer, sorcerer, man-servant, he-bear, female-descendant, cock-sparrow, Mr. Smith, pea-cock, poet, witch, lad, lion, heroine, prince, beau, duke, emperor, queen, husband, papa, negro, mistress, widow, goose, nun, deacon, heir, Jew, patron, governor, administrator, and prophet.

Notice the irregularities in the gender of the nouns in the following sentences, explain each:

1. The ship has lost her rudder.

2. The meek-eyed morn appears, mother of dews.

3. The sun in his glory appears; the moon in her wane hides her face.

4. The nightingale sings her song.

5. The lion meets his foe boldly.

6. The fox made his escape.

7. Heirs are often disappointed.

8. The English are a proud nation.

9. The poets of America should be honored.

10. The bee on its wing
    Never pauses to sing;
    The child in its weakness
    Is master of all.

What property of substantive words depends upon the above noticed distinctions? Define. How many kinds would we have? Why? Define each. Upon what basis is

G—6

this division made?   How are these different kinds of substantive words distinguished?

See Whitney's Essentials, paragraph, 115.
Meiklejohn, pp. 9 and 23.
Lee & Hadley, p. 123.
Southworth & Goddard, pp. 91 and 95.
Indiana Grammar, p. 49.

In the following sentences, state the relations of the objects of thought, expressed by the italicized words, to the
speaker:

1. *I, W. R. Merriam, governor* of *Minnesota,* declare *it* to
be true.

2. *I* hope, *John,* that *you* will remember that *character* is
more precious than *gold.*

3. *Tears* fall sometimes when *hearts* are least willing to
show *grief.*

4. *Mr. Sewell* has the pleasure of informing *Mr. Mason*
that *he* has been elected *president* of the literary *society.*

5. *You* are the *gentleman who* so kindly assisted *me.*

Name and define this property of substantive words.
State the different kinds or classes, and define and illustrate
each.   How is this property indicated in nouns?   How in
pronouns?   Illustrate.

See Welsh Greenwood, p. 67.
Whitney's Essentials of English Grammar, paragraphs 63, 141, 61,
151, 153 to 160, 164, and 177.
Lee & Hadley, pp. 112 to 116.
Indiana Grammar, p. 59.

State whether the italicized words, in the following sentences, express one or more than one individual:

1. *We* shall start for *California* in the *morning.*

2. *We* went from *New York* to *Philadelphia* in three *hours.*

3. *Birds* of beautiful *plumage* flew around us in great *numbers.*

4. In *my hurry, my foot* slipped, and *I* fell to the *ground.*

5. The cork *oak* grows in large *quantities* in the Spanish *peninsula.*

What is the property of substantive words observed in the preceding sentences called? Divide into classes, define and illustrate.

Write the following words in two columns; in one column, write the singular form of each word, and in the other the plural:

Book, desk, sin, church, witness, glory, sky, money, wife, knife, strife, life, fife, cargo, negro, folio, quarto, trio, no, men, ox, mice, teeth, geese, p, q, 6, 7, +, *, brother-in-law, courtmartial, wagon-load, ox-cart, handful, ipse dixit, tete-a-tetes, piano-forte, man-servant, Knight-templar, Miss Seward, Mr. Casad, Sir Isaac Newton, Dr. Benson, Mrs. Henderson, brother, die, fish, genius, index, penny, pea, Sarah, oh, my, ah, calculus, arcanum, criterion, thesis, analysis, antithesis, parenthesis, nebula, phenomena, calyx, strata, silver, vinegar, hemp, darkness, oil, ashes, assets, bellows, clothes, scissors, shears, tongs, news, molasses, lungs, alms, corps, mumps, measles, odds, riches, series, suds, tidings, wages, ethics, politics, mathematics, optics, physics, pedagogics, sheep, deer, couple, salmon, trout, gross, hose, yoke, hiss, adz, sash, embryo, grotto, oratorio, buffalo, mosquito, tomato, potato, valley, chimney, money, duty, spy, cow, foot, bandit, cherub, formula, memorandum, focus, terminus, erratum, medium, axis, genus, automaton, hypothesis, basis, crisis, elipsis, Mrs., Mr., eaves, custom, letter, number, pain, part, liberty, virtue, vices, attorney-general, head, belief, brief, bluff, cliff, staff, ditty, daisy, baby, buoy, turkey, berry, fairy, soliloquy, tray, Chinese, Japanese, forget-me-not.

How is this property indicated in nouns? State the general rule. State five or six special rules for the formation of plurals. What class of nouns change form and retain their identity? What classes may properly have this property and retain their identity? Illustrate.

See Whitney, par. 121 to 131.
Welsh-Greenwood, p. 72.
Southworth & Goddard, p. 163.
Lee & Hadley, p. 117 to 123.
Indiana Grammar, p. 49.

In the following sentences, state the relation of each italicized word to the other words in the sentence:

1. *Blue-Island* is a *town*, situated on a *bluff*, which rises abruptly from a *prairie*.

2. The best *features* of *King James's translation* of the *Bible* are derived from *Tyndale's version.*

3. *They* scaled *Mont Blanc*—the great *mountain*.

4. *St. Paul*, the *apostle*, was beheaded in the *reign* of *Nero*.

5. This *house* was *Longfellow*, the *poet's home*.

6. *James*, the *student*, is a *writer*—a *journalist*.

7. *You*, a *farmer*, may be a *scholar*.

8. *Children*, be honest and true.

9. *We* spoke of *Tennyson*, the dead *poet*.

10. *Blaine* died in *Washington City*, the *capital* of the *United States*.

11. *He* gave *me* the *book*.

12. *They* walked ten *miles*, a long *distance*.

13. *They* wished *him* to study *law*.

14. *His* being ill prevented *our* going.

15. The *law* of the *Lord* is perfect, rejoicing the *heart*.

Name and define the different kinds of relations which you have found substantive words to have in the preceding sentences. Bring to class one good example of the noun and one of the pronoun used in each of these possible relations.

How is the possessive case of the noun indicated?

Correct the spelling of nouns used in the possessive case in the following sentences:

1. The sailors life was in danger.
2. Mens destinies are in their own hands.
3. Childrens plays should be made a means of educating them.
4. Daniel Websters speeches are marvels of oratory.
5. The Bishop of Dublin palace was destroyed by fire.
6. Baker and Watsons store has been sold.
7. Webster and Worcesters Dictionaries are much in demand.
8. Her Majesty, Queen Victorias government has been much disturbed.
9. The captain of the Elbes wife was lost when the vessel sank.
10. The Knight-Templars costume was the most costly.
11. My brother-in-laws house was destroyed by fire.
12. Do no wrong for conscience sake.
13. "For goodness sake!" exclaimed the woman, "spare me my child!"
14. She had taken them all into her great heart—the boys sorrows and the girls cares.
15. Mrs. Cass' appearance gave life to the occasion.
16. Jonas Russ' slate made the noise.
17. I got the money changed at Sloan the druggist.

18. His character stands out when you compare it with his uncle Henry of Hanover.

19. I would not have taken anybody else word for it.

20. I have granted your request but not anybody else; who elses could I grant?

21. We frequently buy books at the book shop of Mr. Horns, on the Circle.

22. In spite of the guards precautions, the prisoner escaped.

23. Harris exposition of Hegels Logic will be found helpful to students.

24. James task was finished early.

25. Moses law was formal.

26. Frances share of the fortune was badly managed.

27. Xerxes army was victorious.

28. The woman would accept neither her neighbors nor the countys offers of assistance.

29. Joris strength failed before he got to Aix.

30. I arranged for the money at Hill the Banker.

See Foundations of Rhetoric, A. S. Hill, pp. 41 and 42.

Read the following references:

Composition Grammar, Bain, p. 20.
Lee & Hadley, pp. 128 to 137 inclusive.        •
Meiklejohn, p. 19.
Whitney, paragraphs 68 to 76.
Southworth & Goddard, pp. 193 and 168.
Indiana Grammar, p. 59.

What is meant by inflection?    Illustrate.

From the expressions inclosed in the marks of parenthesis in each of the following sentences, select the correct one:

1. I had a full understanding of (the fact's significance, the significance of the fact).

2. (Congress' act, the act of congress) was approved by the people.

3. (My wife's picture, picture by my wife) became famous.

4. He is a stranger (in the midst of us, in our midst).

5. Do not remain (on our account, on account of us).

6. He carried (a dice, die) in his vest pocket as a mascot.

7. The millennium is yet a long (way, ways) off.

8. The news (was, were) received with great demonstration.

9. (This, these) news created great consternation.

10. He rose to distinction between the twenty-fourth and twenty-fifth (year, years) of his life.

11. Are you an (alumni, alumnus) of this school?

12. When I looked, I saw a (bacterium, bacteria).

13. Do you approve the change in the (curricula, curriculum)?

14. (This, these) scanty data (is, are) not sufficient.

15. Agassiz's (dictum, dicta) was, "Study the fish."

16. This (phenomenon, phenomena) was observed many times.

17. Did you see the (harpist, harper) who played the beautiful air?

18. Do you expect a (rise, raise) in wages?

19. Is this the (person, party) in question?

20. We are not looking at the question from the same (point of view, standpoint).

Note.—The students should be given general exercises in writing different forms for the noun and pronoun, used in expressing gender, person, number, and case.

Sum up with an outline, indicating all you have learned concerning the noun.

### The Pronoun.

In the following sentences, point out the pronouns and state the relation between the object of thought, expressed by each one, and the speaker. Or state whether the object of thought, expressed by the pronoun, is the speaker, the person spoken to, or the person or thing spoken of. State what it is in the sentence or the word which gives you this information :

1. I am a poor man myself, and I can sympathize with him.
2. Nathan said to him, " Thou art the man."
3. He, himself, acknowledged his fault to me.
4. The book which the child has is not worth reading.
5. The point was well stated by the child, when he saw it.
6. You who are blest with plenty should be kind to the poor.
7. They who sow in folly shall reap in sorrow.
8. · Blessed are they that mourn, for they shall be comforted.
9. Freely ye have received ; freely give.
10. Lay not up for yourselves treasures on earth.
11. We, ourselves, are at fault.
12. Who killed Cock Robin?
13. Our fathers, where are they ?
14. Which did you enjoy more, Fiske or Ridpath?

Separate the pronouns into classes. Give the basis of the division. Define and illustrate each class. State how the pronoun is like the noun, and how it differs from it. What is meant by antecedent? Give literal meaning of the word. Name all the pronouns in each class and give all their forms.

State the antecedents of the following italicized pronouns. State the gender, person, and number of the pronouns. How do you determine these properties?  State any irregularity which you may discover.  Give the rule in the case:

1.  Each soldier drew *his* battle blade.
2.  He liveth long *who* liveth well.
3.  One's manners show *his* breeding.
4.  The person who doeth good has *his* reward.
5.  If any person in the audience objects, *he* will please stand.
6.  The poor widow lost *her* only son.
7.  True to *his* flag, the soldier braved even death.
8.  A pupil *that* is studious will learn.
9.  *He who* runs may read.
10.  *He* desired to pray but *it* was denied *him*.
11.  *He* has squandered *his* money and *he* now regrets *it*.
12.  *You* are here on time, Henry.
13.  *You* are good children.
14.  *Mine* eyes have seen the glory of the coming of the Lord.
15.  *Thine* ears have heard the joyful sound.
16.  " *We* formerly thought differently but now have changed *our* mind," wrote the editor.
17.  *It* thundered as *it* seemed to *me*.
18.  Come and trip *it* on the green.
19.  Which way *I* fly is hell; *myself* am hell.
20.  Try to see *yourself* as others see *you*.

How are the compound personal pronouns formed?  State their uses in the sentence.

21.  Let every pupil use *his own* book.
22.  If any one be found at fault, do unto *him* as you would wish to be done by.
23.  *You, he,* and *I* were boys together.
24.  A friend and *I* were talking the matter over.

25.　*Whoever* comes will take your place.
26.　I must do *whatever* seems best.
27.　I will give you *whatsoever* is right.
28.　They censure *whomever* I commend.
29.　They wist not *what* it was.
30.　I will call *whomever* you ask.

How are the compound relative pronouns formed?　What determines their case forms?

Explain the use of the italicized words in the following sentences:

1.　*Who* discovered America?
2.　*Who* were killed?
3.　*Which* are the boys in trouble?
4.　*Which* is the Jew and *which* the merchant here?
5.　*What* are these people?
6.　*What* is the man?
7.　I know *who* killed Cock Robin.
8.　I will tell you *what* I will take.
9.　I know *which* is most valuable.
10.　I see *which* will come next.

From the expressions enclosed in the marks of parenthesis in each of the following sentences, select the correct one:

1. (Its, it's) tower leaned.
2. Is that friend of (your's, yours) with you yet?
3. He was a man (as, who) could be depended upon.
4. He adopts the same rules in Sunday-school (as, that) he adopts in his day school.
5. Such devices (which, as) you have in mind are important.
6. He now thinks that foolish (which, what) he once thought wise.
7. (What, whatever) can the man want?

8. I cannot~pay (the two of, both of) them.

9. Oh, if it had only been (me, I)!

10. You and (I, me) are invited.

11. Our father brought you and (I, me) a present.

12. Wretched people console themselves when they see many who are quite as (bad, badly) off as (them, they).

13. Let (him, he) who made thee, answer this.

14. You are somewhat taller than (me, I).

15. There is no one that I like better than (he, him).

16. I was sure of its being (he, him).

17. I do not mind (his, him) going out evenings.

18. He was associated with Longfellow and other poets for (which, whom) America is noted.

19. (Who, whom) shall the party put forward?

20. Find out (who, whom) the hat belongs to.

21. (Who, whom) could that be?

22. I saw my friend (who, whom) I had once thought would succeed in business, fail.

23. She lived with an aunt (who, whom) she said, treated her shamefully.

24. Then came another man (who, whom) they all declared, was the best of the performers.

25. Under this tree (the bark of which, whose bark) is scarred in many places, Washington took command of the army.

26. This is a point (the consideration of which, whose consideration) has caused much trouble.

27. This is the tree (that, which) was struck by lightning.

28. To come so near winning the prize and yet lose it. I could never stand (it, that).

29. She is a better student than (any one, either) of her three brothers.

30. (Either, any one) of the ten points is worth remembering, but the (latter, last) is most essential.

31. (All, each) of the children took an apple.

32. I am (the one, he, the person) who signaled the train.

33. He gets Emerson's ideas (the ones, those) that are most essential, on first reading.

34. When (one, a person, we) (comes, come) to think of it, (he, one, we) (takes, take) (one's, his, our) (life, lives) in (one's, his, our) (hand, hands) every time (one, he, we) (boards, board) a train.

35. If any one has lost baggage, the matter will be investigated for (you, him) free of charge.

36. Soldier after soldier took up the cry, and added (their, his) voice to the mighty din.

37. Every one was absorbed in (his or her, his, their) own pleasure, or was bitterly resenting the absence of the pleasure (he or she, he, they) expected.

38. Everybody thought it was right to extend (his, their) sympathy.

39. I like to see each of them doing well—in (their, his) own way at least.

40. Anybody can catch trout, if (he, they) can find the trout.

41. Everybody was there, if (he, they) could possibly go.
See Foundations of Rhetoric, A. S. Hill, p. 76.

42. He heard of a man whose life had been spent on the water and (whose, his) record was good.

43. The undersigned is sorry to say that he took a hat from the rack which is not (mine, his).

44. When I close my eyes, I can see pictures like (the ones, those) presented.

45. The two brothers love (one another, each other).

• Fill the following blanks with the proper forms of the compound relative pronoun, *whoever:*

1. The old man put the question to —— he met.
2. I am satisfied with —— you have selected.
3. I am ready to entertain —— may be sent.
4. The Lord loveth —— doeth His will.
5. You must restore —— book you have taken.
6. Make yourself agreeable to —— you meet.
7. Tell the truth to —— asks it.
8. Contest the ground with —— opposes you.
9. The lady inquired of —— she saw.
10. The missionary preached to —— remained.

Read the following references:

Lee & Hadley, pp. 36 and 37, and pp. 130 to 158 inclusive.
Whitney, par. 33, 34, 58, 70, 75, 61, 149, 190, 468, 470, 481, 40, 376.
Welsh-Greenwood, p. 88.
Meikeljohn, pp. 23, 28, 74, 76.
Indiana Grammar, pp. 17, 54 and 59.
Composition Grammar, Bain, p. 5.

Make an outline of the pronoun covering those points given in the outline of the noun.

––––––––

### The Adjective.

Point out the adjectives in the following sentences. Divide them into as many different classes as the fundamental differences among them would indicate. State your basis of division in each case. Define and illustrate each kind:

1. A beautiful, pink sea-shell was found by little Mary on the sandy beach.
2. Large and small streams flow from great mountains.
3. Fine feathers do not make fine birds.

4. Bob looked with longing eyes at the red cranberry sauce and steaming turkey.

5. Soft, fleecy clouds o'er hung the sky.

6. Give us this day our daily bread.

7. The children are having a gala time.

8. The fresh-looking youth was very much embarrassed.

9. The new-born babe received the gifts of the wise men.

10. Those islands belong to the United States.

11. These rude instruments were used by this savage people.

12. All the government officials are well paid.

13. Yonder pond contains fish.

14. That book was written by John Fiske.

15. This proposition is unreasonable.

15. Which way did he go?

17. What book do you most prefer?

18. I know which way the deer went.

19. I see what books are needed.

See Whitney, Par. 210.

20. A few ducks were seen by the sportsmen.

21. Some money was earned by the boy.

22. Each warrior drew his battle blade.

23. Every man stood to his post.

24. Neither man was right, and yet I would not censure either one.

25. We were interested in watching two large prairie fires.

26. Fifty men were in line.

27. James is the third pupil in the row.

28. Washington was the first President of the United States.

29. This is a threefold punishment.

30. Let us make a double house.

Explain the use of the following italicized expressions. How do they differ? What is the cause of this difference?

1. *Tall* trees are easily blown over.
2. I am *taller* than my father.
3. The *tallest* boy in the room is also the *best* scholar.
4. The boy is a *good* scholar.
5. To be is *better* than to seem.
6. A teacher may be *pleasant* and at the same time *strict ;* in fact, the *more pleasant* she is, the *more strict* she can afford to be.
7. While she is the *most strict* mother I know, she is also the *most pleasant* with her children.

What is this difference among adjectives, which you have just been explaining, called? Define it. What classes or kinds do you discover? State the basis of your division. Define and illustrate each kind. When is each kind used? Observe, in the above sentences, how this property of adjectives is indicated. State the different ways and illustrate each.

State the use of the italicized expressions in the following sentences:

1. The *white* rose is *beautiful.*
2. He who dares stand for the right, though he stand alone, is *truly* brave.
3. The river is a *mile* broad.
4. The girl is cruel to *her pets.*
5.                 A child's kiss
Set on thy *sighing* lips, shall make thee *glad ;*
A *poor* man served by thee, shall make thee *rich ;*
A *sick* man helped by thee, shall make thee *strong ;*
Thou shalt be served thyself by *every* sense
Of service which thou renderest.

State the uses of the adjective and modifiers which may belong to it.    Illustrate.

State the meaning of each of the following words when used as adjectives.    Compare the words in cases in which such comparison will help to bring out the meaning more clearly :

| each | this | which | few |
|------|------|-------|-----|
| every | these | what | less |
| either | that | the | only |
| neither | those | a or an | |
| each other | | one another | |

See Foundations of Rhetoric, A. S. Hill, p. 32.

Use the following adjectives correctly, in sentences : Beautiful, magnificent, pretty, handsome, awful, dreadful, lovely, those, drowned, fewer, less, healthy, healthful, much, most, nice, well, mad, angry, vexed, plenty, quite a, a considerable, a great, a large, real, elegant, opposite, contrary.

From the expressions enclosed in the marks of parenthesis in each of the following sentences, select the correct one :

1. The boy was permitted to go (everywhere, everywheres).

2. My daughter may be described as (having a light complexion, being light-complected).

3. We thus had more, not (less, fewer) friends.

4. One can hardly think of a man (more, better) suited to the place.

5. The people had never seen a (costlier, more costlier) equipage.

6. This is true of (most, almost) all my friends.

7. Nobody was (like, likely) to see him.

8. The town was (quite, plenty) large enough.

9. There isn't a (sightlier, finer) place in town.

10. Do you like (this, these) sort of books?

11. How do you like (that, those) kind of gowns?

12. This point is (easiest, most easily) seen.

13. My conscience feels (easily, easy).

14. The girl looked (prettily, pretty).

15. The teacher feels (bad, badly) to-day.

16. The party went (solid, solidly) for free trade.

17. She was not (only, alone) a true woman, but a kind friend also.

18. The boy (only) tried (only) three times.

19. That they use money is true of (both, each) (parties, party).

20. (Each, every) dog has his day.

21. (Each, every) day in the year should be the happiest day.

22. We should avoid (many, much) of the baser struggles of life.

23. He has caught (many, much) fish to-day.

24. Will (all, the whole) finance ministers and upholsterers and confectioners of modern Europe undertake, in joint-stock company, to make one shoe-black happy?

25. Of the states of the union named, the (first four, four first) were the last admitted.

26. He says some very (aggravating, irritating) things.

27. In consequence of (aggravating, irritating) circumstances, he was punished severely.

28. The statement seems hardly (creditable, credible).

29. Here, too, Sydney Carton is an (exceptional, exceptionable) man.

30. I shall not go (further, farther).

G—7

31. Rice is (healthy, healthful, wholesome) food.

32. The scene from the window was (luxuriant, luxurious).

33. The boy told a (pitiable, pitiful) story.

34. The spider spins a (subtle, subtile) web.

35. There is a (continual, continuous) hurry to be off.

36. The sky gradually became (cloudless, more and more cloudless).

37. The shouts gradually became (more and more inaudible, inaudible).

38. In this characteristic, Coleridge is (unique, most unique).

39. The vote was (so nearly unanimous, so unanimous) that the crowd shouted.

40. We go about, professing openly (total isolation, the totalist isolation).

See Elements of Composition and Grammar, Southworth & Goddard, p. 60, etc.

The Dictionary.

The Study of Words, Trench, p. 248, etc.

Indiana Grammar, pp. 21 and 65.

Make a complete outline of the adjective, showing definition, classes on different bases, properties and syntax.

***

### The Verb.

In the following sentences, state the use of each italicized expression. Note how one differs from the other and classify them. Name and define each class:

1. The sun *is* ninety-two millions of miles away.

2. The soldier *was* without food for three days.

3. Tom Brown *has been* in many escapades.
4. The sun *gives* light and heat.
5. The general *gave* his orders in a very loud tone.
6. Leland Stanford *has given* a great deal of money to found a university at Palo Alto.
7. The minister frequently *quotes* from the Talmud.
8. The speaker *quoted* Webster in support of his view.
9. The attorney *has quoted* much that is not to the point.
10. Not to know me, *argues* yourself unknown.
11. They *argued* the point an hour.
12. I *have argued* the question from every point of view.

Be able to give the principal parts of the following verbs:

| | | | | |
|---|---|---|---|---|
| abide | do | lead | shake | stick |
| awake | draw | lean | shall | sting |
| be | dream | leap | shear | stink |
| bear | drink | learn | shed | stride |
| beat | drive | leave | shine | strike |
| begin | dwell | lend | shoe | string |
| bend | eat | let | shoot | strive |
| bereave | fall | lie | show | strow,-ew |
| beseech | feed | light | shred | swear |
| bid | feel | lose | shrink | sweat |
| bind | fight | make | shut | sweep |
| bite | find | may | sing | swim |
| bleed | flee | mean | sink | swing |
| blow | fling | meet | sit | take |
| break | fly | mote | slay | teach |
| breed | forsake | must | sleep | tear |
| bring | freeze | need | slide | tell |
| build | freight | ought | sling | think |
| burn | get | pen | slink | thrive |

| | | | | |
|---|---|---|---|---|
| burst | gild | put | slit | throw |
| buy | gird | quit | smell | thrust |
| can | give | quoth | smite | tread |
| cast | go | read | sow | wake |
| catch | grind | reave | speak | wax |
| chide | grow | rend | speed | wear |
| choose | hang | rid | spell | weave |
| cleave | have | ride | spend | weep |
| cling | hear | ring | spill | wend |
| clothe | heave | rise | spin | wet |
| come | hide | run | spit | whet |
| cost | hit | say | split | will |
| creep | hold | see | spoil | win |
| crow | hurt | seek | spread | wind |
| cut | keep | seethe | spring | wit |
| dare | kneel | sell | stand | work |
| deal | knit | send | stave | wring |
| dig | know | set | steal | write |

See Elements of Composition and Grammar, Southworth & Goddard, p. 236.

Whitney, p. 135 and read the references there given.

Conklin's English Grammar and Composition, par. 738.

English Grammar, Meiklejohn, p. 44.

Lee & Hadley, p. 181.

Studies in English Grammar, Welsh-Greenwood, p, 121.

Indiana Grammar, p. 84.

Be able to fill the following blanks with any appropriate verb from the preceding list. Omit the word, *it*, if necessary to make the form suit the meaning of the verb:

1. I —— it now.
2. I —— it a week ago.
3. I have —— it lately.
4. He —— it now.

5. He —— it a week ago.
6. He has —— it lately.
7. They may —— to-day.
8. They —— yesterday.
9. They had —— before you came.

Fill the following blanks with the proper forms of *speak* and *write:*

1. She —— very well.
2. You have —— too soon.
3. I should have —— sooner.
4. Have they —— to you?
5. Has James —— to you about it?
6. Who said you had —— about it?

Supply the proper forms of *do:*

1. I —— as I was told.
2. My work is——.
3. Who —— the mischief?
4. The boy has —— his work well.
5. Who said I —— that?
6. Sarah —— it herself.
7. Mary —— her example.

Insert the proper forms of *choose.*

1. I — the blue pencil.
2. Americans —— freedom of thought.
3. I —— to go ashore.
4. Henry was —— first.
5. My sister herself —— the goods.
6. He should have been ——.
7. Will you —— first?

Insert the proper forms of *raise* or *rise* in the following:

1. He —— from the chair.

   2. I have —— as early as five.

   3. He that would thrive must —— by five.

   4. Have you —— the window?

   5. Have you —— from your chair?

   6. What makes the bread ——?

   7. Yeast —— the bread.

   8. The sun —— at six.

   9. The river has —— a great deal.

  10. I saw the sun —— this morning.

  11. I cannot —— this window.

  12. The sun —— at five this morning.

  13. The sun has ——.

  14. I wish you would —— from the floor.

In the following sentences, fill the blanks with the proper forms of *lie, lay, sit, set, teach, learn, seem, appear, love,* or *like:*

   1. The boy —— up straight.

   2. I have —— up long enough.

   3. —— the lamp on the table and —— by me.

   4. James —— for his picture to-day.

   5. I can —— my lesson.

   6. Will you —— me to write?

   7. How long will it take you to —— me?

   8. I cannot —— my lesson.

   9. Will you —— me to skate?

  10. Do not ask me to —— you.

  11. You will not —— me to swim.

  12. He —— down to rest.

  13. He —— the book down.

  14. He had —— down to rest.

  15. He had —— the book down.

  16. He has —— the book down.

  17. I will —— down and rest.

18. I will —— my pen down.
19. A man is —— on the porch.
20. James is —— out tomato plants.
21. The sun is just ——.
22. I am —— still.
23. I am tired of —— so still.
24. She is —— near the window.
25. The —— sun looks red.
26. Belle is —— under a tree in the yard.
27. She is —— to be satisfied.
28. The dress —— to be new.
29. The day —— fine.
30. Did she —— to be contented?
31. The moon —— over the hill.
32. How did he —— to be?
33. It —— to be red.
34. The man —— to be well pleased.
35. I hope you will —— well.
36. I can —— well if I wish to.
37. The storm —— to be passing over.
38. The sun —— between the clouds.
39. I —— my brother.
40. The boy —— his sister.
41. Do you —— oranges.
42. The child —— its parents, who are dead.
43. I —— his appearance very much.
44. Do you —— amusements?
45. They —— Nat Goodwin.

Note.—Other devices requiring the pupils to use the different forms of irregular verbs in sentences, should be invented by the teacher. For example, the teacher, rising from her chair, says:

"What do I do, Kate?"

Kate : " You rise from your chair."

Teacher : " What did I do, Tom ?"

Tom : " You rose from your chair."

Teacher : " What have I done, Ned ?"

Ned : " You have risen from your chair."

The teacher then breaks a piece of chalk, or writes on the board, or chooses a book, or speaks loudly, etc., etc., and asks the same questions. The exercise may be continued at will.

Classify the following italicized expressions on the basis previously discovered. State how the attributes expressed differ. State what classes of verbs we have on basis of this difference. Define and illustrate each class :

1. *Hitch* your wagon to a star.

2. Fulton *invented* the steamboat.

3. The robin *picked* the crumbs after hopping in at the window.

4. We *heard* a highly instructive lecture.

5. We *walked* along the fragrant lanes.

6. We *talked* of pleasant times in olden days.

7. We *journeyed* through the fields together.

8. John Anderson, my jo John,

   We *clam* the hills thegither ;

   And mony a canty day, John,

   We've *had* wi' ane anither :

   Now we *maun totter* down, John,

   But hand in hand we'll *go ;*

   And *sleep* thegither at the foot,

   John Anderson, my jo.

State how the following italicized expressions differ from the other verbs with which you have been dealing. What are such verbs called ? Define and illustrate further :

1. " It *snows ?*" cries the schoolboy.

Mäetzner's Eng. Grammar, Vol. II., p. 14.

2. It *rains* the livelong day, and mournful is the house.

3. They *die* the death of the righteous.

New English Grammar, H. Sweet, p. 91.

4. I have *fought* a good fight; I have finished the faith.

5. He *blew* a blast upon the winding horn.

6. I will *run* as far as God has any ground.

7. You *call* me unbeliever, cut-throat dog,
And *spit* upon my Jewish garberdine,
And all for use of that which is mine own.

8. I will *buy* with you, *sell* with you, *talk* with you, *walk* with you, and so following, but I will not *eat* with you, *drink* with you, nor *pray* with you.

9. If I *forget* thee, O Jerusalem, let my right hand forget her cunning.

10. I *will* never leave thee, nor *forsake* thee.

11. I *may* never see you again.

12. I *may* neither choose whom I would nor refuse whom I dislike.

13. Is it not hard, Nerissa, that I *cannot* choose one nor refuse none?

14. "By my troth," *quoth* he, "you're a bold man."

15. It *must* not be.

16. One *ought* to love his neighbor as himself.

17. Every one *owes* himself an education.

18. He *forces* himself to be generous.

New English Grammar, H. Sweet, p. 92.
Mäetzner's English Grammar, Vol. I., p. 322.

19. Christ *made* the water wine.

New English Grammar, H. Sweet, pp. 95 and 96.

20. The traveler *walked* himself weary.

21. The singer *sang* her throat hoarse.

22. The lightning *struck* him dead.

23. He *has* told the story many times.

24. This above all: to thine own self be true,
    And it *must* follow, as the night the day,
    Thou *canst* not then be false to any man.

25. Child, thou *wilt* not leave thy mother so?

26. Thou *shalt* not bear false witness against thy neighbor.

27. We *do* reject the offer.

28. What *should* such fellows as I do crawling between earth and heaven?

29. He *does* confess he feels himself distracted;
    But from what cause, he *will* by no means speak.

Get the literal meaning of the following words: have, can, may, must, do, be, shall, and will. (See Century Dictionary.)

Fill the following blanks with *may* or *can:*

1. —— I ask a question?

2. I —— start yet to-night.

3. Please, —— I take your book?

4. The boy —— do better work.

5. How far —— you ride?

6. The eagle —— carry off a child.

7. —— you see where you are going?

8. You —— take a walk.

9. —— stars be suns?

10. How —— you bear to leave?

State the difference between the meaning of the auxiliaries *may* and *can.*

Composition Grammar, Bain, p. 197.
Lee and Hadley's Grammar, pp. 189-190.
Reed and Kellogg's Grammar, Lesson 31.
Metcalf's Grammar, p. 245.

Maxwell's Grammar, p. 227.
Whitney's Grammar, par. 369, 370.
Miietzner's English Grammar, Vol. I., p. 322.
How To Parse, Abbott, p. 91.

State the meaning conveyed by the following italicized expressions:

1. I *shall* see Salvini.
2. I *shall* be drowned; no one can save me.
3. You *shall* go.    "
4. He *shall* return at once.
5. *Shall* I assist you in mounting?
6. *Shall* I be obliged to pay the debt for him?
7. *Shall* you be at school this afternoon?
8. *Shall* you suffer for his offense?
9. *Shall* the boy bring the carriage?
10. "I *will* be revenged," said Philip.
11. I *will* be a good boy.
12. You *will* find me there.
13. You *will* obey me.
14. He *will* leave to-morrow.
15. He *will* apologize to you.
16. *Will* I give up my principle?
17. *Will* you persist in your reckless course?
18. *Will* the deed return to the doer?
19. *Will* he let you have your choice?
20. *Will* the house that is built upon a rock fall?

See, "Shall and Will," by Sir Edward Head.
How To Parse, Abbott, pp. 68, 118, 151.
Foundations of Rhetoric, A. S. Hill, p. 83.
Composition Grammar, Bain, p. 179.
Public School Journal, Jan., '95, p. 242.

Fill the following blanks with the proper forms of *shall* or *will*:

1. He —— preach in the evening.
2. —— you go with us?
3. You —— have your way.
4. You can learn, if you —— study.
5. We —— vote early.
6. We —— go in spite of you.
7. They —— go, if they can.
8. She —— not be allowed to go home alone.
9. You —— have gone before we arrive.
10. We —— be avenged.
11. If you see him, you —— find him busy.
12. —— you dine with us to-morrow?
13. I —— read awhile.
14. —— I see him?
15. —— I read to you?
16. You —— have your money to-day.
17. He —— be punished for it.
18. I —— be happy to accept.
19. I —— die ere I —— obey him.
20. God —— not give us any more truth than we are willing to live.

Composition Grammar, Bain, p. 197.

State the relation in each case, in the following sentences, between the thought expressed by the sentence, and the fact in the external world. State whether the thought expressed by the sentence is a reality; or whether there is some doubt in the mind as to its reality; or whether it is a mere supposition, and there is no fact in the external world corresponding to it; or if the thought in the mind corresponds to the fact in the external world on account of necessity in external circumstances, or will, outside of that of the actor:

1. I can see the towers of London.

2. Blessed is the man that walketh not in the counsels of the ungodly.

3. The mill will never grind with the water that is past.

4. My soul to-day is far away,
   Sailing the Vesuvian bay.

5. The pen is mightier than the sword.

6. His work, in many respects, is very imperfect.

7. Slovenliness and indelicacy of character generally go together.

8. When thy friend is denounced openly and boldly, espouse his cause.

9. Plutarch calls lying the vice of slaves.

10. An upright mind will never be at a loss to discern what is just and true, lovely, honest, and of good report.

11. If 't were done when 't is done, then 't were well,
    It were done quickly.

12. If he has been here, I have not seen him.

13. I he were here, I should like to meet him.

14. If thou hadst been here, my brother had not died.

15. If thou be brave, I will conduct thee through this wilderness.

16. Were it not for leaving thee, my child, I could die happy.

17. He may study his lessons.

18. He may take my book.

19. If thou hadst said him nay, it had been sin.

20. It must be true.

21. Give me your hand.

22. Let this cup pass from me.

23. Down, slave, behold the governor!
    Down, Down! and beg for mercy.

24. Thou shalt not steal.

25. Turn ye! Turn ye again, O Israel!

What property of the verb is illustrated in the preceding sentences? Define. State the different kinds or classes and illustrate each.

Composition Grammar, Bain, pp. 168, 177.

See Whitney, par. 233 to 235 inclusive, 478 and 480.

Elements of Composition and Grammar, Southworth & Goddard, par. 441 to 448 inclusive.

Brown's Grammar of English Grammars, pp. 336-340.

Studies in English Grammar, Welsh-Greenwood, p. 127.

Lee & Hadley, p. 198.

Indiana Grammar, pp. 72 and 76.

How To Parse, Abbott, pp. 69, 112, 224, 198.

State whether the relation seen to exist between the thought subject and thought predicate, as expressed in each of the following sentences, is a relation which is seen to exist in present time, or past time, or future time. State whether we use one or more than one of these periods of time in locating the relation:

1. The leaves tremble in the wind.

2. The sun is shining brightly.

3. Columbus discovered America in 1492.

4. We saw General Grant.

5. We shall attend the World's Fair.

6. Will you permit that I shall stand condemned?

7. Feelest thou not, O world, the earthquake of his chariot thundering up Olympus?

8. How sleep the brave, that sink to rest
    By all their country's wishes blest!

9. My sister was gathering flowers.

10. Be aye sticking in a tree, Jack; it'll be growing while ye're sleeping.

11. I have cautioned you frequently.

12. Wilfred had roused him to reply.

13. When I shall have brought them into the land, then will they turn to other gods.

14. I have sung my song.

15. I had sung the song before you arrived.

16. I shall have sung the song before you arrive.

17. By slow degrees the whole truth has come out.

18. Matilda had taken her accustomed place in the window-seat.

19. I shall have seen all the wonders, when I write to you.

20. Plans and elevations of their palace have been made for them, and are now being engraved for the public.

State the property of the verb illustrated in the preceding sentences. Define. State the different classes or kinds, and define and illustrate each.

State the tense of each verb in the following sentences; state the time in which the relation between thought subject and thought predicate is seen to exist:

1. He hears his daughter's voice.

2. Man is mortal.

3. The man travels for Hermand and Knox.

4. My brother goes to New York to-morrow on business.

5. They cross the river; they fire the town; they form under the cover of the smoke; they advance up the hill; they are driven back.

6. I see the nation gathering her forces for the mighty struggle; they put forth one mighty effort and the end comes.

7. The little birds sang gayly in the trees.

8. He preached in this little hamlet for many years.

9. If I should be there, you would be surprised.

10. If my sister were here, she would enjoy the lecture.

11. The teachers will go to Denver the coming summer.

12. He will wander in the woods day after day.

13. Milton has given us Comus.

14. The hour shall not strike till I have gained my point.

15. He had written the poem before this book appeared.

16. If I had walked rapidly, I should have overtaken you.

17. At the close of this year, I shall have finished my course.

18.   The truth itself is not believed
      From one who often has deceived.

See Reed and Kellogg, Lesson 138.

See Whitney, par. 64, 213, 256, and 279 to 305 inclusive.

Lee & Hadley, p. 176.

Reed & Kellogg, Lessons 131 and 138.

Studies in English grammar, Welsh-Greenwood, pp. 129 and 188.

Southworth & Goddard, par. 431, 440, 508, 511, 608, 494, 434, 437, 479, 482 and 489–494.

Indiana Grammar, pp. 72 and 75.

State concerning the verbs in the following sentences, whether the attribute expressed by them is an attribute exerted by the thought subject and directed away from it, or whether it is exerted by some other object of thought and is directed toward or exerted upon the thought subject:

1.   The engine draws the train.

2.   The story has been told by many writers.

3.   England had taxed the colonies unjustly.

4.   Marco Polo tells us strange stories.

5.   The Mississippi was discovered by De Soto in 1541.

6.   The prudent neither waste time nor money.

7.   Paris was besieged by the Prussians in 1871.

8.   Every patriot will defend the flag.

9.   Our friends came last week.

10.   We were entertained in royal style.

11. The singer was fatigued by his exertions.
12. The traveler was weary.
13. The minister was fatigued.
14. I go where duty calls me.
15. The soldier was sleepy and tired.

Name and define the property of the verb illustrated in the preceding sentences. State the different kinds or classes. Define and illustrate each class. State and illustrate the different ways in which the passive voice may be formed from the active. When does the combination of the past participle with the different forms of the verb, *be*, form the passive voice; when does it not form the passive voice?

See Whitney, par. 302.
Indiana Grammar, p. 87.

State all the uses of the passive voice. Illustrate each by two or more examples.

In the following sentences, state whether the verbs are active or passive:

1. If she hate me, then believe,
   She shall die ere I will grieve.
2. Where shall we dine to-day?
3. He that complies against his will
   Is of the same opinion still.
4. Frequently the exordium is too long, and the peroration interminable.
5. The mother loves her child.
6. The speaker corrected himself.
7. I hold it true with him who sings,
   To one clear harp in divers tones,
   That men may rise on stepping-stones,
   Of their dead selves to higher things.

G—8

8.   The train was wrecked at midnight.
9.   The slave was devoted to his master.
10.   The truth, conned from the book by many readers, was carried away in their hearts.

See Lee & Hadley, p. 193.
Whitney, paragraphs 301 to 306 inclusive.
Southworth & Goddard, par. 499 and 504.
Studies in English Grammar, Welsh-Greenwood, p. 140.
Reed & Kellogg, pp. 229–233, Lessons 129 and 130.

Notice the person and number of each subject in the following sentences.   Note the change in the verb to accommodate the change in the subject :

1.   I know that my Redeemer liveth.
2.   He knows where the wild flowers grow.
3.   They know how the wild flowers grow.
4.   The scissors are dull.
5.   Evil news rides post, while good news baits.
6.   The tongs are hot.
7.   The sheep was fast in the fence.
8.   The sheep were driven to the pond and washed.
9.   The school was dismissed for the holidays.
10.   The school were not all present.
11.   Henry, William, and Charles were kings.
12.   The boy or his father is at fault.
13.   Each man, woman, and child was given a prize.
14.   Every boy and every girl is expected to be obedient.
15.   The officers and not the private were at fault.
16.   The children, or the servant, or I am to blame.
17.   Red, white, and blue makes a pretty flag.
18.   Grace and beauty is a desirable combination.
19.   "Paint me as I am," said Cromwell.

20. "You are excused," said the teacher, in a pleasant voice.

21. He is the freeman, whom the truth makes free.

22. Thou art a pretty fellow!

23. The storm was dreadful along the Atlantic coast.

24. The islands were beautiful as we sailed in and out among them.

25. 'Tis as easy as lying.

26. He prayeth best who loveth best
All things, both great and small.

27. Thou standst on the threshold of life.

28. Thou waitest for the coming of thy mate.

29. Thou pretty child, why weepest thou?

30. I dare do all that may become a man;
Who dares do more is none.

What is meant by person and number in the verb? In what sense may it be said to be a property of the verb? What changes in form does the verb undergo to denote person and number? By observing the preceding sentences, state the different kinds of subjects and how the verb accommodates itself in form, to the form of the subject.

Read Whitney, par. 59 to 64 inclusive, and 228 to 231 inclusive.
Reed & Kellogg, pp. 234, 235, and 260 to 263 inclusive, Lessons 131 and 142.
Southworth & Goddard, par. 449–455.
Indiana Grammar, p. 69.

Fill the following blanks with suitable verbs:

1. Either of you —— able to do it.
2. Each of the —— studied the lesson.
3. Neither of the prisoners —— guilty of the charge.
4. No one of the animals —— dangerous.
5. Neither of them —— ten years old.

6. No one of the men —— escaped.

7. Every man, woman, and child —— lost.

8. Neither of the boats —— injured.

9. The ashes —— light.

10. Oats —— a good price.

11. The molasses —— fine.

12. The news —— bad.

13. Politics —— his delight.

14. The deer —— pursued by the hunter.

15. Truth and Mercy —— met in the way.

16. Righteousness and Peace —— kissed each other.

17. The lion and the lamb —— lain down together.

18. Elegance and ease —— a combination which pleases.

Give the literal meaning of the word, *conjugation*. What is meant by the conjugation of the verb? Illustrate with any verb.

See Whitney, par. 239, etc.

Give the literal meaning of the word, *synopsis*. What is meant by the synopsis of the verb? Illustrate with any verb.

Observe the form of the verb in each of the following sentences. State how the forms differ. What difference in meaning does this difference in form indicate? Name, define, and illustrate the different forms which the verb may have:

1. I study my lessons carefully before coming to recitation.

2. Men rise above their animal natures and become divine.

3. I was studying when you called.

4. The sun was rising as we started.

5. The boy does study diligently.

6. I do rise betimes.

7. Do you study Astronomy?

8. Do men rise in the world by mere chance?

9. I do not study when I should be sleeping.

10. Men do not rise in the world, because they do not put forth an effort to do so.

11. A bad man can have no possessions that are fire proof.

12. No man is right on any question unless the side he takes is God's side.

13. The man gains nothing who loses his character and saves his money.

14. For every fault we see in others, we have two of our own which we overlook.

15. He who thinks loosely will write loosely.

See Whitney, par. 295.

Studies in English Grammar, Welsh-Greenwood, pp. 134 and 140.

Indiana Grammar, p. 77.

Make a complete outline of the verb, including definition, classes, properties, etc.

From the expressions enclosed in the marks of parenthesis in each of the following sentences, select the correct one:

1. The passenger (allows, admits, declares) that the time for starting has come.

2. The child (did, done) it.

3. Tom (dove, dived) to the bottom several times.

4. Silver has (flowed, flown) into the treasury.

5. Have you (hanged, hung) the clothes out?

6. The prisoner was sentenced to be (hung, hanged).

7. I'll (learn, teach) a man to swim for five dollars.

9. He would't (let, leave) me go.

9. I can (lend, loan) you some money.

10. He (lit, alighted) from his horse with great agility.

11. The child (plead, pleaded) so hard that the teacher let him off.

12. Trumbull had been used to having every attention (shown, showed) him.

13. It is (talked, said) privately that the bank is ruined.

14. The plant has (took, taken) root there.

15. I could have (gone, went).

16. In the afternoon, I (lied, lay) down.

17. He (laid, lay) down and fell into a heavy sleep.

18. I recalled the times I had (laid, lain) awake.

19. Orlando (lay, laid) Adam down carefully, and told him that he would soon return with food.

20. Scott often gives us the picture of some old ruined abbey, (lying, laying) cold and deserted in the moonlight.

21. There let him (lay, lie).

22. If you had a strong fire, and your steam (was, were) inclined to (rise, raise) what (would, should) you do?

23. More skilled to (rise, raise) the wretched than to (raise, rise).

24. Orville (seated, sat) her in the big chair.

25. She (sat, set) before the fire.

26. Did she (sit, set) still?

27. You (are n't, aint) so tall as your sister.

28. As it (don't, does n't) suit you, never mind.

29. He (does n't, don't) know me.

30. You (ought not to, should not, had n't ought to) whisper in the class.

31. You (were, was) in Boston then, (was n't, were n't) you?

32. How infinitely good you (was, were) to poor Mrs. Goldsworthy!

33. "Sir, said the King, " was it not when you (were, was,) opposing me?"

34. (Can, may) I help you to the fruit?

35. If an author's ideas are original, he (can, may) safely fail in all other requirements.

36. I (shall, will) bring him over to the manor, if I (can, may). I don't say, if I (can, may).

37. Here we encountered an opposition which (must, had to) be overcome.

38. They met a friend and one of them (had to, must) return with him to show him the way.

39. Never (shall, will) I see her more—never (will, shall) I see her more, till she is married.

40. We (shall, will) do our best to make you happy and hope that we (will, shall) succeed.

41. We (shall, will) be killed together.

42. We (shall, will) have to go.

43. I leave early, and, accordingly (shall, will) be there.

44. Is the time coming when we (will, shall) desert Thackeray?

45. I (will, shall) be happy to see you there.

46. If we proceed on this principle, we (will, shall) lose everything.

47. "Not pay it!" says he, "but you (will, shall) pay it! ay, ay, you (will, shall) pay it!"

48. You (shall, will) be elected, whoever may be your opponent.

49. Thou (shall, wilt) not steal.

50. *Sicinius.*  It is a mind
    That (shalt, will) remain a poison where it is,
    Not poison any further.

*Coriolanus.* Shall remain!—
Hear you this Triton of the minnows? Mark you
His absolute ("shall," "will")?

51. I am afraid that I (shall, will) not be there, and that you and he (shall, will) obtain the place.

52. He thinks that he (will, shall) come out with a profit.

53. If I (rise, raise) early enough, I (shall, will) see the sun (raise, rise).

54. He is afraid that he (will, shall) not pass his examination.

55. While he is wondering how long he (shall, will) live in this condition, a boat appears.

56. Surely goodness and mercy (will, shall) follow me all the days of my life, and I (will, shall) dwell in the house of the Lord forever.

57. The time is coming when the English language (shall, will) be the language of the globe.

58. (Will, shall) you bear the message? Or (shall, will) I?

59. Shall, will) I speak to him? Or (shall, will) you?

60. (Shall, will) you be there?

61. Where (shall, will) I see the man?

62. How long (shall, will) we need to stay?

63. When our friends (would, should) walk out, they (would, should) always go down by the lake.

64. The train (should, would) make better time than it does.

65. If it (should, would) be very cold, he (would, should) not start.

66. I knew that we (should, would) either go to the bottom together or that she (would, should) be the making of me.

67. If I had not gone on the excursion, I (should, would) have needed money.

68. I (should, would) be pleased to meet your friend.

69. Taking this for granted, we (would, should) expect to find gold in every hill.

70. I (should, would) think that we (should, would) likely find the man at his home.

71. Thackeray says that he (should, would) have been proud (to be, to have been) Shakespeare's boot-black or Addison's errand-boy.

72. We thought that in taking this course we (would, should) escape criticism.

73. We hoped that she (should, would) soon visit us again.

74. As a friend, I (would, should) like to warn you.

75. I (would, should) be willing to go, if it were not for my friends.

76. If we (were, was) consulted, we (should, would) not want a change.

77. We (should, ought to) assist our friends.

78. He had always thought he (would, should) like to go west.

79. He (bid, bade) them farewell.

80. The commander (bid, bade) the soldiers fire.

81. The man (bade, bid) one dollar for the book.

82. The water has not been (drank, drunk).

83. The weary traveler (drank, drunk) eagerly.

84. He (ate, eat) a hearty meal.

85. Before I had (got, gotten) my breath, men (came, come) running after me.

86. The lamp was (lit, lighted) early.

87. The statement has been (proven, proved).

88. I have (rode, ridden) only a short (way, ways).

89. I have (awaked, awoke) in time.

90. Mr. Conklin regrets that a previous engagement (prevents, will prevent) him from accepting Mrs. Waller's invitation to dinner Tuesday.

91. Mr. Curtis (accepts with pleasure, will be happy to accept) Mrs. Long's kind invitation for Saturday evening.

92. It (is, was) the duty of history to record inventions as well as wars.

93. It has always been a question with me whether scientific tastes (denote, denoted) a higher type of mind than aesthetic tastes.

94. It was (the business of Harvard, Harvard's business) (to be, to have been) on the lookout, and (to secure, to have secured) all the glory it could.

95. Every bill shall be presented to the governor; if he (approve, approves), he (shall, will) sign it.

96. Whether the encounter (alienate, alienates) friends or (raise, raises) up enemies, whether it (be fraught, is fraught) with physical risk or moral danger, whether it (lead, leads) to defeat or to total ruin, the editor who is worthy of the name will not shrink from the contest.

97. How terrible it would be if you (were, was) a saint!

98. If your home (were, was) not in Italy, you would feel as I do.

99. My wife is apt to look as if she (was, were) going to cry.

100. If I (was, were) you, I (should, would) let it pass.

101. The frigate now came tearing along as if she (were, was) alive and (were, was) feeling the fever of the chase.

102. If it (is, be) discouraging to notice (your own, one's own) faults in the second generation, it is still more so to en-

counter idiosyncrasies with which you have no association.

103. Three centuries of New England climate (has, have) made him quick-witted.

104. The persecutions of the chapel bell, sounding its unwelcome summons to six o'clock prayers, (interrupt, interrupts) my slumbers no more.

105. The gayety and the enthusiasm of the soul (recall, recalls) the last loiterer in the supper-room.

106. With two of his companions, he entered and (was, were) conducted through the place.

107. The mother, with two young children, (has, have) gone abroad.

108. The religion of this period, as well as that of the early Christains, (was, were) entirely opposed to any such belief.

109. The Rev. Goldust, accompanied by his family, (has, have) left the city.

110. The whole system of mind-reading, mesmerism, and spiritualism (seem, seems) to be connected.

111. The formation of paragraphs (are, is) very important.

112. All that they could see of the mysterious person (was, were) his boots.

113. What (are, is) wanted (is, are) not more teachers, but better trained teachers.

114. Since this matter has been discussed, there (have, has) been many inquiries.

115. In the evening, there (was, were) always some social games.

116. In literature (is, are) embalmed the short stories of the day.

117. No one of these forty English words (were, was) in use before the battle of Hastings.

118. While either of these (is, are) hungry, nothing will ever give (them, him) sleep.

119. Neither of the girls (was, were) very much at (their, her) ease.

120. Neither the Bishop nor a recent writer in the *Spectator* (has, have) arrived at the truth.

121. She is one of the writers who (is, are) destined to be immortal. .

122. We lament the excessive delicacy of his ideas, which (prevents, prevent) one from grasping them.

123. The number of exercises (is, are) not great.

124. The majority of Indian marriages (is, are) happy.

125. A multitude of heads, hats, fans, (were, was) waving.

126. One hundred dollars (has, have) been added.

127. The Chamber of Commerce of Columbus (request, requests) your presence at its First Annual Dinner.

128. The committee (has called, have called) for more witnesses.

129. Thackeray gives Swift a much better character (than Johnson, than Johnson does).

130. The government (has not and will not enter, has not entered and will not enter) into negotiations.

131. He (liked, loved) to wander through the woods.

132. The bill was (championed, supported) by senator Logan.

133. I did not (calculate, intend) to insult any one by the remarks.

134. They (carried, fetched, brought) water from a spring near by.

135. Mrs. Masters (claims, declares) that she is satisfied.

136. The senator (claims, wants) the floor.

137. We (admit, confess) the truth of that statement.

138. My friend failed to (materialize, appear).

139. The man (was shocked by electricity, received an electric shock).

140. This (shows the measure of, sizes up) the man.

141. He (states, says) that he was hungry.

142. I am (stopping, staying, living) at the hotel.

143. The rumors of what (had taken place, occurred, transpired) were spread abroad.

144. I gladly (except, accept) your offer.

145. He grants all (accept, except) the last point.

146. She (expects, suspects) her brother to-morrow.

147. I (expect, suspect, think) you will find bad roads.

148. He completely (vanquished, downed) his opponent.

149. A beautiful doll came out and (gestured, gesticulated) solemnly.

150. The two men (were never neighborly, never neighbored), much to the regret of the Quaker.

151. Why do you (resurrect, revive) that old question?

152. She (went to work as a clerk, began clerking) in a store.

153. People (are not very enthusiastic, don't enthuse) on the subject.

154. He (summoned, summonsed) me to his office.

155. Mr. Jackson was asked (to act as umpire, to umpire the game).

156. A vote of thanks was extended to Mr. Temple for (refereeing the game, acting as referee of the game).

157. This ruling does not (effect, affect) the case of the prisoner at the bar.

158. They sailed away without (affecting, effecting) their purpose

159. The attribute expressed by a transitive verb directly effects, affects) an object.

160. Has it (cultured, cultivated), the popular sensibilities?

---

### The Adverb.

State the use of each italicized word in the following:

1. The mountain stream flows *rapidly*.
2. The sentence is *undoubtedly* a just one.
3. The girl is *exceedingly* lonesome.
4. The vessel was wrecked when it was *almost* over the ocean.
5. We shall all meet *there*.
6. The method is slow at first but will *rapidly* grow easier.
7. *Occasionally* written exercises should be substituted for the oral, *when* the teacher wishes to test the progress of the class.
8. I shall be glad to see you *whenever* you may stop).
9. I saw the place *where* the World's Fair buildings are to stand.
10. The young man was greatly respected in the town *where* he was born.
11. No spot on earth, do I love *more sincerely*,
    Than old Virginia, the place *where* I was born.
12. He speaks *most sincerely when* in private conversation.
13. I *sincerely* hope for your success.
14. The prisoner begged *hard* for mercy.
15. The boy studies *harder* than his sister.
16. It rained *hardest just* after we started.
17. *Now* will we deal *worse* with thee than with them.

18. He is *much* taller than I.
19. He is *more* polite than his brother.
20. He is the *most* industrious boy in school.
21. The soul lives on *forever.*
22. We shall no doubt meet *often hereafter.*
23. I cannot believe *otherwise.*
24. The lady was *greatly* distressed by the news.
25. *When* shall we three meet *again.*
26. *Where* do the people congregate?
27. I know *why* you have come.
28. I see *how* you made the mistake.
29. I can tell *why* the sun appears to rise and set.

30. *There* is the same reason for the study of language that *there* is for the study of thought. The careful study of language cannot fail to make the student acquainted with the laws of the human mind.

Define adverb. State the different classes which you have discovered in the preceding sentences. Define and illustrate in each case. State the basis of classification. State all the adverbial ideas which may be expressed by the adverb and give one example of each. Discuss comparison in connection with the adverb. Compare the adverb with the adjective with regard to comparison. State all the uses of the adverb and illustrate each. Name the modifiers which may belong to the adverb and give an example of each. Make out a list of errors most frequently made in the use of the adverb. Read the following references:

Whitney, par. 508-518.

Elements of Composition and Grammar, Southworth & Goddard, par. 536-558.

Studies in English Grammar, Welsh-Greenwood. pp. 148-156.

Indiana Grammar, p. 95, etc.

How to Parse, Abbott, p. 329.

From the expressions enclosed in the marks of parenthesis in the following sentences, select the correct one:

1. He will (probably, likely) be here this evening.
2. That poem I like (better than, most of) any other single piece.
3. He was (nowhere, not nearly so) prolific a writer as Wordsworth.
4. The outside of the earth, after it had cooled (some, somewhat) was hard and solid.
5. There is (first, firstly) the distinction mentioned before.
6. The child was treated (ill, illy).
7. The statement amused the court (much, muchly).
8. He reasoned (thus, thusly).
9. Pope didn't translate the Iliad (accurate, accurately).
10. These poor people were not so (bad, badly) off.
11. Swift treated his child as (mean, meanly) as a child could be treated.
12. Byron could be (terrible, terribly) scathing.
13. Trilby was (uncommon, uncommonly) tall.
14. Even his friends looked (coldly, cold) upon him.
15. The coat goes on (easy, easily).
16. The girl danced (graceful, gracefully).
17. We learned to appreciate a (real, really) clear day.
18. (Relative to her population, England has—England has, relative to her population) nearly four times as many railway passengers as the United States.
19. The girl was (too much surprised, too surprised) to answer.
20. The statement is not (likely, liable) to convince any one.
21. (As soon as, directly) I came, the child knew me.

22. (As soon as she had said, immediately she said) this, she was sorry for it.

23. (After, once) the apology was made, he felt better.

24. He is not (as, so) old as you.

25. The house is not (so, as) dark as we thought it to be.

26. The boy was (rather, quite) tall for his age.

27. We had (quite a, a protracted) discussion in the meeting.

28. I remained until I heard (quite a number of, several) speeches.

29. Their misery impressed the minister (strongly; quite a great deal).

30. He dwelt on the point for (some time, quite a time).

31. The teacher's opinion was (much, very) respected.

32. I cannot walk (further, farther).

33. He wrote articles (which were even envied, which were envied even) by his teachers.

34. Lane told them (not to shoot, to not shoot).

35. You've no idea what a bother it is (to be always, to always be) neat and in order.

36. He moved (that the subject be indefinitely postponed, to indefinitely postpone the subject).

37. The birds sing (beautiful, beautifully).

38. He spoke (clear and distinct, clearly and distinctly).

39. The moon shines (bright, brightly).

40. The old man looks (sad, sadly).

## The Infinitive.

Explain the use of the following italicized expressions:

1. *To be good is to be great.*
2. *To forgive is to be charitable.*

3. The noblest revenge is *to forgive.*
4. My friend is about *to depart.*
5. All desire *to live* long but no one would be old.
6. It is easy *to find* fault.
7. The lion, *to speak* figuratively. is the king of beasts.
8. My child is anxious *to go* to school.
9. My friend failed *to appear.*

See Whitney. par. 448.

10. We believe in the life *to come.*
11. Time *to come* is called future time.
12. The children are *to sing.*
13. We are *to have* a jolly time.
14. We eat *to live* and do not live *to eat.*
15. I know him *to be* a man.
16. They made *Victoria queen.*
17. The boy grew *to be* useful.
18. To learn a lesson *accurately* is difficult.
19. I love to read *good books.*
20. He loves to send *presents* to *his friends.*
21. To coast, *sliding,* is fine sport.
22. To die, *sleeping always,* is not much to be dreaded.
23. Man never is but always *to be blest.*
24. *To err* is human.
25. *To obey* is *to enjoy.*
26. He loves *to play.*
27. He is trying *to learn.*
28. *To spend money recklessly* is criminal.
29. *To report* a speech *correctly* is difficult.
30. I study *to learn.*
31. They bade him *depart.*
32. I saw him *fall.*
33. I hoped *to see you.*

34. I intended *to call for you.*

35. He expected *to see you yesterday.*

36. *To do justice* and *judgment* is more acceptable to the Lord than sacrifice.

37. It is our duty *to try* and our determination *to succeed.*

38. They had dared *to think for themselves.*

39. Flee from the wrath *to come.*

40. I heard him *declaim.*

41. He went *to see* the World's Fair.

42. The gods are hard *to reconcile.*

43. The rain threatening *to fall,* we left early.

44. He told me when *to come.*

45. They tried *to cheat, rob,* and *murder* him.

46. I come not here *to talk.*

47. In sooth, deceit maketh no mortal *gay.*

48. It is better *to fight* for the good than *to rail* at the ill.

49. Let the great world *spin* forever down the ringing grooves of change.

50. I saw along the winter snow a spectral column *pour.*

Composition Grammar, Bain, pp. 168, 177.
How to Parse, Abbott, p. 224.

Define infinitive. State all the uses and modifiers which the infinitive may have.

---

### The Participle.

State the use of the italicized expressions in the following:

1. *Walking* rapidly develops the muscles.

2. *Boxing* is not *fighting.*

3. I heard the *rushing* of the storm.

4. He is anxious for *learning.*

5. We learn to do by *doing.*

6. That sport, *racing*, is dangerous.

7. His conduct, generally *speaking*, was honorable.

8. His master *being* away, the work was neglected.

9. The *howling* storm swept by us.

10. The plants are *growing* nicely.

11. I saw him *coming* to town.

12. The child grew *interested* in the story.

13. The rain came *dashing* down.

14. The horse came *trotting* down the road.

15. Your mother *being* sick, I came.

16. I thought about his *being* tired.

17. I came, *being* sick.

18. He stood, *being hesitating* in his manner.

19. *Spelling, naming the letters of the word*, is difficult.

20. We did not like *his singing.*

21. The boy is *bringing the carriage.*

22. *Speaking to the boy*, he said, "Go quickly."

23. *Good singing* is very attractive.

24. *Thinking rapidly* requires presence of mind.

25. The regiment, *moving* the battery to the hill, renews the engagement.

26. The class will soon be *reading.*

27. The soldier, *deceived* by the enemy, was *slain.*

28. The carriage *being broken*, we could not go farther.

29. *Having lost* our guide, we were unable to reach the village.

30. The money having been stolen, the bank closed its doors.

31. A penny *given willingly* is of greater value than a pound *given grudgingly.*

32. The spider, *spinning his web*, was an inspiration to Bruce.

33. The messenger, *waving the packet to the crowd*, appeared in the distance.

34. Christ, *walking* on the sea, came to his disciples.

35. John, the Baptist, came *eating* and *drinking*.

Define participle; state all its uses in the sentence; and all the modifiers it may have. Make an outline of the infinitive and participle, showing definitions, uses, and modifiers. Compare and contrast the infinitive and participle.

Composition Grammar, Bain, p. 171.
Read Chapter XV, p. 211, Whitney's Grammar.
Reed & Kellogg, pp. 78 to 85, Lessons 40 to 44; and pp. 72 to 76. Lessons 37 to 40.
Studies in English Grammar, Welsh-Greenwood, pp. 119 to 120.
Lee & Hadley, pp. 48, 211, 45, and 174.
How to Parse, Abbott, pp. 48, 234.
Indiana Grammar, p. 77.

Point out the infinitives and participles in the following sentences and give the use of each:

1. Thoughts shut up, want air,
   And spoil like bales unopened to the sun.

2. Let us be content in work,
   To do the the thing we can, and not presume
   To fret because it's little.

3. One day with life and heart,
   Is more than time enough to find a world.

4. Needful auxiliars are our friends, to give
   To social man true relish of himself.

5. Learn well to know how much need not be known,
   And what that knowledge which impairs your sense.

6. Let him not violate kind nature's laws,
   But own man born to live as well as die.
7. The blood more stirs
   To rouse a lion than to start a hare.
8. He that lacks time to mourn lacks time to mend.
   Eternity mourns that.
9. It is the curse of kings to be attended
   By slaves that take their humors for a warrant
   To break within the bloody house of life,
   And on the winking of authority,
   To understand a law.
10. Have you brave sons?   Look in the next fierce brawl
    To see them die.   Have ye fair daughters?   Look
    To see them live, torn from your arms, distained,
    Dishonoured, and if ye dare call for justice,
    Be answered by the lash.

Dispose of the infinitives and participles in the sentences beginning on page 225, Whitney.

––––––––––

### The Preposition.

State the use of each italicized expression in the following sentences:

1. He was brave *on* the field of battle.
2. He triumphed *in* his death.
3. The boy is very popular *with* his playmates.
4. Samuel offered his seat *to* the lady.
5. The teacher gave the book *to* Sarah.
6. The slave was very grateful *to* his master.
7. The paths of glory lead but *to* the grave.
8. The curfew tolls the knell *of* parting day.
9. Good deeds return *to* bless him who does them.

10. *To* waste *in* youth is *to* want *in* old age.

Define the class of words with which you have been dealing. State and illustrate the uses of the class. Name the principal words belonging to this class. Make out a list of the principal errors, made in the use of these words.

Make a complete outline of this class of words.

Read the following references:

Elements of Composition and Grammar, Southworth & Goddard, pp. 270-274.

Whitney, par. 319-326.

Lee & Hadley, pp. 253-261.

Indiana Grammar, p. 97.

From the expressions enclosed in the marks of parenthesis in each of the following sentences, select the correct one:

1. The vessel will arrive (within, inside of) two weeks.

2. He did not remember (saying, of saying) that the thief was tall.

3. She replied, "Not that I (remember, remember of)."

4. Is your father (at, to) home?

5. The greatest masters of critical learning differ (among, from, with) one another.

6. They danced (round, around) the pole.

7. He was not successful, as a rule, (with, at) narrative.

8. There was the old man in the forest (back of, behind) the barn.

9. (Behind, back of) his falsehood there is a truth.

10. I have no decided preference (between, among) these five authors.

11. There is some trouble (among, between) the teacher and his pupils.

12. She made a resolution (with, between) every mouthful, never to say one word to that magpie again.

13. He interfered with her sister's attachment (to, for) Mr. Bingley.

14. The old clock on the stairs frightened us (by, in) striking two.

15. Judged (from, by) this (standpoint, point of view) he was wanting.

16. He put the water (in, within) reach of the dog.

17. He went (in, into) the house.

18. He was thrown (into, in) the mud.

19. This merging of self (into, in) mankind is noble.

20. Put money (in, into) thy purse.

31. This discovery I made as soon as I was fairly (in, into) the room.

22. "Parcelsus" shows Browning's clever insight (into, of) man.

23. You have an advantage (of, over) me in that you know my name.

24. The difference (in, of) character (between, of) the two men (affected, effected) their writings.

25. There is no use (in, of) my trying to get ready.

26. The remainder of his wages (is, are) deposited (on, to( his credit.

27. A lady who did not belong to some church, would be looked (on, at) askance.

28. The vessel was blown (on, onto) the rocks.

29. This was brought about (by, through) the services of friends.

30. His longer poems are of a very different stamp (than, from) his shorter ones.

31. Wordsworth's "Skylark" is altogether different (to, from) Shelley's.

32. A difference arose (between, among) the two in their correspondence (with, to) each other.

33. Your decision accords (to, with) mine.

34. Gladstone set out (for, to) London.

35. The vessel sank far out (at, to) sea.

36. I believe, (on, to) the contrary, that Washington was the greatest of good men and the best of great men.

37. Byron's "Farewell" was written after his separation (from, with) his wife.

38. He was accompanied (by, with) his wife.

39. I differ (from, with) you.

40. We parted (from, with) him at the corner.

41. He was fully alive to the advantages of foreign methods (as well as to the necessity of using them, as well as the necessity of using them).

42. I wrote (to him, him) in May.

43. I went to Chicago and (from thence, thence) to St. Louis.

44. They (pondered, pondered over) the question.

45. One calamity (follows, follows after) another.

46. The teacher (examined, examined into) the subject carefully.

## The Conjunction.

State the use of the italicized expressions in the following sentences:

1. Truth makes man free *but* error binds him in endless chains.

2. Sincerity *and* modesty are essential to good character.

3. The blue *and* white flower is a pansy.

4. Goodness *and* mercy shall follow me all the days of my life.

5. I shall not proceed *for* danger lurks in my course.

6. I will have the heart of him *if* he forfeit.

7. I know *that* you will be pleased with my friends.

8. I see *that* you are disappointed in the book.

9. Bread *and* butter is palatable food.

10. I shall be sure to see you *for* I live in the town.

11. Swearing is *neither* profitable *nor* pleasant.

12. You will have to study *or* you will get behind your class.

13. I have seen other people make the same mistake, *therefore*, I warn you.

14. Cunning may succeed for a time, *but* in the end, murder will out.

15. I oft delivered from his forfeitures
    Many that have at times made moan to me;
    *Therefore* he hates me.

Define the class of words illustrated in the preceding sentences. What different kinds do you discover? Name and define each. State and illustrate the use of each class.

Make a complete outline of this class of words.

Read the following references:

Studies in English Grammar, Welsh-Greenwood, pp. 162–167.

Lee & Hadley, pp. 262–270.

Whitney, par. 327–331.

Indiana Grammar, p. 99.

From the expressions enclosed in the marks of parenthesis in each of the following sentences, select the correct one:

1. I am not sure (as, that) either my brother or my friend can help you.

2. Then (as, like) all rich men do, he appealed to the public.

3. They were told not to leave (unless, without) they were sent for.

4. Then these same ministers of mercy are bathing the hot head (or, and) binding up the broken limb.

5. At that time he was going (and, or) coming twice a day.

6. My father is a wise (but, and) cautious man.

7. (Since, as) you are going my way, I might as well ride.

8. I loved Lincoln (as, because) he was a true man.

9. I consider him a superior man in (both, all) intellect, feeling and courage.

10. They regret (how, that) they left school.

11. They told us (how, that) they had just visited Switzerland and (how, that) they had thought of boarding the Elbe.

12. (Though, if) science has made much progress, there are still many problems.

13. I am sure that it was neither my father (or, nor) my mother.

14. The book was neither so interesting (or, nor) so helpful as we had hoped to find it.

15. I have no word from the vessel (or, nor) do I expect any to-day.

16. (Though alone in the house, I was alone in the house but) I was not frightened.

17. He looked at me curiously (as if, as though) he knew me.

18. Very soon, (though, however), the sun appeared.

19. I smiled and tried to make myself agreeable (when, though) my head was almost bursting.

20. (While, when) walking out this morning, I found several dainty anemones.

21. To learn the subjects is a difficult task, (while, but) to teach them is much more difficult.

22. She was under the large tree in the yard, (while, and) beside her was her book.

For my part, I am convinced that the method of teaching which approaches most nearly to the method of investigation is incomparably the best; since, not content with serving up a few barren and lifeless truths, it leads to the stock on which they grew.—*Burke.*

# PART II.

# INTRODUCTION TO THE SECOND PART.

The preceding pages deal largely with the scientific phase of the subject of grammar. If the student has mastered the work there presented, the subject of grammar appears to him in its logical relations; he has seen and understands the four circles of work, mentioned in the introduction; he sees the relation of each circle of the work to every other circle, and to the subject as a whole; and may be said to have organized the subject of grammar.

This knowledge is necessary to any conscious mastery of language as an instrument in expressing thought. It is especially necessary for the teacher, who is to direct the child in the formation of language habits; for, how can she hope to guide the child aright in the formation of language habits, unless she knows the principles which underlie correct language forms?

But the great weakness in the language power of the graduates of our public and high schools, lies not in their knowledge of the science side, but in their *use* of the language. It is not that they do not know principles, but they do not use the language in accordance with the principles. They know that a pronoun which is used in the nominative relation, should have the nominative form; and they can "rattle off" the principal parts of irregular verbs fast enough to make an ordinary mortal dizzy; but at the same time, they go right on saying, "It was not me who done it."

What can we put into a text-book on grammar that will

help students use the language in accordance with the principles which they have learned ? How can we help students to become proficient in the art of grammar?

Some devices and suggestions looking to this end have been given in the preceding pages. In addition to efforts of this kind, the student's language should be carefully watched and corrected by the teacher at all times. But the teacher has the students in language only a small part of the time. Can she, in this brief period, counteract the influence of the incorrect language they use in the recitations of all other subjects; of that which they hear and use upon the street, the play-ground, and at home? Unless the teacher can see to it that the students use good language in their recitations in history, geography, arithmetic, etc., either by carefully watching over their language herself, if she teaches the other subjects, or by obtaining the cooperation of her associates in the matter, if other teachers have charge of the work in these other subjects, surely she must be content with a low degree of proficiency, on the part of her pupils, in the use of our language. As teachers of English, we do not make enough of this point.

More can be accomplished in the way of giving a student a mastery of the art side of language in one year's careful supervision of his oral and written language, than can be accomplished by five year's text-book work as it is usually done in the public schools. We encourage and fix inaccuracies in language every time a student makes a mistake in our hearing, and we do not call his attention to it. We encourage and fix bad habits in language every time we call for written work of any kind, and do not hold the pupil responsible for the language he uses; especially is this true with pupils of the grades in our public schools.

Another cause of the pupil's weakness in the use of the language is the fact that our recitations in school are scrappy and disconnected. The pupil talks only in reply to the teachers questions, and then makes only one statement at a time, and this, too often, consists of only a single word. He hasn't much opportunity to show the teacher his bad habits in the use of language. We rarely ask a pupil to stand and talk continuously for even five minutes. We do not ask pupils to talk and write enough.

But if students are to talk and write they must have something about which to talk and write. They do not care to thresh over old straw; they will not talk and write well, if they are compelled to say something that every one knows; they want something new and fresh. The greatest weakness in our composition work is that we do not furnish pupils a motive for writing. We tell the boy to write a composition of three pages on the horse. He has no interest in the horse; knows nothing new about it; does not care to say what everybody knows; has no other motive for writing than to get the three pages full, and his composition will always show it. But if the boy is really interested in something; if he can find out something new about it, or see some new thought in connection with it, he will write much better.

It is to supply the material, to some extent, for such work as is indicated above, that the following pages are given. Let the students analyze and discuss the selections; let them discover the idea which the author is setting forth; the purpose in the selection; and let them see how all parts of the selection contribute to the accomplishment of this purpose. Let them notice the beauty of the language and its appropriateness to express the thought. Let them discuss characters, scenes, and events; and let them write frequently about

G 10

them.   Let them pursue mythological and historical references and write little stories in explanation of them.

It is hoped that the following selections may serve at least four purposes:

1. They will furnish abundant sentences of sufficient variety to illustrate amply the work given in the first part of this book.

2. In dealing with the selections, the students will become familiar with the language of the author and will unconsciously imitate it.

3. The consideration of the correspondence between the thought of the selection and the language in which it is expressed, will enable the student to see the beauty, appropriateness, and strength of the language, thus furnishing him an ideal with which he can compare his own language.

4. They will furnish interesting topics which will help the teacher to supply the student with a motive for talking and writing.

# WESTMINSTER ABBEY.

" When I behold, with deep astonishment,
  To famous Westminster how there resorte,
Living in brasse or stoney monument,
  The princes and the worthies of all sorte :
Doe not I see reformde nobilitie,
  Without contempt, or pride, or ostentation,
And looke upon offenseless majesty,
  Naked of pomp or earthly domination ?
And how a play-game of a painted stone
Contents the quiet now and silent sprites,
Whome all the world which late they stood upon
Could not content nor quench their appetites,
  Life is a frost of cold felicitie,
  And death the thaw of all our vanitie."
                    CHRISTOLERO'S *Epigrams*, BY T. B., 1598.

On one of those sober and rather melancholy days, in the
latter part of autumn, when the shadows of morning and
evening almost mingle together, and throw a gloom over the
decline of the year, I passed several hours in rambling about
Westminster Abbey.    There was something congenial to the
season in the mournful magnificence of the old pile ; and as
I passed its threshold, it seemed like stepping back into the
regions of antiquity, and losing myself among the shades of
former ages.

I entered from the inner court of Westminster School,
through a long, low, vaulted passage, that had an almost
subterranean look, being dimly lighted in one part by cir-
cular perforations in the massive walls.    Through this dark
avenue I had a distant view of the cloisters, with the figure
of an old verger, in his black gown, moving along their
shadowy vaults, and seeming like a spectre from one of the
neighboring tombs.

The approach to the abbey through these gloomy monastic remains, prepares the mind for its solemn contemplation. The cloisters still retain something of the quiet and seclusion of former days. The gray walls are discolored by damps, and crumbling with age; a coat of hoary moss has gathered over the inscriptions of the mural monuments, and obscured the death's-heads, and other funereal emblems. The sharp touches of the chisel are gone from the rich tracery of the arches; the roses which adorned the key-stones have lost their leafy beauty; everything bears marks of the gradual dilapidations of time, which yet has something touching and pleasing in its very decay.

The sun was pouring down a yellow autumnal ray into the square of the cloisters, beaming upon a scanty plot of grass in the centre, and lighting up an angle of the vaulted passage with a kind of dusky splendor. From between the arcades, the eye glanced up to a bit of blue sky, or a passing cloud, and beheld the sun-gilt pinnacles of the abbey towering into the azure heaven.

As I paced the cloisters, sometimes contemplating this mingled picture of glory and decay, and sometimes endeavoring to decipher the inscriptions on the tombstones which formed the pavement beneath my feet, my eye was attracted to three figures, rudely carved in relief, but nearly worn away by the footsteps of many generations. They were the effigies of three of the early abbots: the epitaphs were entirely effaced; the names alone remained, having no doubt been renewed in later times (Vitalis. Abbas. 1082, and Gislebertus. Crispinus. Abbas. 1114, and Laurentius. Abbas. 1176). I remained some little while, musing over these casual relics of antiquity, thus left like wrecks upon this distant shore of time, telling no tale but that such be-

ings had been and had perished; teaching no moral but the
futility of that pride which hopes still to exact homage in
its ashes, and to live in an inscription. A little longer and
even these faint records will be obliterated, and the monument will cease to be a memorial. Whilst I was yet looking
down upon these grave stones, I was roused by the sound
of the abbey clock, reverberating from buttress to buttress,
and echoing among the cloisters. It is almost startling to
hear this warning of departed time sounding among the
tombs, and telling the lapse of the hour, which, like a bil-
low, has rolled us onward towards the grave.

I pursued my walk to an arched door opening to the interior of the abbey. On entering here, the magnitude of the
building breaks fully upon the mind, contrasted with the
vaults of the cloisters. The eyes gaze with wonder at clust-
ered columns of gigantic dimensions, with arches springing
from them to such an amazing height; and man wandering
about their bases, shrunk into insignificance in comparison
with his own handiwork. The spaciousness and gloom of
this vast edifice produce a profound and mysterious awe.
We step cautiously and softly about, as if fearful of disturb-
ing the hallowed silence of the tomb; while every footfall
whispers along the wall, and chatters among the sepulchres,
making us more sensible of the quiet we have interrupted.

It seems as if the awful nature of the place presses down
upon the soul, and hushes the beholder into noiseless reverence. We feel that we are surrounded by the congregated
bones of the great men of past times, who have filled history
with their deeds, and the earth with their renown. And yet
it almost provokes a smile at the vanity of human ambition,
to see how they are crowded together, and jostled in the
dust; what parsimony is observed in doling out a scanty

nook, a gloomy corner, a little portion of earth, to those whom, when alive, kingdoms could not satisfy; and how many shapes and forms and artifices are devised to catch the casual notice of the passenger, and save from forgetfulness, for a few short years, a name which once aspired to occupy ages of the world's thought and admiration.

I passed some time in Poet's Corner, which occupies an end of one of the transepts or cross aisles of the abbey. The monuments are generally simple; for the lives of literary men afford no striking themes for the sculptor. Shakespeare and Addison have statues erected to their memories; but the greater part have busts, medallions, and sometimes mere inscriptions. Notwithstanding the simplicity of these memorials, I have always observed that the visitors to the abbey remained longest about them. A kinder and fonder feeling takes the place of that cold curiosity or vague admiration with which they gaze on the splendid monuments of the great and heroic. They linger about these as about the tombs of friends and companions; for indeed there is something of companionship between the author and the reader. Other men are known to posterity only through the medium of history, which is continually growing faint and obscure; but the intercourse between the author and his fellow-men is ever new, active, and immediate. He has lived for them more than for himself; he has sacrificed surrounding enjoyments, and shut himself up from the delights of social life, that he might the more intimately commune with distant minds and distant ages. Well may the world cherish his renown; for it has been purchased, not by deeds of violence and blood, but by the diligent dispensation of pleasure. Well may posterity be grateful to his memory; for he has left it an inheritance, not of empty names and sounding actions, but whole treasures of wisdom, bright gems of thought, and golden veins of language.

From Poet's Corner I continued my stroll towards that part of the abbey which contains the sepulchres of the kings. I wandered among what once were chapels, but which are now occupied by the tombs and monuments of the great. At every turn, I met with some illustrious name, or the cognizance of some powerful house renowned in history. As the eye darts into these dusky chambers of death, it catches glimpses of quaint effigies; some kneeling in niches, as if in devotion; others stretched upon the tombs, with hands piously pressed together: warriors in armor, as if reposing after battle; prelates, with crosiers and mitres; and nobles in robes and coronets, lying as it were in state. In glancing over this scene, so strangely populous, yet where every form is so still and silent, it seems almost as if we were treading a mansion of that fabled city, where every being had been suddenly transmuted into stone.

I paused to contemplate a tomb on which lay the effigy of a knight in complete armor. A large buckler was on one arm; the hands were pressed together in supplication upon the breast; the face was almost covered by the morion; the legs were crossed in token of the warrior's having been engaged in the holy war. It was the tomb of a crusader,—of one of those military enthusiasts, who so strangely mingled religion and romance, and whose exploits form the connecting link between fact and fiction, between the history and the fairy-tale. There is something extremely picturesque in the tombs of these adventurers, decorated as they are with rude armorial bearings and Gothic sculpture. They comport with the antiquated chapels in which they are generally found; and in considering them, the imagination is apt to kindle with the legendary associations, the romantic fictions, the chivalrous pomp and pageantry, which poetry has spread over the wars for the Sepulchre of Christ. They are the relics of times utterly gone by, of beings passed from recollection, of customs and manners with which ours have no affinity. They are like objects from some strange and distant land of which we have no certain knowledge, and about which all our conceptions are vague and visionary. There is something extremely solemn and awful in those effigies on Gothic tombs, extended as if in the sleep of death, or in the supplication of the dying hour. They have an effect infinitely more impressive on my feelings than the fanciful attitudes, the over-wrought conceits, and allegorical groups which abound on modern monuments. I have been struck, also, with the superiority of many of the old sepulchral inscriptions. There was a noble way, in former times, of saying things simply, and yet saying them proudly; and I do not know an epitaph that breathes a loftier consciousness of family worth and honorable lineage, than one which affirms, of a noble house, that "all the brothers were brave, and all the sisters virtuous."

In the opposite transept to Poet's Corner, stands a monument which is among the most renowned achievements of modern art; but which to me appears horrible rather than sublime. It is the tomb of Mrs. Nightingale, by Roubillac. The bottom of the monument is represented as throwing open its marble doors and a sheeted skeleton is starting forth. The shroud is falling from his fleshless frame as he launches his dart at his victim. She is sinking into her affrighted husband's arms, who strives, with vain and frantic effort, to avert the blow. The whole is executed with terrible truth and spirit; we almost fancy we hear the gibbering yell of triumph, bursting from the distended jaws of the spectre. But why should we thus seek to clothe death with unnecessary terrors, and to spread horrors round the tomb of those we love? The grave should be surrounded by everything that might inspire tenderness and veneration for the dead, or that might win the living to virtue. It is the place, not of disgust and dismay, but of sorrow and meditation.

While wandering about these gloomy vaults and silent aisles, studying the records of the dead, the sound of busy existence from without occasionally reaches the ear,—the rumbling of the passing equipage, the murmur of the multitude, or perhaps the light laugh of pleasure. The contrast is striking with the death-like repose around: and it has a strange effect upon the feelings, thus to hear the surges of active life hurrying along and beating against the very walls of the sepulchre.

I continued in this way to move from tomb to tomb, and from chapel to chapel. The day was gradually wearing away: the distant tread of loiterers about the abbey grew less and less frequent; the sweet-tongued bell was summoning to evening prayers; and I saw at a distance the choristers, in their white surplices, crossing the aisle and entering the choir. I stood before the entrance to Henry the Seventh's chapel. A flight of steps leads up to it, through a deep and gloomy, but magnificent arch. Great gates of brass, richly and delicately wrought, turn heavily upon their hinges as if proudly reluctant to admit the feet of common mortals into this most gorgeous of sepulchres.

On entering, the eye is astonished by the pomp of architecture, and the elaborate beauty of sculptured detail. The very walls are wrought into universal ornament, encrusted with tracery, and scooped into niches, crowded with the statues of saints and martyrs. Stone seems, by the cunning labor of the chisel, to have been robbed of its weight and density, suspended aloft, as if by magic, and the fretted roof achieved with the wonderful minuteness and airy security of a cobweb.

Along the sides of the chapel are the lofty stalls of the Knights of the Bath, richly carved of oak, though with the grotesque decorations of Gothic architecture. On the pinacles of the stalls are affixed the helmets and crests of the knights, with their scarfs and swords; and above them are suspended their banners, emblazoned with their armorial bearings, and contrasting the splendor of gold and purple and crimson, with the cold gray fretwork of the roof. In the midst of this grand mausoleum stands the sepulchre of its founder,—his effigy, with that of his queen, extended on a sumptuous tomb, and the whole surrounded by a superbly wrought brazen railing.

There is a sad dreariness in this magnificence; this strange mixture of tombs and trophies; these emblems of living and aspiring ambition, close beside mementos which show the dust and oblivion in which all must, sooner or later, terminate. Nothing impresses the mind with a deeper feeling of loneliness, than to tread the silent and deserted scene of former throng and pageant. On looking round on the vacant stalls of the knights and their esquires, and on the rows of dusty but gorgeous banners that were once borne before them, my imagination conjured up the scene when this hall was bright with the valor and beauty of the land, glittering with the splendor of jeweled rank and military array, alive with the tread of many feet, and the hum of an admiring multitude. All had passed away; the silence of death had settled again upon the place, interrupted only by the casual

chirping of birds, which had found their way into the
chapel, and built their nests among its friezes and pendants,
—sure signs of solitariness and desertion. When I read the
names inscribed on the banners, they were those of men
scattered far and wide about the world; some tossing upon
distant seas, some under arms in distant lands, some mingling in the busy intrigues of courts and cabinets; all seeking
to deserve one more distinction in this mansion of shadowy
honors,—the melancholy reward of a monument.

Two small aisles on each side of this chapel present a
touching instance of the equality of the grave, which brings
down the oppressor to a level with the oppressed, and
mingles the dust of the bitterest enemies together. In one
is the sepulchre of the haughty Elizabeth; in the other is
that of her victim, the lovely and unfortunate Mary. Not
an hour in the day but some ejaculation of pity is uttered
over the fate of the latter, mingled with indignation at her
oppressor. The walls of Elizabeth's sepulchre continually
echo with the sighs of sympathy heaved at the grave of her
rival.

A peculiar melancholy reigns over the aisle where Mary
lies buried. The light struggles dimly through windows
darkened by dust. The greater part of the place is in deep
shadow, and the walls are stained and tinted by time and
weather. A marble figure of Mary is stretched upon the
tomb, round which is an iron railing, much corroded, bearing her national emblem,—the thistle. I was weary with
wandering, and sat down to rest myself by the monument,
revolving in my mind the checkered and disastrous story of
poor Mary.

The sound of casual footsteps had ceased from the abbey.
I could only hear, now and then, the distant voice of the

priest repeating the evening service, and the faint responses of the choir; these paused for a time, and all was hushed. The stillness, the desertion and obscurity that were gradually prevailing around, gave a deeper and more solemn interest to the place:

> " For in the silent grave no conversation,
> No joyful tread of friends, no voice of lovers,
> No careful father's counsel,—nothing's heard,
> For nothing is, but all oblivion,
> Dust, and an endless darkness."

Suddenly the notes of the deep-laboring organ burst upon the ear, falling with doubled and redoubled intensity, and rolling, as it were, huge billows of sound. How well do their volume and grandeur accord with this mighty building! With what pomp do they swell through its vast vaults, and breathe their awful harmony through these caves of death, and make the silent sepulchre vocal! And now they rise in triumphant acclamation, heaving higher and higher their accordant notes, and piling sound on sound. And now they pause, and the soft voices of the choir break out into sweet gushes of melody; they soar aloft, and warble along the roof, and seem to play about these lofty vaults like the pure airs of heaven. Again the pealing organ heaves its thrilling thunders, compressing air into music, and rolling it forth upon the soul. What long-drawn cadences! What solemn sweeping concords! It grows more and more dense and powerful,—it fills the vast pile, and seems to jar the very walls; the ear is stunned, the senses are overwhelmed. And now it is winding up in full jubilee,—it is rising from the earth to heaven,—the very soul seems rapt away, and floated upwards on this swelling tide of harmony!

I sat for some time lost in that kind of reverie which a strain of music is apt sometimes to inspire; the shadows of

evening were gradually thickening around me ; the monu-
ments began to cast deeper and deeper gloom ; and the distant clock again gave token of the slowly waning day.

I arose, and prepared to leave the abbey. As I descended
the flight of steps which lead into the body of the building,
my eye was caught by the shrine of Edward the Confessor,
and I ascended the small staircase that conducts to it, to take
from thence a general survey of this wilderness of tombs.
The shrine is elevated upon a kind of platform, and close
around it are the sepulchres of various kings and queens.
From this eminence the eye looks down between pillars and
funereal trophies to the chapels and chambers below, crowded
with tombs; where warriors, prelates, courtiers, and statesmen lie mouldering in their "beds of darkness." Close by
me stood the great chair of coronation, rudely carved of oak,
in the barbarous taste of a remote and Gothic age. The
scene seemed almost as if contrived, with theatrical artifice,
to produce an effect upon the beholder. Here was a type
of the beginning and the end of human pomp and power; here
it was literally but a step from the throne to the sepulchre.
Would not one think that these incongruous mementos
had been gathered together as a lesson to living greatness?
—to show it, even in the moment of its proudest exaltation,
the neglect and dishonor to which it must soon arrive; how
soon that crown which encircles its brow must pass away,
and it must lie down in the dust and disgraces of the tomb,
and be trampled upon by the feet of the meanest of the multitude? For, strange to tell, even the grave is here no longer
a sanctuary. There is a shocking levity in some natures,
which leads them to sport with awful and hallowed things ;
and there are base minds, which delight to revenge on the
illustrious dead the abject homage and grovelling servility

which they pay to the living. The coffin of Edward the
Confessor has been broken open, and his remains despoiled
of their funereal ornaments; the sceptre has been stolen
from the hand of the imperious Elizabeth, and the effigy of
Henry the Fifth lies headless. Not a royal monument but
bears some proof how false and fugitive is the homage of
mankind. Some are plundered, some mutilated; some covered with ribaldry and insult,—all more or less outraged and
dishonored!

The last beams of day were now faintly streaming through
the painted windows in the high vaults above me; the lower
parts of the abbey were already wrapped in the obscurity of
twilight. The chapel and aisles grew darker and darker.
The effigies of the kings faded into shadows; the marble figures of the monuments assumed strange shapes in the uncertain light; the evening breeze crept through the aisles like
the cold breath of the grave; and even the distant footfall
of a verger, traversing the Poet's Corner, had something
strange and dreary in its sound. I slowly retraced my morning's walk, and as I passed out at the portals of the cloisters,
the door, closing with a jarring noise behind me, filled the
whole building with echoes.

I endeavored to form some arrangement in my mind of
the objects I had been contemplating, but found they were
already falling into indistinctness and confusion. Names,
inscriptions, trophies, had all become confounded in my recollection, though I had scarcely taken my foot from off the
threshold. What, thought I, is this vast assemblage of sepulchres but a treasury of humiliation, a huge pile of reiterated homilies on the emptiness of renown, and the certainty of oblivion? It is, indeed, the empire of Death,—his
great shadowy palace, where he sits in state, mocking at the

relics of human glory, and spreading dust and forgetfulness on
the monuments of princes. How idle a boast, after all, is
the immortality of a name! Time is ever silently turning
over his pages; we are too much engrossed by the story of
the present, to think of the characters and anecdotes that
gave interest to the past; and each age is a volume thrown
aside to be speedily forgotten. The idol of to-day pushes
the hero of yesterday out of our recollection; and will, in
turn, be supplanted by his successor of to-morrow. "Our
fathers," says Sir Thomas Browne, "find their graves in our
short memories, and sadly tell us how we may be buried in
our survivors." History fades into fable; fact becomes cloud-
ed with doubt and controversy; the inscription moulders
from the tablet; the statue falls from the pedestal. Columns,
arches, pyramids,—what are they but heaps of sand, and
their epitaphs but characters written in the dust? What is
the security of a tomb, or the perpetuity of an embalment?
The remains of Alexander the Great have been scattered to
the winds, and his empty sarcophagus is now the mere curiosity of a museum. "The Egyptian mummies, which Cam-
byses or time hath spared, avarice now consumeth; Mizraim
cures wounds, and Pharaoh is sold for balsams."

What, then, is to insure this pile, which now towers above
me from sharing the fate of mightier mausoleums? The
time must come when its gilded vaults which now spring so
loftily, shall lie in rubbish beneath the feet; when, instead
of the sound of melody and praise, the wind shall whistle
through the broken arches, and the owl hoot from the shat-
tered tower,—when the garish sunbeam shall break into these
gloomy mansions of death, and the ivy twine round the
fallen column, and the fox-glove hang its blossoms about
the nameless urn, as if in mockery of the dead. Thus man

passes away ; his name perishes from record and recollection ; his history is as a tale that is told, and his very monument becomes a ruin.

## SCHEME FOR THE STUDY OF A SELECTION.

I.   THE IDEA TREATED.

What is the idea about which the author is writing in this selection ?  What is the idea treated by the author ?  What is the subject of the selection ?  What idea is the author trying to put before us ?

II.   THE PURPOSE EMBODIED IN THE SELECTION.

What is the purpose embodied in the selection ?  What effect is produced on our minds by this selection ?  Think how you felt before you read this selection, then how you feel since you have read it ; what change has it made in you ?  Is there a lesson taught by the selection ; if so, what is the lesson ?  What do you think the author hoped to accomplish by writing this selection ?

III.   THE MEANS EMPLOYED IN THE ACCOMPLISHMENT OF THE PURPOSE.

Mention one point that the author has presented about the idea treated.  Why did he tell us this ?  How does it help to accomplish the purpose ?  Read the first paragraph. Why does the author tell us that which is expressed in it ? How does this help to accomplish the purpose ?  Show how the thought of each paragraph helps to accomplish the purpose.  Has the author told all that could be written about the idea treated ?  Mention some things which he has not told us.  Why does he not tell us these things ?  Would they help to accomplish the purpose ?  Suppose he had left out the fourth paragraph, would the selection be complete ? Why ?  Suppose he had written the sixth paragraph before the third, would the purpose be just as well accomplished ? Why ?  Is it necessary that the thought of the first paragraph be presented first ; the second, next ; the third, next, etc., to the end: or could the purpose be accomplished just as well, if the points were presented in a different order? Why? Show what you think the author must have done in writing this selection. If you were writing a composition, what would you need to do first, second, third?

NOTE.—It will be seen that the preceding outline may be used in dealing with any selection. The teacher should first work out all the points carefully with the children in recitation. The questions in the outline have been repeated and stated in many different ways in order to make them clear to the children. Perhaps, with some classes, the teacher will need to make them still more simple. It will take several lessons to work out the thought of the selection well in this way. After this has been carefully done, the teacher may ask the pupils to write a paper embodying the following points: (1). The idea treated in the selection. (2). The purpose embodied in the selection. (3). The means employed in the accomplishment of the purpose. Perhaps it will be more simple to tell them to write a paper, stating the idea treated in the selection; the purpose embodied in the selection; and showing how the author has accomplished this purpose.

Teach children a neat form for their compositions, the proper margins, the idea of the paragraph, and require *neat work* of them at all times. (See the author's elementary book, "Language Work for the Grades.")

Notice the punctuation, spelling, use of capitals, sentence construction, etc. Read and correct the compositions in class, rewrite them, etc., always holding the children strictly responsible for all the work you require of them.

## CHRISTMAS EVE.

### WASHINGTON IRVING.

It was a brilliant moonlight night, but extremely cold; our chaise whirled rapidly over the frozen ground; the post-boy smacked his whip incessantly, and a part of the time his horses were on a gallop. "He knows where he is going,"

G—11

said my companion, laughing. "and is eager to arrive in time
for some of the merriment and good cheer of the servants'
hall. My father, you must know, is a bigoted devotee of the
old school, and prides himself upon keeping up something of
old English hospitality. He is a tolerable specimen of what
you will rarely meet with nowadays in its purity,—the old
English country gentleman; for our men of fortune spend so
much of their time in town. and fashion is carried so much
into the country, that the strong rich peculiarities of ancient
rural life are almost polished away. My father, however,
from early years, took honest Peacham for his text-book,
instead of Chesterfield: he determined in his own
mind, that there was no condition more truly honorable and enviable than that of a country gentleman
on his paternal lands, and therefore passes the whole of his
time on his estate. He is a strenuous advocate for the
revival of the old rural games and holiday observances, and
is deeply read in the writers, ancient and modern, who have
treated on the subject. Indeed, his favorite range of reading
is among the authors who flourished at least two centuries
since; who. he insists, wrote and thought more like true
Englishmen than any of their successors. He even regrets
sometimes that he had not been born a few centuries earlier,
when England was itself, and had its peculiar manners and
customs. As he lives at some distance from the main road,
in rather a lonely part of the country, without any rival
gentry near him, he has that most enviable of all blessings
to an Englishman, an opportunity of indulging the bent of
his own humor without molestation. Being representative
of the oldest family in the neighborhood, and a great part of
the peasantry being his tenants, he is much looked up to,
and, in general, is known simply by the appellation of 'the

Squire,' a title which has been accorded to the head of the family since time immemorial. I think it best to give you these hints about my worthy old father, to prepare you for any eccentricities that might otherwise appear absurd.''

We had passed for some time along the wall of a park, and at length the chaise stopped at the gate. It was in a heavy, magnificent old style, of iron bars, fancifully wrought at top into flourishes and flowers. The huge square columns that supported the gate were surmounted by the family crest. Close adjoining was the porter's lodge, sheltered under dark fir-trees, and almost buried in shrubbery.

The postboy rang a large porter's bell, which resounded through the still frosty air, and was answered by the distant barking of dogs, with which the mansion-house seemed garrisoned. An old woman immediately appeared at the gate. As the moonlight fell strongly upon her, I had a full view of a little primitive dame, dressed very much in the antique taste, with a neat kerchief and stomacher, and her silver hair peeping from under a cap of snowy whiteness. She came curtesying forth, with many expressions of simple joy at seeing her young master. Her husband, it seemed, was up at the house keeping Christmas eve in the servants' hall; they could not do without him, as he was the best hand at a song and story in the household.

My friend proposed that we should alight and walk through the park to the hall, which was at no great distance, while the chaise should follow on. Our road wound through a noble avenue of trees, among the naked branches of which the moon glittered as she rolled through the deep vault of a cloudless sky. The lawn beyond was sheeted with a slight covering of snow, which here and there sparkled as the moonbeams caught a frosty crystal; and at a distance might be seen a thin transparent vapor, stealing up from the low grounds and threatening gradually to shroud the landscape.

My companion looked around him with transport. "How often," said he, "have I scampered up this avenue, on returning home on school vacations! How often have I played under these trees when a boy! I feel a degree of filial reverence for them, as we look up to those who have cherished us in childhood. My father was always scrupulous in exacting our holidays, and having us around him on family festivals. He used to direct and superintend our games with the strictness that some parents do the studies of their children. He was very particular that we should play the old English games according to their original form, and consulted old books for precedent and authority for every 'merrie disport'; yet I assure you there never was pedantry so delightful. It was the policy of the good old gentleman to make his children feel that home was the happiest place in the world; and I value this delicious home-feeling as one of the choicest gifts a parent could bestow."

We were interrupted by the clamor of a troop of dogs of all sorts and sizes, "mongrel, puppy, whelp and hound, and curs of low degree," that, disturbed by the ring of the porter's bell and the rattling of the chaise, came bounding, open-mouthed, across the lawn.

> " 'The little dogs and all,
> Tray, Blanch, and Sweetheart, see,
> They bark at me!' "

cried Bracebridge, laughing. At the sound of his voice, the bark was changed into a yelp of delight, and in a moment he was surrounded and almost overpowered by the caresses of the faithful animals.

We had now come in full view of the old family mansion,

partly thrown in deep shadow, and partly lit up by the cold moonshine. It was an irregular building, of some magnitude, and seemed to be of the architecture of different periods. One wing was evidently very ancient, with heavy stone-shafted bow-windows, jutting out and overrun with ivy. from among the foliage of which the small diamond-shaped panes of glass glittered with the moonbeams. The rest of the house was in the French taste of Charles the Second's time, having been repaired and altered, as my friend told me, by one of his ancestors, who returned with that monarch at the Restoration. The grounds about the house were laid out in the old formal manner of artificial flower-beds, clipped shrubberies, raised terraces, and heavy stone balustrades, ornamented with urns, a leaden statue or two, and a jet of water. The old gentleman, I was told, was extremely careful to preserve this obsolete finery in all its original state. He admired this fashion in gardening; it had an air of magnificence, was courtly and noble, and befitting good old family style. The boasted imitation of nature in modern gardening had sprung up with modern republican notions, but did not suit a monarchical government; it smacked of the leveling system. I could not help smiling at this introduction of politics into gardening, though I expressed some apprehension that I should find the old gentleman rather intolerant in his creed. Frank assured me, however, that it was almost the only instance in which he had ever heard his father meddle with politics; and he believed that he had got this notion from a member of parliament who once passed a few weeks with him. The squire was glad of any argument to defend his clipped yew-trees and formal terraces, which had been occasionally attacked by modern landscape gardeners.

As we approached the house, we heard the sound of music, and now and then a burst of laughter, from one end of the building.  This, Bracebridge said, must proceed from the servants' hall, where a great deal of revelry was permitted, and even encouraged, by the squire, throughout the twelve days of Christmas, provided everything was done conformably to ancient usage.  Here were kept up the old games of hoodman blind, shoe the wild mare, hot cockles, steal the white loaf, bob-apple, and snap-dragon; the Yule clog and Christmas candle were. regularly burnt, and the mistletoe, with its white berries, hung up, to the imminent peril of all the pretty housemaids.

So intent were the servants upon their sports, that we had to ring repeatedly before we could make ourselves heard.  On our arrival being announced, the squire came out to receive us, accompanied by his two other sons: one a young officer in the army, home on leave of absence; the other an Oxonian, just from the university.  The squire was a fine healthy-looking old gentleman, with silver hair curling lightly round an open florid countenance; in which the physiognomist, with the advantage, like myself, of a previous hint or two, might discover a singular mixture of whim and benevolence.

The family meeting was warm and affectionate; as the evening was far advanced, the squire would not permit us to change our travelling dresses, but ushered us at once to the company, which was assembled in a large old-fashioned hall.  It was composed of different branches of a numerous family connection, where there were the usual proportion of old uncles and aunts, comfortable married dames, super-annuated spinsters, blooming country cousins, half-fledged striplings, and bright-eyed boarding-school hoydens.  They were variously occupied: some at a round game of cards; others conversing around the fireplace; at one end of the hall was a group of the young folks, some nearly grown up, others of a more tender and budding age, fully engrossed by a merry game; and a profusion of wooden horses, penny trumpets, and tattered dolls, about the floor, showed traces of a troop of little fairy beings, who, having frolicked through a happy day, had been carried off to slumber through a peaceful night.

While the mutual greetings were going on between young Bracebridge and his relatives, I had time to scan the apartment. I have called it a hall, for so it had certainly been in old times, and the squire had evidently endeavored to restore it to something of its primitive state. Over the heavy projecting fire-place was suspended a picture of a warrior in armor, standing by a white horse, and on the opposite wall hung a helmet, buckler, and lance. At one end an enormous pair of antlers was inserted in the wall, the branches serving as hooks on which to suspend hats, whips, and spurs: and in the corners of the apartment were fowling-pieces, fishing-rods, and other sporting implements. The furniture was of the cumbrous workmanship of former days, though some articles of modern convenience had been added, and the oaken floor had been carpeted; so that the whole presented an odd mixture of parlor and hall.

The grate had been removed from the wide overwhelming fire-place, to make way for a fire of wood, in the midst of which was an enormous log glowing and blazing, and sending forth a vast volume of light and heat. This I understood was the Yule clog, which the squire was particular in having brought in and illumined on a Christmas eve, according to ancient custom.

It was really delightful to see the old squire seated in his hereditary elbow-chair, by the hospitable fire-place of his ancestors, and looking around him like the sun of a system, beaming warmth and gladness to every heart. Even the very dog that lay-stretched at his feet, as he lazily shifted his position and yawned, would look fondly up in his master's face, wag his tail against the floor, and stretch himself again to sleep, confident of kindness and protection. There is an emanation from the heart in genuine hospitality which cannot be described, but is immediately felt, and puts the stranger at once at his ease. I had not been seated many minutes by the comfortable hearth of the worthy old cavalier, before I found myself as much at home as if I had been one of the family.

Supper was announced shortly after our arrival. It was served up in a spacious oaken chamber, the panels of which shone with wax, and around which were several family portraits decorated with holly and ivy. Besides the accustomed lights, two great wax tapers, called Christmas candles, wreathed with greens, were placed on a highly polished buffet among the family plate. The table was abundantly spread with substantial fare; but the squire made his supper of frumenty, a dish made of wheat cakes boiled in milk, with rich spices, being a standing dish in old times for Christmas eve. I was happy to find my old friend, minced pie, in the retinue of the feast; and finding him to be perfectly orthodox, and that I need not be ashamed of my predilection, I greeted him with all the warmth wherewith we usually greet an old and very genteel acquaintance.

The mirth of the company was greatly promoted by the humors of an eccentric personage whom Mr. Bracebridge always addressed with the quaint appellation of Master

Simon. He was a tight, brisk little man, with the air of an arrant old bachelor. His nose was shaped like the bill of a parrot; his face slightly pitted with the small-pox, with a dry perpetual bloom on it, like a frost-bitten leaf in autumn. He had an eye of great quickness and vivacity, with a drollery and lurking waggery of expression that was irresistible. He was evidently the wit of the family, dealing very much in sly jokes and innuendoes with the ladies, and making infinite merriment by harpings upon old themes; which, unfortunately, my ignorance of the family chronicles did not permit me to enjoy. It seemed to be his great delight during supper to keep a young girl next to him in a continual agony of stifled laughter, in spite of her awe of the reproving looks of her mother, who sat opposite. Indeed, he was the idol of the younger part of the company, who laughed at everything he said or did, and at every turn of his countenance. I could not wonder at it, for he must have been a miracle of accomplishments in their eyes. He could imitate Punch and Judy; make an old woman of his hand, with the assistance of a burnt cork and pocket handkerchief; and cut an orange into such a ludicrous caricature, that the young folks were ready to die with laughing.

I was let briefly into his history by Frank Bracebridge. He was an old bachelor, of a small independent income, which, by careful management, was sufficient for all his wants. He revolved through the family system like a vagrant comet in its orbit; sometimes visiting one branch, and sometimes another quite remote,—as is often the case with gentlemen of extensive connections and small fortunes in England. He had a chirping buoyant disposition, always enjoying the present moment; and his frequent change of scene and company prevented his acquiring those rusty un-

accommodating habits with which old bachelors are so
uncharitably charged. He was a complete family chronicle,
being versed in the genealogy, history, and intermarriages of
the whole house of Bracebridge, which made him a great
favorite with the old folks; he was the beau of all the elder
ladies and superannuated spinsters, among whom he was habitually considered rather a young fellow, and he was master
of the revels among the children; so that there was not a
more popular being in the sphere in which he moved than
Mr. Simon Bracebridge. Of late years he had resided almost
entirely with the squire, to whom he had become a factotum,
and whom he particularly delighted by jumping with his
humor in respect to old times, and by having a scrap of an
old song to suit every occasion. We had presently a specimen of his last-mentioned talent, for no sooner was supper
removed, and spiced wines and other beverages peculiar to
the season introduced, than Master Simon was called on for
a good old Christmas song. He bethought himself for a
moment, and then, with a sparkle of the eye, and a voice
that was by no means bad, excepting that it ran occasionally
into a falsetto, like the notes of a split reed, he quavered
forth a quaint old ditty.

> " Now Christmas is come,
> Let us beat up the drum,
> And call our neighbors together,
> And when they appear,
> Let us make them such cheer
> As will keep out the wind and the weather," etc.

The supper had disposed every one to gayety, and an old
harper was summoned from the servants' hall, where he had
been strumming all the evening, and to all appearance com-
forting himself with some of the squire's home-brewed. He
was a kind of hanger-on, I was told, of the establishment,

and, though ostensibly a resident of the village, was oftener
to be found in the squire's kitchen than his own home, the
old gentleman being fond of the sound of " harp in hall."

The dance, like most dances after supper, was a merry one;
some of the older folks joined in it, and the squire himself
figured down several couple with a partner, with whom he
affirmed he had danced at every Christmas for nearly half a
century. Master Simon, who seemed to be a kind of connecting link 'between the old times and the new, and to be
withal a little antiquated in the taste of his accomplishments,
evidently piqued himself on his dancing, and was endeavoring to gain credit by the heel and toe, rigadoon, and other
graces of the ancient school; but he had unluckily assorted
himself with a little romping girl from boarding-school, who,
by her wild vivacity, kept him continually on the stretch,
and defeated all his sober attempts at elegance:—such are
the ill-assorted matches to which antique gentlemen are
unfortunately prone!

The young Oxonian, on the contrary, had led out one of
his maiden aunts, on whom the rogue played a thousand
little knaveries with impunity; he was full of practical jokes,
and his delight was to tease his aunts and cousins; yet, like
all madcap youngsters, he was a universal favorite among
the women. The most interesting couple of the dance was
the young officer and a ward of the squire, a beautiful blush-
ing girl of seventeen. From several shy glances which I had
noticed in the course of the evening, I suspected there was a
little kindness growing up between them; and, indeed, the
young soldier was just the hero to captivate a romantic girl.
He was tall, slender, and handsome, and, like most young
British officers of late years, had picked up various small
accomplishments on the continent: he could talk French

and Italian, draw landscapes, sing very tolerably, dance divinely, but above all, he had been wounded at Waterloo. What girl of seventeen, well read in poetry and romance, could resist such a mirror of chivalry and perfection?

The moment the dance was over he caught up a guitar, and, lolling against the old marble fireplace, in an attitude which I am half inclined to suspect was studied, began the little French air of the Troubadour. The squire, however, exclaimed against having anything on Christmas eve but good old English; upon which the young minstrel, casting up his eye for a moment, as if in an effort of memory, struck into another strain, and, with a charming air of gallantry, gave Herrick's "Night-Piece to Julia."

> " Her eyes the glow-worm lend thee,
> The shooting stars attend thee,
>   And the elves also,
>   Whose little eyes glow
> Like the sparks of fire, befriend thee.
>
> " No will-o'-the-wisp mislight thee ;
> Nor snake nor slow-worm bite thee ;
>   But on, on thy way,
>   Not making a stay,
> Since ghost there is none to affright thee.
>
> " Then let not the dark thee cumber ;
> What though the moon does slumber,
>   The stars of the night
>   Will lend thee their light,
> Like tapers clear without number.
>
> " Then, Julia, let me woo thee,
> Thus, thus to come unto me ;
>   And when I shall meet
>   Thy silvery feet,   ·
> My soul I'll pour into thee."

The song might or might not have been intended in compliment to the fair Julia, for so I found his partner was called ; she, however, was certainly unconscious of any such application, for she never looked at the singer, but kept her eyes cast upon the floor. Her face was suffused, it is true, with a beautiful blush, and there was a gentle heaving of the bosom, but all that was doubtless caused by the exercise of the dance ; indeed so great was her indifference, that she amused herself with picking to pieces a choice bouquet of hot-house flowers, and by the time the song was concluded the nosegay lay in ruins on the floor.

The party now broke up for the night with the kind-hearted old custom of shaking hands. As I passed through the hall, on my way to my chamber, the dying embers of the Yule clog still sent forth a dusky glow, and had it not been the season when "no spirit dares stir abroad," I should have been half tempted to steal from my room at midnight, and peep whether the fairies might not be at their revels about the hearth.

My chamber was in the old part of the mansion, the ponderous furniture of which might have been fabricated in the days of the giants. The room was panelled, with cornices of heavy carved work, in which flowers and grotesque faces were strangely intermingled; and a row of black-looking portraits stared mournfully at me from the walls. The bed was of rich though faded damask, with a lofty tester, and stood in a niche opposite a bow-window. I had scarcely got into bed when a strain of music seemed to break forth in the air just below the window. I listened, and found it proceeded from a band, which I concluded to be the waits from some neighboring village. They went round the house, playing under the windows. I drew aside the curtains to hear them more distinctly. The moonbeams fell through the upper part of the casement, partially lighting up the antiquated apartment. The sounds, as they receded, became more soft and aerial, and seemed to accord with the quiet

and moonlight.   I listened and listened: they became more
and more tender and remote, and, as they gradually died
away, my head sank upon the pillow and I fell asleep.

---

## THE GREAT STONE FACE.

### NATHANIEL HAWTHORNE.

One afternoon, when the sun was going down, a mother
and her little boy sat at the door of their cottage, talking
about the Great Stone Face.   They had but to lift their
eyes, and there it was plainly to be seen, though miles away,
with the sunshine brightening all its features.

And what was the Great Stone Face?

Embosomed amongst a family of lofty mountains, there
was a valley so spacious that it contained many thousand
inhabitants.   Some of these good people dwelt in log huts,
with the black forest all around them, on the steep and
difficult hillsides.   Others had their homes in comfortable
farm-houses, and cultivated the rich soil on the gentle slopes
or level surfaces of the valley.   Others, again, were congregated into populous villages, where some wild, highland
rivulet, tumbling down from its birthplace in the upper
mountain region, had been caught and tamed by human
cunning and compelled to turn the machinery of cotton-
factories.   The inhabitants of this valley, in short, were
numerous, and of many modes of life.   But all of them,
grown people and children, had a kind of familiarity with
the Great Stone Face, although some possessed the gift of
distinguishing this grand natural phenomenon more perfectly than many of their neighbors.

The Great Stone Face, then, was a work of nature in her mood of majestic playfulness, formed on the 'perpendicular side of a mountain by some immense rocks, which had been thrown together in such a position as, when viewed at a proper distance, precisely to resemble the features of the human countenance. It seemed as if an enormous giant, or a Titan, had sculptured his own likeness on the precipice. There was the broad arch of the forehead, a hundred feet in height; the nose, with its long bridge; and the vast lips, which, if they could have spoken, would have rolled their thunder accents from one end of the valley to the other. True it is, that if the spectator approached too near, he lost the outline of the gigantic visage, and could discern only a heap of ponderous and gigantic rocks, piled in chaotic ruin one upon another. Retracing his steps, however, the wondrous features would again be seen; and the farther he withdrew from them, the more like a human face, with all its original divinity intact, did they appear; until, as it grew dim in the distance, with the clouds and glorified vapor of the mountains clustering about it, the Great Stone Face seemed positively to be alive.

It was a happy lot for children to grow up to manhood or womanhood with the Great Stone Face before their eyes, for all the features were noble, and the expression was at once grand and sweet, as if it were the glow of a vast, warm heart, that embraced all mankind in its affections, and had room for more. It was an education only to look at it. According to the belief of many people, the valley owed much of its fertility to this benign aspect that was continually beaming over it, illuminating the clouds, and infusing its tenderness into the sunshine.

As we began with saying, a mother and her little boy sat

at their cottage-door, gazing at the Great Stone Face, and talking about it. The child's name was Ernest.

"Mother," said he, while the Titantic visage smiled on him, "I wish that it could speak, for it looks so very kindly that its voice must needs be pleasant. If I were to see a man with such a face I should love him dearly."

"If an old prophecy should come to pass," answered his mother, "we may see a man, some time or other, with exactly such a face as that."

"What prophecy do you mean, dear mother?" eagerly inquired Ernest. "Pray tell me all about it!"

So his mother told him a story that her own mother had told to her, when she herself was younger than little Ernest; a story, not of things that were past, but of what was yet to come; a story, nevertheless, so very old, that even the Indians, who formerly inhabited this valley, had heard it from their forefathers, to whom, as they affirmed, it had been murmured by the mountain streams, and whispered by the wind among the tree-tops. The purport was, that, at some future day, a child should be born hereabouts, who was destined to become the greatest and noblest personage of his time, and whose countenance, in manhood, should bear an exact resemblance to the Great Stone Face. Not a few old-fashioned people, and young ones likewise, in the ardor of their hopes, still cherished an enduring faith in this old prophecy. But others, who had seen more of the world, had watched and waited till they were weary, and had beheld no man with such a face, nor any man that proved to be much greater or nobler than his neighbors, concluded it to be nothing but an idle tale. At all events, the great man of the prophecy had not yet appeared.

"O mother, dear mother!" cried Ernest, clapping his hands above his head, "I do hope that I shall live to see him!"

His mother was an affectionate and thoughtful woman, and felt that it was wisest not to discourage the generous hopes of her little boy. So she only said to him, "Perhaps you may."

And Ernest never forgot the story that his mother told him. It was always in his mind, whenever he looked upon the Great Stone Face. He spent his childhood in the log cottage where he was born, and was dutiful to his mother, and helpful to her in many things, assisting her much with his little hands, and more with his loving heart. In this manner, from a happy yet often pensive child, he grew up to be a mild, quiet, unobtrusive boy, and sun-browned with labor in the fields, but with more intelligence brightening his aspect than is seen in many lads who have been taught at famous schools. Yet Ernest had had no teacher, save only that the Great Stone Face became one to him. When the toil of the day was over, he would gaze at it for hours, until he began to imagine that those vast features recognized him, and gave him a smile of kindness and encouragement, responsive to his own look of veneration. We must not take upon us to affirm that this was a mistake, although the Face may have looked no more kindly at Ernest than at all the world besides. But the secret was, that the boy's tender and confiding simplicity discerned what other people could not see; and thus the love, which was meant for all, became his peculiar portion.

About this time there went a rumor throughout the valley, that the great man, foretold from ages long ago, who was to bear a resemblance to the Great Stone Face, had appeared at last. It seems that, many years before, a young man had

G—12

migrated from the valley and settled at a distant seaport, where, after getting together a little money, he had set up as a shop keeper.   His name—but I could never learn whether it was his real one, or a nickname that had grown out of his habits and success in life—was Gathergold.   Being shrewd and active and endowed by Providence with that inscrutable faculty which develops itself in what the world calls luck, he became an exceedingly rich merchant, and owner of a whole fleet of bulky-bottomed ships.   All the countries of the globe appeared to join hands for the mere purpose of adding heap after heap to the mountainous accumulation of this one man's wealth.   The cold regions of the north, almost within the gloom and shadow of the Arctic Circle, sent him their tribute in the shape of furs; hot Africa sifted for him the golden sands of her rivers, and gathered up the ivory tusks of her great elephants out of the forests; the East came bringing him the rich shawls, and spices, and teas, and the effulgence of diamonds, and the gleaming purity of large pearls.   The ocean, not to be behindhand with the earth, yielded up her mighty whales, that Mr. Gathergold might sell their oil, and make a profit on it.   Be the original commodity what it might, it was gold within his grasp.   It might be said of him, as of Midas in the fable, that whatever he touched with his finger immediately glistened, and grew yellow, and was changed at once into sterling metal, or, which suited him still better, into piles of coin.   And, when Mr. Gathergold had become so very rich that it would have taken him a hundred years only to count his wealth, he bethought himself of his native valley, and resolved to go back thither, and end his days where he was born.   With this purpose in view, he sent a skillful architect to build him such a palace as should be fit for a man of his vast wealth to live in.

As I have said above, it had already been rumored in the valley that Mr. Gathergold had turned out to be the prophetic personage so long and vainly looked for, and that his visage was the perfect and undeniable similitude of the Great Stone Face. People were the more ready to believe that this must needs be the fact, when they beheld the splendid edifice that rose, as if by enchantment, on the site of his father's old weather beaten farm-house. The exterior was of marble, so dazzingly white that it seemed as though the whole structure might melt away in the sunshine, like those humbler ones which Mr. Gathergold, in his young play-days, before his fingers were gifted with the touch of transmutation, had been accustomed to build of snow. It had a richly ornamented portico, supported by tall pillars, beneath which was a lofty door, studded with silver knobs, and made of a kind of variegated wood that had been brought from beyond the sea. The windows, from the floor to the ceiling of each stately apartment, were composed, respectively, of but one enormous pane of glass, so transparently pure that it was said to be a finer medium than even the vacant atmosphere. Hardly anybody had been permitted to see the interior of this palace; but it was reported, and with good semblance of truth, to be far more gorgeous than the outside, insomuch that whatever was iron or brass in other houses was silver or gold in this; and Mr. Gathergold's bedchamber, especially, made such a glittering appearance that no ordinary man would have been able to close his eyes there. But, on the other hand, Mr. Gathergold was now so inured to wealth, that perhaps he could not have closed his eyes unless where the gleam of it was certain to find its way beneath his eyelids.

In due time, the mansion was finished; next came the

upholsterers, with magnificent furniture; then a whole troop
of black and white servants, the harbingers of Mr. Gathergold, who, in his own majestic person, was expected to arrive
at sunset.   Our friend Ernest, meanwhile, had been deeply
stirred by the idea that the great man, the noble man, the
man of prophecy, after so many ages of delay, was at length
to be made manifest to his native valley.   He knew, boy as
he was, that there were a thousand ways in which Mr. Gathergold, with his vast wealth, might transform himself into
an angel of beneficence, and assume a control over human
affairs as wide and benignant as the smile of the Great Stone
Face.   Full of faith and hope, Ernest doubted not that what
the people said was true, and that now he was to behold the
living likeness of those wondrous features on the mountain-
side.   While the boy was still gazing up the valley, and
fancying, as he always did, that the Great Stone Face returned his gaze and looked kindly at him, the rumbling of
wheels was heard, approaching swiftly along the winding
road.

"Here he comes!" cried a group of people who were assembled to witness the arrival.    "Here comes the great Mr.
Gathergold!"

A carriage drawn by four horses dashed round the turn
of the road.   Within it, thrust partly out of the window,
appeared the physiognomy of a little old man, with a skin
as yellow as if his own Midas-hand had transmuted it.   He
had a low forehead, small, sharp eyes, puckered about with
innumerable wrinkles, and very thin lips, which he made
still thinner by pressing them forcibly together.

"The very image of the Great Stone Face!" shouted the
people.   "Sure enough, the old phrophecy is true; and here
we have the great man come, at last!"

And, what greatly perplexed Ernest, they seemed actually to believe that here was the likeness which they spoke of. By the roadside there chanced to be an old beggar-woman and two little beggar-children, stragglers from some far-off region, who, as the carriage rolled onward, held out their hands and lifted up their doleful voices, most piteously beseeching charity. A yellow claw—the very same that had clawed together so much wealth—poked itself out of the coach-window, and dropped some copper coins upon the ground; so that, though the great man's name seems to have been Gathergold, he might just as suitably have been nicknamed Scattercopper. Still, nevertheless, with an earnest-shout, and evidently with as much good faith as ever, the people bellowed,—

" He is the very image of the Great Stone Face!"

But Ernest turned sadly from the wrinkled shrewdness of that sordid visage, and gazed up the valley, where, amid a gathering mist, gilded by the last sunbeams, he could still distinguish those glorious features which had impressed themselves into his soul. Their aspect cheered him. What did the benign lips seem to say?

"He will come! Fear not, Ernest; the man will come!"

The years went on, and Ernest ceased to be a boy. He had grown to be a young man now. He attracted little notice from the other inhabitants of the valley; for they saw nothing remarkable in his way of life, save that, when the labor of the day was over, he still loved to go apart and gaze and meditate upon the Great Stone Face. According to their idea of the matter, it was a folly, indeed, but pardonable, inasmuch as Ernest was industrious, kind, and neigborly, and neglected no duty for the sake of indulging this idle habit. They knew not that the Great Stone Face had become a teacher to him, and that the sentiment which was expressed in it would enlarge the young man's heart, and fill it with wider and deeper sympathies than other hearts. They knew not that thence would come a better wisdom than could be learned from books, and a better life than could be moulded on the defaced example of other human lives. Neither did Ernest know that the thoughts and affections which came to him so naturally, in the fields and at the fireside, and wherever he communed with himself, were of a higher tone than those which all men shared with him. A simple soul,—simple as when his mother first taught him the old prophecy,—he beheld the marvelous features beaming adown the valley, and still wondered that their human counterpart was so long in making his appearance.

By this time poor Mr. Gathergold was dead and buried ; and the oddest part of the matter was, that his wealth, which was the body and spirit of his existence, had disappeared before his death, leaving nothing of him but a living skeleton, covered over with a wrinkled, yellow skin. Since the melting away of his gold, it had been very generally conceded that there was no such striking resemblance, after all, betwixt the ignoble features of the ruined merchant and that majestic face upon the mountain-side. So the people ceased to honor him during his lifetime, and quietly consigned him to forgetfulness after his decease. Once in a while, it is true, his memory was brought up in connection with the magnificent palace which he had built, and which had long ago been turned into a hotel for the accomodation of strangers, multitudes of whom came every summer to visit that famous natural curiosity, the Great Stone Face. Thus, Mr. Gathergold being discredited and thrown into the shade, the man of prophecy was yet to come.

It so happened that a native-born son of the valley, many years before, had enlisted as a soldier, and, after a great deal of hard fighting, had now become an illustrious commander. Whatever he may be called in history, he was known in camps and on the battle-field under the nickname of Old Blood-and-Thunder. This war-worn veteran, being now infirm with age and wounds, and weary of the turmoil of a military life, and of the roll of the drum and the clangor of the trumpet, that had so long been ringing in his ears, had lately signified a purpose of returning to his native valley, hoping to find repose where he remembered to have left it. The inhabitants, his old neighbors and their grown-up children, were resolved to welcome the renowned warrior with a salute of cannon and a public dinner; and all the more enthusiastically, it being affirmed that now, at last, the likeness of the Great Stone Face had actually appeared. An aide-de-camp of Old Blood-and-Thunder, travelling through the valley, was said to have been struck with the resemblance. Moreover the schoolmates and early acquaintances of the general were ready to testify, on oath, that to the best of their recollection, the aforesaid general had been exceedingly like the majestic image, even when a boy, only that the idea had never occurred to them at that period. Great, therefore, was the excitement throughout the valley; and many people, who had never once thought of glancing at the Great Stone Face for years before, now spent their time in gazing at it, for the sake of knowing exactly how General Blood-and-Thunder looked.

On the day of the great festival, Ernest, with all the other people of the valley, left their work, and proceeded to the spot where the sylvan banquet was prepared. As he approached, the loud voice of the Rev. Dr. Battleblast was heard, beseeching a blessing on the good things set before them, and on the distinguished friend of peace in whose honor they were assembled.  ·The tables were arranged in a cleared space of the woods, shut in by the surrounding trees, except where a vista opened eastward, and afforded a distant view of the Great Stone Face. Over the general's chair, which was a relic from the home of Washington, there was an arch of verdant boughs, with the laurel profusely intermixed, and surmounted by his country's banner, beneath which he had won his victories. Our friend Ernest raised himself on his tip-toes, in hopes to get a glimpse of the celebrated guest; but there was a mighty crowd about the tables anxious to hear the toasts and speeches, and to catch any word that might fall from the general in reply; and a volunteer company, doing duty as a guard, pricked ruthlessly with their bayonets at any particularly quiet person among the throng. So Ernest, being of an unobtrusive character, was thrust quite into the background, where he could see no more of Old Blood-and-Thunder's physiognomy than if it had been still blazing on the battle-field. To console himself, he turned towards the Great Stone Face, which, like a faithful and long-remembered friend, looked back and smiled upon him through the vista of the forest. Meantime, however, he could overhear the remarks of various individuals, who were comparing the features of the hero with the face on the distant mountain-side.

"'Tis the same face, to a hair!" cried one man, cutting a caper for joy.

"Wonderfully like, that's a fact!" responded another.

"Like! why, I call it Old Blood-and-Thunder himself in a monstrous looking-glass!" cried a third. "And why not? He's the greatest man of this or any other age, beyond a doubt."

And then all three of the speakers gave a great shout, which communicated electricity to the crowd, and called forth a roar from a thousand voices, that went reverberating for miles among the mountains, until you might have supposed that the Great Stone Face had poured its thunder-breath into the cry. All these comments, and this vast enthusiasm, served the more to interest our friend; nor did he think of questioning that now, at length, the mountain-visage had found its human counterpart. It is true, Ernest had imagined that this long-looked-for personage would appear in the character of a man of peace, uttering wisdom, and doing good, and making people happy. But, taking an habitual breadth of view, with all his simplicity, he contended that Providence should choose its own method of blessing mankind, and could conceive that this great end might be effected even by a warrior and a bloody sword, should inscrutable wisdom see fit to order matters so.

"The general! the general!" was now the cry. "Hush! silence! Old Blood-and-Thunder's going to make a speech."

Even so; for, the cloth being removed, the general's health had been drunk amid shouts of applause, and he now stood upon his feet to thank the company. Ernest saw him. There he was, over the shoulders of the crowd, from the two glittering epaulets and embroidered collar upward, beneath the arch of green boughs with intertwined laurel, and the banner drooping as if to shade his brow! And there, too, visible in the same glance, through the vista of the forest, appeared the Great Stone Face! And was there, indeed, such a resemblance as the crowd had testified? Alas, Ernest could not recognize it. He beheld a war-worn and weather-beaten countenance, full of energy and expressive of an iron will; but the gentle wisdom, the deep, broad, tender sym-

pathies, were altogether wanting in Old Blood-and-Thunder's
visage; and even if the Great Stone Face had assumed his
look of stern command, the milder traits would still have
tempered it.

"This is not the man of prophecy," sighed Ernest to
himself, as he made his way out of the throng. "and must
the world wait longer yet?"

The mists had congregated about the distant mountain-
side, and there were seen the grand and awful features of
the Great Stone Face, awful but benignant, as if a mighty
angel were sitting among the hills and enrobing himself in
a cloud-vesture of gold and purple.  As he looked, Ernest
could hardly believe but that a smile beamed over the whole
visage, with a radiance still brightening, although without
motion of the lips.  It was probably the effect of the western
sunshine, melting through the thinly diffused vapors that
had swept between him and the object that he gazed at.
But—as it always did—the aspect of his marvellous friend
made Ernest as hopeful as if he had never hoped in vain.

"Fear not, Ernest," said his heart, even as if the Great
Face were whispering him,—"fear not, Ernest; he will
come."

More years sped swiftly and tranquilly away.  Ernest
still dwelt in his native valley, and was now a man of middle
age.  By imperceptible degrees, he had become known among
the people.  Now, as heretofore, he labored for his bread,
and was the same simple-hearted man that he had always
been.  But he had thought and felt so much, he had given
so many of the best hours of his life to unworldly hopes for
some great good to mankind, that it seemed as though he
had been talking with the angels, and had imbibed a portion
of their wisdom unawares.  It was visible in the calm and

well-considered beneficence of his daily life, the quiet stream
of which had made a wide green margin all along its course.
Not a day passed by that the world was not the better because this man, humble as he was, had lived. He never
stepped aside from his own path, yet would always reach a
blessing to his neighbor. Almost involuntarily, too, he had
become a preacher. The pure and high simplicity of his
thought, which, as one of its manifestations, took shape in
the good deeds that dropped silently from his hand, flowed
also forth in speech. He uttered truths that wrought upon
and moulded the lives of those who heard him. His auditors, it may be, never suspected that Ernest, their own
neighbor and familiar friend, was more than an ordinary
man ; least of all did Ernest himself suspect it ; but, inevita-
bly as the murmur of a rivulet, came thoughts out of his
mouth that no other human lips had spoken.

When the people's minds had had a little time to cool,
they were ready enough to acknowledge their mistake in
imagining a similarity between General Blood-and-Thunder's
truculent physiognomy and the benign visage on the mountain-side. But now, again, there were reports and many
paragraphs in the newspapers, affirming that the likeness of
the Great Stone Face had appeared upon the broad shoulders of a certain eminent statesman. He, like Mr. Gathergold and Old Blood-and-Thunder, was a native of the valley,
but had left it in his early days, and taken up the trades of
law and politics. Instead of the rich man's wealth and the
warrior's sword, he had but a tongue, and it was mightier
than both together. So wonderfully eloquent was he, that
whatever he might choose to say, his auditors had no choice
but to believe him ; wrong looked like right, and right like
wrong; for when it pleased him he could make a kind of

illuminated fog with his mere breath, and obscure the natural daylight with it.  His tongue, indeed, was a magic
instrument; sometimes it rumbled like the thunder; sometimes it warbled like the sweetest music.  It was the blast
of war,—the song of peace; and it seemed to have a heart
in it, when there was no such matter.  In good truth, he
was a wondrous man; and when his tongue had acquired
him all other imaginable success,—when it had been heard
in halls of state, and in the courts of princes and potentates,
—after it had made him known all over the world, even as
a voice crying from shore to shore,— it finally persuaded his
countrymen to select him for the Presidency.  Before this
time,—indeed, as soon as he began to grow celebrated,— his
admirers had found out the resemblance between him and
the Great Stone Face; and so much were they struck by it
that throughout the country this distinguished gentleman
was known by the name of Old Stony Phiz.  The phrase
was considered as giving a highly favorable aspect to his
political prospects; for, as is likewise the case with the Pope-
dom, nobody ever becomes President without taking a name
other than his own.

While his friends were doing their best to make him President, Old Stony Phiz, as he was called, set out on a visit to
the valley where he was born.  Of course, he had no other
object than to shake hands with his fellow-citizens, and
neither thought nor cared about any effect which his progress through the country might have upon the election.
Magnificent preparations were made to receive the illustrious statesman; a cavalcade of horsemen set forth to meet
him at the boundary line of the State, and all the people
left their business and gathered along the wayside to see him
pass.  Among these was Ernest.  Though more than once

disappointed, as we have seen, he had such a hopeful and confiding nature, that he was always ready to believe in whatever seemed beautiful and good. He kept his heart continually open, and thus was sure to catch the blessing from on high, when it should come. So now again, as buoyantly as ever, he went forth to behold the likeness of the Great Stone Face.

The cavalcade came prancing along the road, with a great clattering of hoofs and a mighty cloud of dust, which rose up so dense and high that the visage of the mountain-side was completely hidden from Ernest's eyes. All the great men of the neighborhood were there on horseback; militia officers, in uniform; the member of congress; the sheriff of the county; the editors of newspapers; and many a farmer, too, had mounted his patient steed, with his Sunday coat upon his back. It really was a very brilliant spectacle, especially as there were numerous banners flaunting over the cavalcade, on some of which were gorgeous portraits of the illustrious statesman and the Great Stone Face, smiling familiarly at one another, like two brothers. If the pictures were to be trusted, the mutual resemblance, it must be confessed, was marvellous. We must not forget to mention that there was a band of music, which made the echoes of the mountains ring and reverberate with the loud triumph of its strains; so that airy and soul-thrilling melodies broke out among all the heights and hollows, as if every nook of his native valley had found a voice to welcome the distinguished guest. But the grandest effect was when the far-off mountain precipice flung back the music; for then the Great Stone Face itself seemed to be swelling the triumphant chorus, in acknowledgment that, at length, the man of prophecy was come.

All this while the people were throwing up their hats and shouting, with enthusiasm so contagious that the heart of Ernest kindled up, and he likewise threw up his hat, and shouted, as loudly as the loudest, " Huzza for the great man! Huzza for Old Stony Phiz!" But as yet he had not seen him.

"Here he is now!" cried those who stood near Ernest. "There! There! Look at Old Stony Phiz and then at the Old Man of the Mountain, and see if they are not as like as two twin brothers!"

In the midst of all this gallant array, came an open barouche, drawn by four white horses; and in the barouche, with his massive head uncovered, sat the illustrious statesman, Old Stony Phiz himself.

"Confess it," said one of Ernest's neighbors to him, "the Great Stone Face has met its match at last!"

Now, it must be owned that, at his first glimpse of the countenance which was bowing and smiling from the barouche, Ernest did fancy that there was a resemblance between it and the old familiar face upon the mountain side. The brow, with its massive depth and loftiness, and all the other features, indeed, were boldly and strongly hewn, as if in emulation of a more than heroic, of a Titanic model. But the sublimity and stateliness, the grand expression of a divine sympathy, that illuminated the mountain visage, and etherealized its ponderous granite substance into spirit, might here be sought in vain. Something had been originally left out, or had departed. And therefore the marvellously gifted statesman had always a weary gloom in the deep caverns of his eyes, as of a child that has outgrown its playthings, or a man of mighty faculties and little aims, whose life, with all its high performances, was vague and empty, because no high purpose had endowed it with reality.

Still Ernest's neighbor was thrusting his elbow into his side, and pressing him for an answer.

"Confess! confess! Is not he the very picture of your Old Man of the Mountain?"

"No!" said Ernest, bluntly. "I see little or no likeness."

"Then so much the worse for the Great Stone Face!" answered his neighbor; and again he set up a shout for Old Stony Phiz.

But Ernest turned away, melancholy, and almost despondent; for this was the saddest of his disappointments, to behold a man who might have fulfilled the prophecy, and had not willed to do so. Meantime, the cavalcade, the banners, the music, the barouches swept past him, with the vociferous crowd in the rear, leaving the dust to settle down, and the Great Stone Face to be revealed again, with the grandeur that it had worn for untold centuries.

"Lo, here I am, Ernest!" the benign lips seemed to say. "I have waited longer than thou, and am not yet weary. Fear not; the man will come."

The years hurried onward, treading in their haste on one another's heels. And now they began to bring white hairs, and scatter them over the head of Ernest; they made reverend wrinkles across his forehead, and furrows in his cheeks. He was an aged man. But not in vain had he grown old: more than the white hairs on his head were the sage thoughts in his mind; his wrinkles and furrows were inscriptions that Time had graved, and in which he had written legends of wisdom that had been tested by the tenor of a life. And Ernest had ceased to be obscure. Unsought for, undesired, had come the fame which so many seek, and made him known in the great world, beyond the limits of the valley in which he had dwelt so quietly. College professors, and even the

active men of cities, came from afar to see and converse with
Ernest; for the report had gone abroad that this simple hus-
bandman had ideas unlike those of other men, not gained
from books, but of a higher tone,—a tranquil and familiar
majesty, as if he had been talking with the angels as his
daily friends.  Whether it were sage, statesman, or philan-
thropist, Ernest received these visitors with the gentle sincerity that had characterized him from boyhood, and spoke
freely with them of whatever came uppermost, or lay deep-
est in his heart or their own.  While they talked together
his face would kindle, unawares, and shine upon them, as
with a mild evening light.  Pensive with the fullness of
such discourse, his guests took leave and went their way;
and passing up the valley, paused to look at the Great Stone
Face, imagining that they had seen its likeness in a human
countenance, but could not remember where.

While Ernest had been growing up and growing old, a
bountiful Providence had granted a new poet to this earth.
He, likewise, was a native of the valley, but had spent the
greater part of his life at a distance from that romantic region, pouring out his sweet music amid the bustle and din
of cities.  Often, however, did the mountains which had
been familiar to him in his childhood lift their snowy peaks
into the clear atmosphere of his poetry.  Neither was the
Great Stone Face forgotten, for the poet had celebrated it in
an ode which was grand enough to have been uttered by its
own majestic lips.  The man of genius, we may say, had
come down from heaven with wonderful endowments.  If
he sang of a mountain, the eyes of all mankind beheld a
mightier grandeur reposing on its breast, or soaring to its
summit, than had before been seen there.  If his theme were
a lovely lake, a celestial smile had now been thrown over it,

to gleam forever on its surface. If it were the vast old sea, even the deep immensity of its dread bosom seemed to swell the higher, as if moved by the emotions of the song. Thus the world assumed another and a better aspect from the hour that the poet blessed it with his happy eyes. The Creator had bestowed him, as the last best touch to his own handiwork. Creation was not finished till the poet came to interpret, and so complete it.

The effect was no less high and beautiful when his human brethren were the subject of his verse. The man or woman, sordid with the common dust of life, who crossed his daily path, and the little child who played in it, were glorified if he beheld them in his mood of poetic faith. He showed the golden links of the great chain that intertwined them with an angelic kindred; he brought out the hidden traits of a celestial birth that made them worthy of such kin. Some, indeed, there were, who thought to show the soundness of their judgment by affirming that all the beauty and dignity of the natural world existed only in the poet's fancy. Let such men speak for themselves, who undoubtedly appear to have beeen .spawned forth by nature with a contemptuous bitterness; she having plastered them up out of her refuse stuff, after all the swine were made. As respects all things else, the poet's ideal was the truest truth.

The songs of this poet found their way to Ernest. He read them after his customary toil, seated on the bench before his cottage door, where for such a length of time he had filled his repose with thought, by gazing at the Great Stone Face. And now as he read stanzas that caused the soul to thrill within him, he lifted his eyes to the vast countenance beaming on him so benignantly.

G—13

"O majestic friend," he murmured, addressing the Great Stone Face, "is not this man worthy to resemble thee?"

The Face seemed to smile, but answered not a word.

Now it happened that the poet, though he dwelt so far away, had not only heard of Ernest, but had meditated much upon his character, until he deemed nothing so desirable as to meet this man, whose untaught wisdom walked hand in hand with the noble simplicity of his life. One summer morning, therefore, he took passage by the railroad, and, in the decline of the afternoon, alighted from the cars at no great distance from Ernest's cottage. The great hotel, which had formerly been the palace of Mr. Gathergold, was close at hand, but the poet, with his carpet-bag on his arm, inquired at once where Ernest dwelt, and was resolved to be accepted as his guest.

Approaching the door, he there found the good old man, holding a volume in his hand, which alternately he read, and then, with a finger between the leaves, looked lovingly at the Great Stone Face.

"Good evening," said the poet. "Can you give a traveler a night's lodging?"

"Willingly," answered Ernest; and then he added, smiling, "methinks I never saw the Great Stone Face look so hospitably at a stranger."

The poet sat down on the bench beside him, and he and Ernest talked together. Often had the poet held intercourse with the wittiest and the wisest, but never before with a man like Ernest, whose thoughts and feelings gushed up with such a natural freedom, and who made great truths so familiar by his simple utterance of them. Angels, as had been so often said, seemed to have wrought with him at his labor in the fields; angels seemed to have sat with him by the fireside; and, dwelling with angels as friend with friends, he had imbibed the sublimity of their ideas, and imbued it with the sweet and lowly charm of household words. So thought the poet. And Ernest, on the other hand, was moved and agitated by the living images which the poet flung out of his mind, and which peopled all the air about the cottage door with shapes of beauty, both gay and pensive. The sympathies of these two men instructed them with a profounder sense than either could have attained alone. Their minds accorded into one strain, and made delightful music which neither of them could have claimed as all his own, nor distinguished his own share from the other's. They led one another, as it were, into a high pavilion of their thoughts, so remote, and hitherto so dim, that they had never entered it before, and so beautiful that they desired to be there always.

As Ernest listened to the poet, he imagined that the Great Stone Face was bending forward to listen too. He gazed earnestly into the poet's glowing eyes.

" Who are you, my strangely gifted guest ? " he said.

The poet laid his finger on the volume that Ernest had been reading.

" You have read these poems," said he. " You know me, then,— for I wrote them."

Again, and still more earnestly than before, Ernest examined the poet's features; then turned towards the Great Stone Face : then back, with an uncertain aspect, to his guest. But his countenance fell; he shook his head, and sighed.

" Wherefore are you sad ? " inquired the poet.

" Because," replied Ernest, " all through life I have awaited the fulfillment of a prophecy; and, when I read these poems. I hoped that it might be fulfilled in you."

" You hoped," answered the poet, faintly smiling, " to find in me the likeness of the Great Stone Face.  And you are disappointed, as formerly with Mr. Gathergold, and Old Blood-and-Thunder, and Old Stony Phiz.  Yes, Ernest, it is my doom.  You must add my name to the illustrious three, and record another failure of your hopes.  For — in shame and sadness do I speak it, Ernest — I am not worthy to be typified by yonder benign and majestic image."

"And why?" asked Ernest.  He pointed to the volume. "Are not those thoughts divine?"

"They have a strain of the Divinity," replied the poet. " You can hear in them the far-off echo of a heavenly song. But my life, dear Ernest, has not corresponded with my thought.  I have had grand dreams, but they have been only dreams, because I have lived — and that, too, by my own choice — among the poor and mean realities.  Sometimes even — shall I dare to say it? — I lack faith in the grandeur, the beauty, and the goodness, which my own works are said to have made more evident in nature and in human life.  Why, then, pure seeker of the good and true, shouldst thou hope to find me in yonder image of the divine?"

The poet spoke sadly, and his eyes were dim with tears. So, likewise, were those of Ernest.

At the hour of sunset, as had long been his frequent custom, Ernest was to discourse to an assemblage of the neighboring inhabitants in the open air.  He and the poet, arm in arm, still talking together as they went along, proceeded to the spot.  It was a small nook among the hills, with a gray precipice behind, the stern front of which was relieved by the pleasant foliage of many creeping plants, that made a tapestry for the naked rock, by hanging their festoons from all its rugged angles.  At a small elevation above the ground, set in a rich framework of verdure, there appeared a niche, spacious enough to admit a human figure, with freedom for such gestures as spontaneously accompany earnest thought and genuine emotion. Into this natural pulpit Ernest ascended, and threw a look of familiar kindness around upon his audience. They stood, or sat, or reclined upon the grass, as seemed good to each, with the departing sunshine falling obliquely over them, and mingling its subdued cheerfulness with the solemnity of a grove of ancient trees, beneath and amid the boughs of which the golden rays were constrained to pass. In another direction was seen the Great Stone Face, with the same cheer, combined with the same solemity, in its benignant aspect.

Ernest began to speak, giving to the people of what was in his heart and mind. His words had power, because they accorded with his thoughts; and his thoughts had reality and depth, because they harmonized with the life which he had always lived. It was not mere breath that this preacher uttered; they were the words of life, because a life of good deeds and holy love was melted into them. Pearls, pure and rich, had been dissolved into this precious draught. The poet, as he listened, felt that the being and character of Ernest were a nobler strain of poetry than he had ever written. His eyes glistening with tears, he gazed reverentially at the venerable man, and said within himself that never was there an aspect so worthy of a prophet and a sage as that mild, sweet, thoughtful countenance, with the glory of white hair diffused about it. At a distance, but distinctly to be seen, high up in the golden light of the setting sun, appeared the Great Stone Face, with hoary mists around it, like the white hairs around the brow of Ernest. Its look of grand beneficence seemed to embrace the world.

At that moment, in sympathy with a thought which he was about to utter, the face of Ernest assumed a grandeur of expression, so imbued with benevolence, that the poet, by an irresistible impulse, threw his arms aloft, and shouted,—

"Behold! Behold! Ernest is himself the likeness of the Great Stone Face!"

Then all the people looked and saw that what the deep-sighted poet said was true. The prophecy was fulfilled. But Ernest, having finished what he had to say, took the poet's arm, and walked slowly homeward, still hoping that some wiser and better man than himself would by and by appear, bearing a resemblance to the GREAT STONE FACE.

---

## THE RED MANTLE.

### A GERMAN LEGEND.

There was a German merchant in the days of old who used to travel with costly jewels from city to city. His name was Berthold. He was an earnest, warm-hearted man, but he had a fiery temper and a sharp tongue.

One day, towards night, he was journeying through a black forest. The winds were sighing in the pines; there were scudding clouds; a great shade came down on the forest, and the rain seemed about to fall. Berthold saw that he could not reach the city that evening. He was alone in the wild forest with his portmanteau of jewels. What was he to do?

Night came on. The moon rose, and was darkened. The forest roared with the wind. Around him were beasts of prey. What could he do?

He stumbled on. At last he saw a gleam of light. It came from a window in the forest. He hastened towards it, and rapped on the door.

The door slowly opened. A grey-haired old woman with a beautiful face stood before him.

"Who lives here?" asked Berthold.

"A poor collier and his family. Why do you come?"

"I am a traveler, belated and lost. Will you give me food and lodging for the night?"

"I will give you food, but I cannot give you lodging, though loth I would be to refuse a stranger a roof on such a night as this."

Her husband now appeared, holding a light over her shoulder.

"It hurts my heart to refuse a stranger," said he, "but you would be better off in the woods than here. How the wind roars! There, the light has blown out! Come in!"

The merchant entered. The great log room had an open fire, and around it sat the most beautiful children he had ever seen. The woman spread the table. As he finished the meal he said, "You surely would not send me out into the forest on such a night as this?"

"Stranger," said the collier, "you may stay, at your peril—though if you will obey what I tell you, no harm will come."

The table was cleared, and the good woman brought out the musical glasses. She tuned them, and when the children touched them the most beautiful music arose, and the father and mother clasped their hands, and the family sang, "Now the woods are all reposing," but still the wind was wild.

"Now," said the father, "we must pray." They all knelt down, the merchant with them.

As the collier was praying, the door slowly opened, and the fresh air fanned the fire. The merchant looked up—what was at the door? What indeed!

A little dwarf stood there, in a red mantle. He seemed withered and pinched up, and his eyes were like coals of fire. He cast an evil look at the merchant, and slowly closed the door. The merchant wondered.

"Now," said the collier, rising, "I will show you to your chamber. But listen! If anything enters your room in the night, think holy thoughts; and no harm will come. Do not be angry; do not utter any evil words. If you do not obey me, you will bring trouble upon me—"

"And we would have to live all those years over again," said the woman with a look of distress. "Think holy thoughts, whatever may happen!"

The merchant went up to his chamber, and, placing his portmanteau on his bed, laid himself down to rest. He was nigh asleep, when the door of his chamber flew open, and the little dwarf with the red mantle and fiery eyes entered. The merchant started. The dwarf approached the bed, his eyes gleaming in the darkness. He stood for a time looking at the merchant. Then laid his hands on the portmanteau. The merchant's anger kindled, and he uttered a fearful oath.

The dwarf began to grow!

The merchant bade him go, with more profane words.

The dwarf grew at every evil word, taller and taller, more dreadful in form end feature.

"Help!" shrieked the merchant. His voice awoke the house.

The dwarf, now a giant, rushed down the stairs.

The collier and his wife appeared.

"What have you done to our house spirit?" cried the collier. "You have not been thinking holy thoughts. You have made him grow to the demon he was of old! We have lived him down by righteous lives, and he had become smaller and smaller, and we hoped to see him disappear."

"And now," cried the collier's wife, bursting into tears, "we will have to live all those years over again!"

The moon was now shining in a still sky, and the merchant took his portmanteau and hurried away.

Ten years passed, when night overtook the merchant, Berthold, in the same forest again. It was a pleasant night, and the merchant bethought himself of the collier. He saw a light in the same house, and went to the door and knocked.

"Come, in God's name, and welcome," said a voice.

He entered. The family had tuned the musical glasses, and were kneeling down to pray. The merchant knelt with them. Then he listened for the door to open. But the room was still. And, instead of the dwarf, there came as it were a beautiful light into the room. The merchant looked up. There was a glorious face forming in the shadows, and as the collier prayed on, it grew more and more distinct, and came and hovered over them, with a golden circle above the head and with glistening wings. It was the face of an angel!

The merchant told the family who he was.

"Stay with us, we pray you," said the collier's wife. "There is nothing to fear; we have lived him down, and now, praised be the Lord, there is an angel in the house. Did you know—one may live so as to change an evil into an angel?"

---

## ABOU BEN ADHEM.

### LEIGH HUNT.

Abou Ben Adhem (may his tribe increase!)
Awoke one night from a deep dream of peace,
And saw, within the moonlight in his room,

Making it rich, and like a lily in bloom,
An angel writing in a book of gold:—
Exceeding peace had made Ben Adhem bold,
And to the presence in the room he said,
'What writest thou?'—The vision raised its head,
And with a look made all of sweet accord,
Answered, 'The names of those who love the Lord!'
'And is mine one?' said Abou.  'Nay, not so,'
Replied the angel.  Abou spoke more low,
But cheerl'y still; and said, 'I pray thee, then,
Write me as one that loves his fellowmen.'
The angel wrote and vanished.  The next night
It came again with great awak'ning light;
And showed the names whom love of God had blessed,
And lo! Ben Adhem's name led all the rest.

---

## WORK.

### JOHN RUSKIN.

*Delivered before the Working Men's Institute, at Camberwell.*

MY FRIENDS,—I have not come among you to-night to
endeavor to give you an entertaining lecture; but to tell you
a few plain facts, and ask you a few plain questions.  I have
seen and known too much of the struggle for life among our
laboring population, to feel at ease, under any circumstances,
in inviting them to dwell on the trivialties of my own studies; but, much more, as I meet to-night, for the first time, the
members of a working Institute established in the district
in which I have passed the greater part of my life, I am
desirous that we should at once understand each other, on
graver matters.  I would fain tell you, with what feelings,
and with what hope, I regard this Institute, as one of many

such, now happily established throughout England, as well as in other countries; and preparing the way for a great change in all the circumstances of industrial life; but of which the success must wholly depend upon our clearly understanding the conditions, and above all, the necessary *limits* of this change. No teacher can truly promote the cause of education, until he knows the mode of life for which that education is to prepare his pupil. And the fact that he is called upon to address you, nominally, as a "Working Class," must compel him, if he is in any wise earnest or thoughtful, to inquire in the outset, on what you yourselves suppose this class distinction has been founded in the past, and must be founded in the future. The manner of the amusement, and the matter of the teaching, which any of us can offer you, must depend wholly on our first understanding from you, whether you think the distinction heretofore drawn between workingmen and others is truly or falsely founded. Do you accept it as it stands? do you wish it to be modified? or do you think the object of education is to efface it, and make us forget it forever?

Let me make myself more distinctly understood. We call this — you and I — a "Working Men's" Institute, and our college in London, a "Working Men's" College. Now, how do you consider that these several institutes differ, or ought to differ from "idle men's" institutes and "idle men's" colleges? Or by what other word than "idle" shall I distinguish those whom the happiest and wisest of working men do not object to call the "Upper Classes"? Are there necessarily upper classes? necessarily lower? How much should those always be elevated, how much these always depressed? And I pray those among my audience who chance to occupy, at present, the higher position, to forgive me what offense there may be in what I am going to say. It is not *I* who wish to say it. Bitter voices say it; voices of battle and of famine through all the world, which must be heard some day, whoever keeps silence. Neither, as you well know, is it to *you* specially that I say it. I am sure that most now present know their duties of kindness, and fulfill them, better perhaps than I do mine. But I speak to you as representing your whole class, which errs, I know, chiefly by thoughtlessness, but not therefore the less terribly. Willful error is limited by the will, but what limit is there to to that of which we are unconscious?

Bear with me, therefore, while I turn to these workmen, and ask them what they think the "upper classes" are, and ought to be, in relation to them. Answer, you workmen who are here, as you would among yourselves, frankly; and tell me how you would have me call your employers. Am I to call them—would *you* think me right in calling them— the idle classes? I think you would feel somewhat uneasy, and as if I were not treating my subject honestly, or speaking from my heart, if I proceeded in my lecture under the supposition that all rich people were idle. You would be both unjust and unwise if you allowed me to say that;—not less unjust than the rich people who say that all the poor are idle, and will never work if they can help it, or more than they can help.

For indeed the fact is, that there are idle poor and idle rich; and there are busy poor and busy rich. Many a beggar is as lazy as if he had ten thousand a year; and many a man of large fortune is busier than his errand-boy, and never would think of stopping in the street to play marbles. So that, in a large view, the distinction between workers and idlers, as between knaves and honest men, runs through the very heart and innermost nature of men of all ranks and in all positions. There is a working class—strong and happy, —among both rich and poor; there is an idle class—weak, wicked, and miserable,—among both rich and poor. And the worst of the misunderstandings arising between the two orders come of the unlucky fact that the wise of one class [how little wise in this!] habitually contemplate the foolish of the *other.* If the busy rich people watched and rebuked the idle rich people, all would be right among *them*: and if the busy poor people watched and rebuked the idle poor people, all would be right among *them.* But each looks for the faults of the other. A hard working man of property is particularly offended by an idle beggar; and an orderly, but poor, workman is naturally intolerant of the licentious luxury of the rich. And what is severe judgment in the minds of the just men of either class, becomes fierce enmity in the unjust—but among the unjust *only.* None but the dissolute among the poor look upon the rich as their natural enemies, or desire to pillage their houses and divide their property. None but the dissolute among the rich speak in opprobrious terms of the vices and follies of the poor.

There is, then, no worldly distinction between idle and industrious people; and I am going to-night to speak only of the industrious. The idle people we will put out of our thoughts at once—they are mere nuisances—what ought to be done with *them,* we'll talk of at another time. But there are class distinctions among the industries themselves; tremendous distinctions, which rise and fall to every degree in the infinite thermometer of human pain and of human power,—distinctions of high and low, of lost and won, to the whole reach of man's soul and body.

These separations we will study, and the laws of them,

among energetic men only, who, whether they work or whether they play, put their strength into the work, and their strength into the game; being in the full sense of the word "industrious," one way or another,—with purpose, or without.

And these distinctions are mainly four:—

I. Between those who work, and those who play.

II. Between those who produce the means of life, and those who consume them.

III. Between those who work with the head, and those who work with the hand.

IV. Between those who work wisely, and those who work foolishly.

For easier memory, let us say we are going to oppose, in our examination,—

      I. Work to play;

      II. Production to consumption;

      III. Head to hand; and,

      IV. Sense to nonsense.

I. First, then, of the distinction between the classes who work and the classes who play. Of course we must agree upon a definition of these terms,—work and play,—before going farther. Now, roughly, not with vain subtlety of definition, but for plain use of the words, "play" is an exertion of body or mind, made to please ourselves, and with no determined end; and work is a thing done because it ought to be done, and with a determined end. You play, as you call it, at cricket, for instance. That is as hard work as anything else; but it amuses you, and it has no result but the amusement. If it were done as an ordered form of exercise, for health's sake, it would become work directly. So, in like manner, whatever we do to please ourselves, and only for the sake of the pleasure, not for an ultimate object, is "play," the "pleasing thing," not the useful thing. Play may be useful in a secondary sense (nothing is indeed more useful or necessary); but the use of it depends on its being spontaneous.

Let us, then, inquire together what sort of games the playing class in England spend their lives in playing at.

The first of all English games is making money. That is an all-absorbing game; and we knock each other down oftener in playing at that than at football, or any other roughest sport; and it is absolutely without purpose; no one who engages heartily in that game ever knows why. Ask a great moneymaker what he wants to do with his money— he never knows. He doesn't make it to do anything with it. He gets it only that he *may* get it. "What will you make of what you have got?" you ask. "Well, I'll get more," he says. Just as, at cricket, you get more runs. There's no use in the runs, but to get more of them than other people is the game. And there's no use in the money, but to have more of it than other people is the game. So all that great foul city of London there,—rattling, growling, smoking, stinking,—a ghastly heap of fermenting brickwork, pouring out poison at every pore,—you fancy it is a city of work? Not a street of it! It is a great city of play; very nasty play, and very hard play, but still play. It is only Lord's cricket ground without the turf,—a huge billiard table without the cloth, and with pockets as deep as the bottomless pit; but mainly a billiard table, after all.

Well, the first great English game is this playing at counters. It differs from the rest in that it appears always to be producing money, while every other game is expensive. But it does not always produce money. There's a great difference between "winning" money and "making" it; a great difference between getting it out of another' man's pocket into ours, or filling both.

Our next great English games, however, hunting and shooting, are costly altogether; and how much we are fined for them annually in land, horses, game keepers, and game laws, and the resultant demoralization of ourselves, our children, and our retainers, and all else that accompanies that beautiful and special English game, I will not endeavor to count now: but note only that, except for exercise, this is not merely a useless game, but a deadly one, to all connected with it. For through horse-racing, you get every form of what the higher classes everywhere call "Play," in distinction from all other plays; that is, gambling; and through game-preserving, you get also some curious laying out of ground; that beautiful arrangement of dwelling-house for man and beast, by which we have grouse and black-cock —so many brace to the acre, and men and women—so many brace to the garret. I often wonder what the angelic builders and surveyors—the angelic builders who build the "many mansions" up above there; and the angelic surveyors, who measured that four-square city with their measuring reeds—I wonder what they think, or are supposed to think, of the laying out of the ground by this nation.

Then, next to the gentlemen's game of hunting, we must put the ladies' game of dressing. It is not the cheapest of games. And I wish I could tell you what this "play" costs, altogether, in England, France, and Russia annually. But it is a pretty game, and on certain terms I like it; nay, I don't see it played quite as much as I would fain have it. You ladies like to lead the fashion:—by all means lead it—lead it thoroughly,—lead it far enough. Dress yourselves nicely,

and dress everybody else nicely.  Lead the *fashions for the
poor* first; make *them* look well, and you yourselves will look,
in ways of which you have now no conception, all the better.
The fashions you have set for some time among your peasantry are not pretty ones; their doublets are too irregularly
slashed, or as Chaucer calls it "all to-slittered," though not
for "queintise," and the wind blows too frankly through them.

Then there are other games, wild enough, as I could show
you if I had time.

There's playing at literature, and playing at art;—very
different, both, from working at literature, or working at art,
but I've no time to speak of these.  I pass to the greatest of
all—the play of plays, the great gentlemen's game, which
ladies like them best to play at,—the game of War.  It is
entrancingly pleasant to the imagination; we dress for it,
however, more finely than for any other sport; and go out
to it, not merely in scarlet, as to hunt, but in scarlet and
gold, and all manner of fine colors; of course we could fight
better in gray, and without feathers; but all nations have
agreed that it is good to be well dressed at this play.  Then
the bats and balls are very costly ; our English and French
bats, with the balls and wickets, even those which we don't
make any use of, costing, I suppose, now, about fifteen
millions of money annually to each nation; all which you
know is paid for by hard laborer's work in the furrow and
furnace.  A costly game!—not to speak of its consequences
I will say at present nothing of these.  The mere immediate
cost of all these plays is what I want you to consider; they
are all paid for in deadly work somewhere, as many of us
know too well .  The jewel-cutter, whose sight fails over the
diamonds; the weaver, whose arm fails over the webb; the
iron-forger, whose breath fails before the furnace—*they* know

what work is—they, who have all the work, and none of the play, except a kind they have named for themselves down in the north black country, where "play" means being laid up by sickness. It is a pretty example for philologists, of varying dialect, this change in the sense of the word, as used in the black country of Birmingham, and the red and black country of Baden Baden. Yes, gentlemen, and gentlewomen, of England, who think "one moment unamused a misery, not made for feeble man," this is what you have brought the word "play" to mean, in the heart of merry England! You may have your fluting and piping; but there are sad children sitting in the market-place, who indeed cannot say to you, "We have piped unto you, and ye have not danced:" but eternally shall say to you, "We have mourned unto you, and ye have not lamented."

This, then, is the first distinction between the "upper and lower" classes. And this is one which is by no means necessary; which indeed must, in process of good time, be by all honest men's consent abolished. Men will be taught that an existence of play, sustained by the blood of other creatures, is a good existence for gnats and jelly-fish; but not for men: that neither days, nor lives, can be made holy or noble by doing nothing in them: that the best prayer at the beginning of a day is that we may not lose its moments; and the best grace before meat, the consciousness that we have justly earned our dinner. And when we have this much of plain Christianity preached to us again, and cease to translate the strict words, "Son, go work to-day in my vineyard," into the dainty ones: "Baby, go play to-day in my vineyard," we shall all be workers, in one way or another; and this much at least of the distinction between "upper" and "lower" forgotten.

II. I pass then to our second distinction ; between the rich and poor, between Dives and Lazarus,—distinction which exists more sternly, I suppose, in this day, than ever in the world, Pagan or Christian, till now. Consider, for instance, what the general tenor of such a paper as the *Morning Post* implies of delicate luxury among the rich; and then read this chance extract from it :—

"Yesterday morning, at eight o'clock, a woman, passing a dung-heap in the stone-yard near the recently erected alms-houses in Shadwell Gap, High street, Shadwell, called the attention of a Thames police-constable to a man in a sitting position on the dung-heap, and said she was afraid he was dead. Her fears proved to be true. The wretched creature appeared to have been dead several hours. He had perished of cold and wet, and the rain had been beating down on him all night. The deceased was a bone-picker. He was in the lowest stage of poverty, poorly clad, and half-starved. The police had frequently driven him away from the stone-yard, between sunset and sunrise, and told him to go home. He selected a most desolate spot for his wretched death. A penny and some bones were found in his pockets. The deceased was between fifty and sixty years of age. Inspector Roberts, of the K division, has given directions for inquiries to be made at the lodging-houses respecting the deceased, to ascertain his identity if possible."—*Morning Post*, November 25, 1864.

Compare the statement of the finding bones in his pocket with the following, from the *Telegraph* of January 16th of this year :—

"Again, the dietary scale for adult and juvenile paupers was drawn up by the most conspicuous political economists in England. It is low in quantity, but it is sufficient to support nature; yet within ten years of the passing of the Poor Law Act, we heard of the paupers in the Andover Union gnawing the scraps of putrid flesh and sucking the marrow from the bones of horses which they were employed to crush."

You see my reason for thinking that our Lazarus of Christianity has some advantage over the Jewish one. Jewish Lazarus expected, or at least prayed, to be fed with crumbs from the rich man's table; but *our* Lazarus is fed with crumbs from the dog's table.

Now this distinction between rich and poor rests on two bases. Within its proper limits, on a basis which is lawful and everlastingly necessary; beyond them, on a basis unlawful, and everlastingly corrupting the frame-work of society. The lawful basis of wealth is, that a man who works should be paid the fair value of his work; and that if he does not choose to spend it to-day, he should have free leave to keep it, and spend it to-morrow. Thus, an industrious man working daily, and laying by daily, attains at last the possession of an accumulated sum of wealth, to which he has absolute right. The idle person who will not work, and the wasteful person who lays nothing by, at the end of the same time will be doubly poor—poor in possession, and dissolute in moral habit; and he will then naturally covet the money which the other has saved. And if he is then allowed to attack the other, and rob him of his well-earned wealth, there is no more any motive for saving, or any reward for good conduct; and all society is thereupon dissolved, or exists only in systems of rapine. Therefore the first necessity of social life is the clearness of national conscience in enforcing the law—that he should keep who has JUSTLY EARNED.

That law, I say, is the proper basis of distinction between

rich and poor. But there is also a false basis of distinction ; namely, the power held over those who are earning wealth by those who already possess it, and only use it to gain more. There will be always a number of men who would fain set themselves to the accumulation of wealth as the sole object of their lives. Necessarily, that class of men is an unedu- cated class, inferior in intellect, and more or less cowardly. It is physically impossible for a well-educated, intellectual, or brave man to make money the chief object of his thoughts ; just as it is for him to make his dinner the principal object of them. All healthy people like their dinners, but their dinner is not the main object of their lives. So all healthy-• minded people like making money—ought to like it, and to enjoy the sensation of winning it ; but the main object of their life is not money ; it is something better than money. A good soldier, for instance, mainly wishes to do his fighting well. He is glad of his pay—very properly so, and justly grumbles when you keep him ten years without it—still, his main notion of life is to win battles, not to be paid for win- ning them. So of clergymen. They like pew-rents, and baptismal fees, of course ; but yet, if they are brave and well- educated, the pew-rent is not the sole object of their lives,' and the baptismal fee is not the sole purpose of the baptism ; the clergyman's object is essentially to baptise and preach, not to be paid for preaching. So of doctors. They like fees no doubt,—ought to like them ; yet if they are brave and well-educated, the entire object of their lives is not fees. They, on the whole, desire to cure the sick ; and,—if they are good doctors, and the choice were fairly put to them,—would rather cure their patient and lose their fee, than kill him, and get it. And so with all other brave and rightly-trained men ; their work is first, their fees second—very important always, but still *second.*    But in every nation, as I said, there are a vast class who are ill-educated, cowardly, and more or less stupid.    And with these people, just as certainly the fee is first, and the work second, as with brave people the work is first and the fee second.    And this is no small distinction. It is between life and death *in* a man, between heaven and hell *for* him.    You cannot serve two masters;—you *must* serve one or other.    If your work is first with you, and your fee second, work is your master, and the lord of work, who is God.    But if your fee is first with you, and your work second, fee is your master, and the lord of fee, who is the Devil; and not only the Devil, but the lowest of devils—the "least erected fiend that fell."    So there you have it in brief terms; Work first—you are God's servants; Fee first—you are the Fiend's.    And it makes a difference, now and ever, believe me, whether you serve Him who has on His vesture and thigh written, "King of Kings," and whose service is perfect freedom; or him on whose vesture and thigh the name is written, "Slave of Slaves," and whose service is perfect slavery.

However, in every nation there are, and must always be, a certain number of these Fiend's servants, who have it principally for the object of their lives to make money. They are always, as I said, more or less stupid, and cannot conceive of anything else so nice as money.    Stupidity is always the basis of the Judas bargain.    We do great injustice to Iscariot, in thinking him wicked above all common wickedness.    He was only a common money-lover, and, like all money-lovers, did not understand Christ; — could not make out the worth of Him, or meaning of Him.    He never thought He would be killed.    He was horror-struck when he found that Christ would be killed; threw his money away instantly, and hanged himself.    How many of

our present money-seekers, think you, would have the grace
to hang themselves, whoever was killed? But Judas was a
common, selfish, muddle-headed, pilfering fellow; his hand
always in the bag of the poor, not caring for them. Helpless to understand Christ, yet believed in Him, much more
than most of us do; had seen him do miracles, thought He
was quite strong enough to shift for Himself, and he, Judas,
might as well make his own little bye-perquisites out of
the affair. Christ would come out of it well enough, and
he have his thirty pieces. Now, that is the money-seeker's
idea, all over the world. He doesn't hate Christ, but can't
understand Him—doesn't care for Him—sees no good in
that benevolent business; makes his own little job out of it
at all events, come what will. And thus, out of every mass
of men, you have a certain number of bag-men—your "fee-
first," men, whose main object is to make money. And
they do make it—make it in all sorts of unfair ways, chiefly
by the weight and force of money itself, or what is called
the power of capital; that is to say, the power which money,
once obtained, has over the labor of the poor, so that the
capitalist can take all its produce to himself, except the
laborer's food. That is the modern Judas's way of "carrying the bag," and "bearing what is put therein."

Nay, but (it is asked) how is that an unfair advantage?
Has not the man who has worked for the money a right to
use it as he best can? No, in this respect, money is now
exactly what mountain promontories over public roads were
in old times. The barons fought for them fairly:—the
strongest and cunningest got them; then fortified them, and
made everyone who passed below pay toll. Well, capital
now is exactly what crags were then. Men fight fairly (we
will, at least, grant so much, though it is more than we

ought) for their money; but, once having got it, the fortified
millionaire can make everybody who passes below pay
toll to his million, and build another tower of his money
castle. And I can tell you, the poor vagrants by the roadside suffer now quite as much from the bag-baron, as they
ever did from the crag-baron. Bags and crags have just the
same result on rags. I have not time, however, to-night to
show you in how many ways the power of capital is unjust;
but remember this one great principle — you will find it
unfailing — that whenever money is the principal object of
life with either man or nation, it is both got ill, and spent
ill; and does harm both in the getting and spending; but
when it is not the principal object, it and all other things
will be well got and well spent. And here is the test, with
every man, of whether money is the principal object with
him, or not. If in mid-life he could pause and say, "Now
I have enough to live upon, I'll live upon it; and having
well earned it, I will also well spend it, and go out of the
world poor, as I came into it," then money is not principal
with him; but if, having enough to live upon in the manner befitting his character and rank, he still wants to make
more, and to *die* rich, then money is the principal object
with him, and it becomes a curse to himself, and generally
to those who spend it after him. For you know it *must* be
spent some day; the only question is whether the man who
makes it shall spend it, or some one else, and generally it is
better for the maker to spend it, for he will know best its
value and use. And if a man does not choose thus to spend
his money, he must either hoard it or lend it, and the worst
thing he can generally do is to lend it; for borrowers are
nearly always ill-spenders, and it is with lent money that
all evil is mainly done, and all unjust war protracted.

For observe what the real fact is, respecting loans to
foreign military governments, and how strange it is. If
your little boy came to you to ask for money to spend
in squibs and crackers, you would think twice before you
gave it to him, and you would have some idea that it was
wasted, when you saw it fly off in fireworks, even though he
did no mischief with it. But the Russian children and
Austrian children come to you, borrrowing money, not to
spend in innocent squibs, but in cartridges and bayonets to
attack you in India with, and to keep down all noble life in
Italy with, and to murder Polish women and children with;
and *that* you will give at once, because they pay you interest
for it. Now, in order to pay you that interest, they must
tax every working peasant in their dominions; and on that
work you live. You therefore at once rob the Austrian
peasant, assassinate or banish the Polish peasant, and you
live on the produce of the theft, and the bribe for the assas-
sination! That is the broad fact — that is the practical
meaning of your foreign loans, and of most large interest of
money; and then you quarrel with Bishop Colenso, for-
sooth, as if *he* denied the Bible, and you believed it! though,
every deliberate act of your lives is a new defiance of its
primary orders.

III. I must pass, however, now to our third condition of
separation, between the men who work with the hand and
those who work with the head.

And here we have at last an inevitable distinction.
There *must* be work done by the arms, or none of us
could live. There *must* be work done by the brains, or
the life we get would not be worth having. And the
same men cannot do both. There is rough work to be
done, and rough men must do it; there is gentle work to

be done, and gentlemen must do it; and it is physically impossible that one class should do, or divide, the work of the other.   And it is of no use to try to conceal this sorrowful fact by fine words, and to talk to the workman about the honorableness of manual labor, and the dignity of humanity. Rough work, honorable or not, takes the life out of us; and the man who has been heaving clay out of a ditch all day, or driving an express train against the north wind all night, or holding a collier's helm in a gale on a lee-shore, or whirling white-hot iron at a furnace mouth, is not the same man at the end of his day, or night as one who has been sitting in a quiet room, with everything comfortable about him, reading books, or classing butterflies, or painting pictures. If it is any comfort to you to be told that the rough work is the more honorable of the two, I should be sorry to take that much of consolation from you; and in some sense I need not.   The rough work is at all events real, honest, and, generally, though not always, useful; while the fine work is, a great deal of it, foolish and false as well as fine, and therefore dishonorable: but when both kinds are equally well and worthily done, the head's is the noble work, and the hand's the ignoble.   Therefore, of all hand work whatsoever, necessary for the maintenance of life, those old words, " In the sweat of thy face thou shalt eat bread," indicate that the inherent nature of it is one of calamity : and that the ground, cursed for our sake, casts also some shadow of degradation into our contest with its thorn and its thistle; so that all nations have held their days honorable or "holy," and constituted them "holydays" or "holidays," by making them days of rest; and the promise, which, among all our distant hopes, seems to cast the chief brightness over death, is that blessing of the dead who die in the Lord, that "they rest from their labors, and their works do follow them."

And thus the perpetual question and contest must arise, who is to do this rough work? and how is the worker of it to be comforted, redeemed, and rewarded? and what kind of play should he have, and what rest, in this world, sometimes, as well as in the next? Well, my good laborious friends, these questions will take a little time to answer yet. They *must* be answered: all good men are occupied with them, and all honest thinkers. There's grand head work doing about them; but much must be discovered, and much attempted in vain, before anything decisive can be told you. Only note these few particulars, which are already sure.

As to the distribution of the hard work. None of us, or very few of us, do either hard or soft work because we think we ought; but because we have chanced to fall into the way of it, and cannot help ourselves. Now, nobody does anything well that they cannot help doing: work is only done well when it is done with a will; and no man has a thoroughly sound will unless he knows he is doing what he should, and is in his place. And, depend upon it, all work must be done at last, not in a disorderly, scrambling, doggish way, but in an ordered, soldierly, human way—a lawful or "loyal" way. Men are enlisted for the labor that kills—the labor of war: they are counted, trained, fed, dressed, and praised for that. Let them be enlisted also for the labor that feeds: let them be counted, trained, fed, dressed, praised for that. Teach the plough exercise as carefully as you do the sword exercise, and let the officers of troops of life be held as much gentlemen as the officers of troops of death; and all is done: but neither this, nor any other right thing, can be accomplished—you can't even see your way to it—

unless, first of all, both servant and master are resolved that,
come what will of it, they will do each other justice.

People are perpetually squabbling about what will be best
to do, or easiest to do, or advisablest to do, or profitablest to
do; but they never, so far as I hear them talk, ever ask
what it is *just* to do. And it is the law of Heaven that you
shall not be able to judge what is wise or easy, unless you
are first resolved to judge what is just, and to do it. That
is the one thing constantly reiterated by our Master—the
order of all others that is given oftenest—"Do justice and
judgment." That's your Bible order; that's the "Service of
God,"—not praying nor psalm-singing. You are told, indeed,
to sing psalms when you are merry, and to pray when you
need anything; and, by the perverseness of the Evil Spirit,
we get to think that praying and psalm-singing are "service."
If a child finds itself in want of anything, it runs in and
asks its father for it—does it call that doing its father a
service? If it begs for a toy or a piece of cake—does it call
that serving its father? That, with God, is prayer, and He
likes to hear it: He likes you to ask Him for cake when you
want it; but He doesn't call that "serving Him." Begging
is not serving: God likes mere beggars as little as you do—
he likes honest servants, not beggars. So when a child loves
its father very much, and is very happy, it may sing little
songs about him; but it doesn't call that serving its father;
neither is singing songs about God, serving God. It is
enjoying ourselves, if it's anything; most probably its nothing; but if it's anything, it is serving ourselves, not God.
And yet we are impudent enough to call our beggings and
chantings "Divine service:" we say "Divine service" will
be 'performed'" (that's our word—the form of it gone
through) "at so-and-so o'clock." Alas! unless we perform

Divine service in every willing act of life, we never perform it all. The one Divine work—the one ordered sacrifice—is to do justice; and it is the last we are ever inclined to do. Anything rather than that! As much charity as you choose, but no justice. "Nay," you will say, "charity is greater than justice." Yes, it is greater; it is the summit of justice —it is the temple of which justice is the foundation. But you can't have the top without the bottom; you can not build upon charity. You must build upon justice, for this main reason, that you have not, at first, charity to build with. It is the last reward of good work. Do justice to your brother (you can do that, whether you love him or not), and you will come to love him. But do injustice to him, because you don't love him; and you will come to hate him.

It is all very fine to think you can build upon charity to begin with; but you will find all you will have got to begin with, begins at home, and is essentially love of yourself. You well-to-do people, for instance, who are here to-night, will go to "Divine service" next Sunday, all nice and tidy, and your little children will have their tight little Sunday boots on, and lovely little Sunday feathers in their hats; and you'll think, complacently and piously, how lovely they look going to church in their best! So they do: and you love them heartily, and you like sticking feathers in their hats. That's all right: that *is* charity; but it is charity beginning at home. Then you will come to the poor little crossing-sweeper, got up also,—it, in its Sunday dress,—the dirtiest rags it has,—that it may beg the better! you will give it a penny, and think how good you are, and how good God is to prefer your child to the crossing sweeper and be- stow on it a divine hat, feathers, and boots, and the pleas-

ure of giving pence instead of begging for them. That's
charity going abroad. But what does Justice say, walking
and watching near us? Christian Justice has been strangely
mute, and seemingly blind; and, if not blind, decrepit, this
many a day: she keeps her accounts still, however—quite
steadily—doing them at nights, carefully, with her band-
age off, and through acutest spectacles (the only modern
scientific invention she cares·about). You must put your
ear down ever so close to her lips to hear her speak; and
then you will start at what she first whispers, for it will certainly be, "Why shouldn't that little crossing-sweeper have
a feather on its head, as well as your own child?" Then
you may ask Justice, in an amazed manner, "How she can
possibly be so foolish as to think children could sweep
crossings with feathers on their heads?" Then you stoop
again, and Justice says—still in her dull, stupid way—
"Then, why don't you, every other Sunday, leave your
child to sweep the crossing, and take the little sweeper to
church in a hat and feather?" Mercy on us (you think),
what will she say next? And you answer, of course, that " you
don't, because everybody ought to remain content in the position in which Providence has placed them." Ah, my friends,
that's the gist of the whole question. *Did* Providence put
them in that position or did *you*? You knock a man into
a ditch, and then you tell him to remain content in the
"position in which Providence has placed him." That's
modern Christianity. You say—" *We* did not knock him
into the ditch." We shall never know what you have done
or left undone, until the question with us every morning, is
not how to do the gainful thing, but how to do the just
thing during the day; nor until we are at least so far on the
way to being Christian, as to acknowledge that maxim of

the poor half-way Mahometan , "One hour in the execution
of justice is worth seventy years of prayer."

Supposing, then, we have it determined with appropriate
justice, *who* is to do the hand-work, the next question must
be how the hand-workers are to be paid, and how they are
to be refreshed, and what play they are to have. Now, the
possible quantity of play depends on the possible quantity
of pay; and the quantity of pay is not a matter for consideration to hand-workers only, but to all workers. Generally,
good, useful work, whether of the hand or head, is either
ill-paid, or not paid at all. I don't say it should be so, but
it always is so. People, as a rule, only pay for being
amused or being cheated, not for being served. Five thous-
and a year to your talker, and a shilling a day to your
fighter, digger, and thinker, is the rule. None of the best
head work in art, science, or literature is ever paid for.
How much do you think Homer got for his *Iliad?* or Dante
for his *Paradise?* only bitter bread and salt, and going up
and down other people's stairs. In science, the man who
discovered the telescope, and first saw heaven, was paid with
a dungeon; the man who invented the microscope, and first
saw earth, died of starvation, driven from his home. It is
indeed very clear that God means all thoroughly good work
and talk to be done for nothing. Baruch, the scribe, did
not get a penny a line for writing Jeremiah's second roll for
him, I fancy; and St. Stephen did not get bishop's pay for
that long sermon of his to the Pharisees; nothing but
stones. For, indeed, that is the world-father's proper payment. So surely as any of the world's children work for
the world's good, honestly, with head and heart; and come
to it, saying, "Give us a little bread, just to keep the life in
us," the world-father answers them, "No, my children, not

bread; a stone, if you like, or as many as you need, to keep
you quiet and tell to future ages, how unpleasant you made
yourself to the one you lived in."

But the hand-workers are not so ill off as all this comes
to. The worst that can happen to *you* is to break stones;
not be broken by them. And for you there will come a time
for better payment; we shall pay people not quite so much
for talking in Parliament and doing nothing, as for holding
their tongues out of it and doing something; we shall pay
our ploughman a little more, and our lawyer a little less,
and so on: but, at least, we may even now take care that
whatever work is done shall be fully paid for; and the man
who does it paid for it, not somebody else; and that it shall
be done in an orderly, soldierly, well-guided, wholesome
way, under good captains and lieutenants of labor; and that
it shall have its appointed times of rest, and enough of
them; and that in those times the play shall be wholesome
play, not in theatrical gardens, with tin flowers and gas
sunshine, and girls dancing because of their misery; but in
true gardens, with real flowers, and real sunshine, and
children dancing because of their gladness; so that truly
·the streets shall be full (the "streets," mind you, not the
gutters) of children, playing in the midst thereof. We may
take care that working-men shall have at least as good
books to read as anybody else, when they've time to read
them; and as comfortable firesides to sit at as anybody else,
when they've time to sit at them. This, I think, can be
managed for you, my laborious friends, in the good time.

IV. I must go on, however, to our last head, concerning
ourselves all, as workers. What is wise work, and what is
foolish work? What is the difference between sense and
nonsense, in daily occupation?

There are three tests of wise work:—that it must be honest, useful, and cheerful.

I. It is HONEST. I hardly know anything more strange than that you recognize honesty in play, and you do not in work. In your lightest games, you have always some one to see what you call "fair-play." In boxing you must hit fair; in racing, start fair. Your English watch-word is "fair-*play*," your English hatred, "foul-*play*." Did it never strike you that you wanted another watchword also, "fair-*work*," and another and bitterer hatred—"foul-*work*?" Your prize-fighter has some honor in him yet; and so have the men in the ring round him: they will judge him to lose the match, by foul hitting. But your prize-merchant gains his match by foul selling, and no one cries out against that. You drive a gambler out of the gambling-room who loads dice, but you leave a tradesman in flourishing business who loads scales! For observe, all dishonest dealing *is* loading scales. What difference does it make whether I get short weight, adulterate substance, or dishonest fabric?—unless that flaw in the substance or fabric is the worse evil of the two. Give me short measure of food, and I only lose by you; but give me adulterate food, and I die by you. Here, then, is your chief duty, you workmen and tradesmen—to be true to yourselves, and to us who would help you. We can do nothing for you, nor you for yourselves, without honesty. Get that, you get all; without that, your suffrages, your reforms, your free-trade measures, your institutions of science, are all in vain. It is useless to put your heads together, if you can't put your hearts together. Shoulder to shoulder, right hand to right hand, among yourselves, and no wrong hand to anybody else, and you'll win the world yet.

II. Then, secondly, wise work is USEFUL. No man minds,

or ought to mind. its being hard, if only it comes to something; but when it is hard and comes to nothing; when all our bees' business turns to spiders'; and for honey-comb we have only resultant cobweb, blown away by the next breeze— that is the cruel thing for the worker. Yet do we ever ask ourselves. personally. or even nationally, whether our work is coming to anything or not? We don't care to keep what has been nobly done; still less do we care to do nobly what others would keep; and, least of all, to make the work itself useful instead of deadly to the doer, so as to exert his life indeed, but not to waste it. Of all wastes, the greatest waste that you can commit is the waste of labor. If you went down in the morning into your dairy, and found that your youngest child had got down before you, and that he and the cat were at play together, and that he had poured out all the cream on the floor for the cat to lap up, you would scold the child, and be sorry the cream was wasted. But if, instead of wooden bowls with milk in them, there are golden bowls with human life in them, and instead of the cat to play with—the devil to play with; and you yourself the player; and instead of leaving that golden bowl to be broken by God at the fountain. you break it in the dust yourself, and pour the human life out on the ground for the fiend to lick up—that is no waste!

What! you perhaps think. "to waste the labor of men is not to kill them." Is it not? I should like to know how you could kill them more utterly—kill them with second deaths. seventh deaths, hundredfold deaths? It is the slightest way of killing to stop a man's breath. Nay; the hunger, and the cold, and the whistling bullets—our love-messengers between nation and nation—have brought pleasant messages to many a man before now; orders of sweet release, and leave at last to go where he will be most welcome and most happy. At the worst you do but shorten his life, you do not corrupt his life. But if you put him to base labor, if you bind his thoughts, if you blind his eyes, if you blunt his hopes, if you steal his joys, if you stunt his body, and blast his soul, and at last leave him not so much as strength to reap the poor fruit of his degradation, but gather that for yourself, and dismiss him to the grave, when you have done with him, having, so far as in you lay, made the walls of that grave everlasting; (though, indeed, I fancy the goodly bricks of some of our family vaults will hold closer in the resurrection day than the sod over the laborer's head), this you think is no waste and no sin!

III. Then, lastly, wise work is CHEERFUL, as a child's work is. And now I want you to take one thought home with you, and let it stay with you. Everybody in this room has been taught to pray daily, "Thy kingdom come." Now, if we hear a man swear in the streets, we think it very wrong, and say he "takes God's name in vain." But there's a twenty times worse way of taking His name in vain, than that. It is to *ask God for what we don't want.* He doesn't like that sort of prayer. If you don't want a thing, don't ask for it: such asking is the worst mockery of your King you can insult Him with; the soldiers striking Him on the head with the reed was nothing to that. If you do not wish for His kingdom, don't pray for it. But if you do you must do more than pray for it; you must work for it. And, to work for it, you must know what it is: we have all prayed for it many a day without thinking. Observe, it is a kingdom that is to come to us; we are not to go to it. Also, it is not to be a kingdom of the dead, but of the living. Also, it is not to come all at once, but quietly; nobody knows

how. " The kingdom of God cometh not with observation."
Also, it is not to come outside of us, but in our hearts: " the
kingdom of God is within you." And being within us, it is
not a thing to be seen, but to be felt; and, though it brings
all substance of good with it, it does not consist in that:
" The kingdom of God is not meat and drink, but righteousness, peace, and joy in the Holy Ghost:" joy, that is to say,
in the holy, healthful, and helpful Spirit. Now, if we want
to work for this kingdom, and to bring it, and enter into it,
there's one curious condition to be first accepted. You must
enter it as children, or not at all; " Whosoever will not
receive it as a little child shall not enter therein." And
again, "Suffer little children to come unto me, and forbid
them not, *for of such is the kingdom of heaven.*"

*Of such,* observe. Not of children themselves, but of such
as children. I believe most mothers who read that text
think that all heaven or the earth—when it gets to be like
heaven—is to be full of babies. But that's not so. "Length
of days, and long life and peace," that is the blessing, not to
die, still less to live, in babyhood. It is the *character* of
children we want, and must gain at our peril; let us see,
briefly, in what it consists.

The first character of right childhood is that it is Modest.
A well-bred child does not think it can teach its parents, or
that it knows everything. It may think its father and
mother know everything,—perhaps that all grown-up people
know everything; very certainly it is sure that *it* does not.
And it is always asking questions, and wanting to know
more. Well, that is the first character of a good and wise
man at his work. To know that he knows very little;—to
perceive that there are many above him wiser than he; and
to be always asking questions, wanting to learn, not to teach.

No one ever teaches well who wants to teach, or governs well who wants to govern; it is an old saying (Plato's, but I know not if his, first), and as wise as old.

Then, the second character of right childhood is to be Faithful. Perceiving that its father knows best what is good for it, and having found always, when it has tried its own way against his, that he was right and it was wrong, a noble child trusts him at last wholly, gives him its hand, and will walk blindfold with him, if he bids it. And that is the true character of all good men also, as obedient workers, or soldiers under captains. They must trust their captains;— they are bound for their lives to choose none but those whom they *can* trust. Then, they are not always to be thinking that what seems strange to them, or wrong in what they are desired to do, *is* strange or wrong. They know their captain: where he leads they must follow,—what he bids they must do; and without this trust and faith, without this captain- ship and soldiership, no great deed, no great salvation, is possible to man.

Then the third character of right childhood is to be Loving. Give a little love to a child, and you get a great deal back. It loves everything near it, when it is a right kind of child; would hurt nothing, would give the best it has away, always, if you need it; does not lay plans for get- ting everything in the house for itself, and delights in help- ing people; you can not please it so much as by giving it a chance of being useful, in ever so humble a way.

And because of all these characters, lastly, it is Cheerful. Putting its trust in its father, it is careful for nothing—being full of love to every creature, it is happy always, whether in its play or in its duty. Well, that's the great worker's character also. Taking no thought for the morrow; taking thought only for the duty of the day; trusting somebody else to take care of to-morrow ; knowing indeed what labor is, but not what sorrow is; and always, ready for play—beautiful play.   For lovely human play is like the play of the Sun.   There's a worker for you.   He, steady to his time, is set as a strong man to run his course, but also, he *rejoiceth* as a strong man to run his course.   See how he plays in the morning, with the mists below, and the clouds above, with a ray here and a flash there, and a shower of jewels everywhere; that's the Sun's play; and great human play is like his—all various—all full of light and life, and tender, as the dew of the morning.

So then, you have the child's character in these four things—Humility, Faith. Charity, and Cheerfulness.   That's what you have got to be converted to.   " Except ye be converted and become as liltle children."—You hear much of conversion nowadays; but people always seem to think they have got to be madē wretched by conversion,—to be con verted to long faces.   No, friends, you have got to be converted to short ones ; you have to repent into childhood, to repent into delight and delightsomeness.   You can't go into a conventicle but you'll hear plenty of talk of backsliding. Backsliding, indeed!   I can tell you, on the ways most of us go, the faster we slide back the better.   Slide back into the cradle, if going on is into the grave :—back, I tell you : back—out of your long faces, and into your long clothes. It is among children only, and as children only, that you will find medicine for your healing and true wisdom for your teaching.   There is poison in the counsels of the *men* of this world; the words they speak are all bitterness, "the poison of asps is under their lips," but, "the sucking child shall play by the hole of the asp."   Their is death in the looks of men. "Their eyes are privily set against the poor;" they are as the uncharmable serpent, the cockatrice, which slew by seeing. But "the weaned child shall lay his hand on the cockatrice' den." There is death in the steps of men : "their feet are swift to shed blood; they have compassed us in our steps like the lion that is greedy of his prey, and the young lion lurking in secret places;" but, in that kingdom, the wolf shall lie down with the lamb, and the fatling with the lion, and "a little child shall lead them." There is death in the thoughts of men: the world is one wide riddle to them, darker and darker as it draws to a close; but the secret of it is known to the child, and the Lord of heaven and earth is most to be thanked in that "He has hidden these things from the wise and prudent, and has revealed them unto babes." Yes, and there is death—infinitude of death in the principalities and powers of men. As far as the east is from the west, so far our sins are—*not* set from us, but multiplied around us: the Sun himself, think you he *now* "rejoices" to run his course, when he plunges westward to the horizon, so widely red, not with clouds, but blood? And it will be red more widely yet. Whatever drought of the early and latter rain may be, there will be none of that red rain. You fortify yourselves, you arm yourselves against it in vain; the enemy and avenger will be upon you also, unless you learn that it is not out of the mouths of the knitted gun, or the smooth rifle, but "out of the mouths of babes and sucklings" that the strength is ordained, which shall "still the enemy and avenger."

## THE LITERATURE OF BRITAIN.

*A Speech Delivered at the Opening of the Edinburgh Philosophical Institution, on the 4th of November, 1846.*

### LORD MACAULEY.

I thank you, gentlemen, for this cordial reception. I have thought it right to steal a short time from duties not unimportant for the purpose of lending my aid to an undertaking calculated, as I think, to raise the credit and to promote the best interests of the city which has so many claims on my gratitude.

The Directors of our Institution have requested me to propose to you as a toast the Literature of Britain. They could not have assigned to me a more agreeable duty. The chief object of this Institution is, I conceive, to impart knowledge through the medium of our own language. Edinburgh is already rich in libraries worthy of her fame as a seat of literature and a seat of jurisprudence. A man of letters can here without difficulty obtain access to repositories filled with the wisdom of many ages and of many nations. But something was still wanting. We still wanted a library open to that large, that important, that respectable class which, though by no means destitute of liberal curiosity or of sensibility to literary pleasures, is yet forced to be content with what is written in our own tongue. For that class especially, I do not say exclusively, this library is intended. Our directors, I hope, will not be satisfied, I, as a member, shall certainly not be satisfied, till we possess a noble and complete collection of English books, till it is impossible to seek in vain on our shelves for a single English book which is valuable either on account of matter or on account of manner, which throws any light on our civil, ecclesiastical, intel-

lectual, or social history, which, in short, can afford either
useful instruction or harmless amusement.

From such a collection, placed within the reach of that
large and valuable class which I have mentioned, I am disposed to expect great good. And when I say this I do not
take into the account those rare cases to which my valued
friend, the Lord Provost,* so happily alluded. It is indeed
not impossible that some man of genius who may enrich our
literature with imperishable eloquence and song, or who may
extend the empire of our race over matter, may feel in our
reading room, for the first time, the consciousness of powers
yet undeveloped. It is not impossible that our volumes may
suggest the first thought of something great to some future
Burns, or Watt, or Arkwright.

But I do not speak of these extraordinary cases. What I
confidently anticipate is that, through the whole of that
class whose benefit we have peculiarly in view, there will be
a moral and an intellectual improvement; that many hours,
which might otherwise be wasted in folly or in vice, will be
employed in pursuits which, while they afford the highest
and most lasting pleasure, are not only harmless, but purify-
ing and elevating. My own experience, my own observation,
justifies me in entertaining this hope. I have had opportu-
nities, both in this and in other countries, of forming some
estimate of the effect which is likely to be produced by a
good collection of books on a society of young men.
There is, I will venture to say, no judicious commanding
officer of a regiment who will not tell you that the vicinity of a
valuable library will improve perceptibly the whole character
of a mess. I well knew one eminent military servant of the
East India Company, a man of great and various accom-

*Mr. Adam Black.

plishments, a man honorably distinguished both in war and in diplomacy, a man who enjoyed the confidence of some of the greatest generals and statesmen of our time. When I asked him how, having left his country while still a boy, and having passed his youth at military stations in India, he had been able to educate himself, his answer was, that he had been stationed in the neighborhood of an excellent library, that he had been allowed free access to the books, and that they had, at the most critical time of his life, decided his character, and saved him from being a mere smoking, card-playing, punch-drinking lounger.

Some of the objections which have been made to such institutions as ours have been so happily and completely refuted by my friend, the Lord Provost, and by the Most Reverend Prelate, who has honored us with his presence this evening,* that it would be idle to say again what has been so well said. There is, however, one objection which, with your permission, I will notice. Some men, of whom I wish to speak with great respect, are haunted, as it seems to me, with an unreasonable fear of what they call superficial knowledge. Knowledge, they say, which really deserves the name, is a great blessing to mankind, the ally of virtue, the harbinger of freedom. But such knowledge must be profound. A crowd of people who have a smattering of mathematics, a smattering of astronomy, a smattering of chemistry, who have read a little poetry and a little history, is dangerous to the commonwealth. Such half knowledge is worse than ignorance. And then the authority of Pope is vouched. Drink deep or taste not; shallow draughts intoxicate; drink largely and that will sober you. I must confess that the danger which alarms these gentlemen never seemed

---

*Archbishop Whateley.

to me very serious, and my reason is this: that I never could prevail on any person who pronounced superficial knowledge a curse and profound knowledge a blessing, to tell me what was his standard of profundity. The argument proceeds on the supposition that there is some line between profound and superficial knowledge similar to that which separates truth from falsehood. I know of no such line. When we talk of men of deep science, do we mean that they have got to the bottom or near the bottom of science? Do we mean that they know all that is capable of being known? Do we mean even that they know, in their own especial department, all that the smatterers of the next generation will know? Why, if we compare the little truth that we know with the infinite mass of truth which we do not know, we are all shallow together; and the greatest philosophers that ever lived would be the first to confess their shallowness. If we could call up the first of human beings, if we could call up Newton, and ask him whether, even in those sciences in which he had no rival, he considered himself as profoundly knowing, he would tell us that he was but a smatterer like ourselves, and that the difference between his knowledge and ours vanished, when compared with the quantity of truth still undiscovered, just as the distance between a person at the foot of Ben Lomond and at the top of Ben Lomond vanishes when compared with the distances of the fixed stars.

It is evident then that those who are afraid of superficial knowledge do not mean by superficial knoweldge, knowledge which is superficial when compared with the whole quantity of truth capable of being known. For, in that sense, all human knowledge is, and always has been, and always must be, superficial. What then is the standard? Is it the same two years together in any country? Is it the same, at the

same moment, in any two countries? Is it not notorious
that the profundity of one age is the shallowness of the
next; that the profundity of one nation is the shallowness
of a neighboring nation? Ramohun Roy passed, among the
Hindoos, for a man of profound Western learning; but he
would have been but a very superficial member of this Institute. Strabo was justly entitled to be called a profound geo-
grapher eighteen hundred years ago. But a teacher of geography, who had never heard of America, would now be laughed at
by the girls of a boarding-school. What would now be thought
of the greatest chemist of 1746, or of the greatest geologist
of 1746? The truth is, that in all experimental science,
mankind is, of necessity, constantly advancing. Every generation, of course, has its front rank and its rear rank; but
the rear rank of a later generation occupies the ground
which was occupied by the front rank of a former generation.

You remember Gulliver's adventures. First he is ship-
wrecked in a country of little men; and he is a Colossus
among them. He strides over the walls of their capital: he
stands higher than the cupola of their great temple: he
tugs after them a royal fleet: he stretches his legs; and a
royal army, with drums beating and colours flying, marches
through the gigantic arch: he devours a whole granary for
breakfast, eats a herd of cattle for dinner, and washes down
his meal with all the hogsheads of a cellar. In his next
voyage he is among men sixty feet high. He who, in Lilliput, used to take people up in his hand in order that he
might be able to hear them, is himself taken up in the hands
and held to the ears of his masters. It is all that he can do
to defend himself with his hanger against the rats and mice.
The court ladies amuse themselves with seeing him fight

wasps and frogs: the monkey 'runs off' with him to the chimney top: the dwarf drops him into the cream jug and leaves him to swim for his life. Now, was Gulliver a tall or a short man? Why, in his own house at Rotherhithe, he was thought a man of the ordinary stature. Take him to Lilliput; and he is Quinbus Flestrin, the Man Mountain. Take him to Brobdingnag, and he is Grildrig, the little Manikin. It is the same in science. The pigmies of one society would have passed for giants in another.

It might be amusing to institute a comparison between one of the profoundly learned men of the thirteenth century and one of the superficial students who will frequent our library. Take the great philosopher of the time of Henry the Third of England, or Alexander the Third of Scotland, the man renowned all over the island, and even so far as Italy and Spain, as the first of astronomers and chemists. What is his astronomy? He is a firm believer in the Ptolemaic system. He never heard of the law of gravitation. Tell him that the succession of day and night is caused by the turning of the earth on its axis. Tell him that, in consequence of this motion, the polar diameter of the earth is shorter than the equatorial diameter. Tell him that the succession of summer and winter is caused by the revolution of the earth around the sun. If he does not set you down for an idiot, he lays an information against you before the Bishop, and has you burned for a heretic. To do him justice, however, if he is ill informed on these points, there are other points on which Newton and Laplace were mere children when compared with him. He can cast your nativity. He knows what will happen when Saturn is in the House of Life, and what will happen when Mars is in conjunction with the Dragon's Tail. He can read in the stars whether

an expedition will be successful, whether the next harvest
will be plentiful, which of your children will be fortunate
in marriage, and which will be lost at sea.  Happy the State,
happy the family, which is guided by the counsels of so profound a man!  And what but mischief, public and private,
can we expect from the temerity and conceit of sciolists who
know no more about the heavenly bodies than what they
have learned from Sir John Herschel's beautiful little volume?  But, to speak seriously, is not a little truth better
than a great deal of falsehood?  Is not the man who, in the
evenings of a fortnight, has acquired a correct notion of the
solar system, a more profound astronomer than a man who
has passed thirty years in reading lectures about the *primum
mobile*, and in drawing schemes of horoscopes?

Or take chemistry.  Our philosopher of the thirteenth
century shall be, if you please, an universal genius, chemist
as well as astronomer.  He has perhaps got so far as to know,
that if he mixes charcoal and saltpetre in certain propor-
tions and then applies fire, there will be an explosion which
will shatter all his retorts and aludels; and he is proud of
knowing what will in a later age be familiar to all of the
idle boys in the kingdom.  But there are departments of
science in which he need not fear the rivalry of Black, or
Lavoisier, or Cavendish, or Davy.  He is in hot pursuit of
the philosopher's stone, of the stone that is to bestow wealth,
and health and longevity.  He has a long array of strangely
shaped vessels, filled with red oil and white oil, constantly
boiling.  The moment of projection is at hand; and soon all
his kettles and gridirons will be turned into pure gold.  Poor
Professor Faraday can do nothing of the sort.  I should deceive you if I held out to you the smallest hope that he will
ever turn your halfpence into sovereigns.  But if you can

induce him to give at our Institute a course of lectures such as I once heard him give at the Royal Institution to children in the Christmas holidays, I can promise you that you will know more about the effects produced on bodies by heat and moisture than was known to some alchemists who, in the middle ages, were thought worthy of the patronage of kings.

As it has been in science so it has been in literature. Compare the literary acquirements of the great men of the thirteenth century with those which will be within the reach of many who will frequent our reading room. As to Greek learning, the profound man of the thirteenth century was absolutely on a par with the superficial man of the nineteenth. In the modern languages, there was not, six hundred years ago, a single volume which is now read. The library of our profound scholar must have consisted entirely of Latin books. We will suppose him to have had both a large and a choice collection. We will allow him thirty, nay forty manuscripts, and among them a Virgil, a Terence, a Lucan, an Ovid, a Statius, a great deal of Livy, a great deal of Cicero. In allowing him all this, we are dealing most liberally with him; for it is much more likely that his shelves were filled with treatises on school divinity and canon law, composed by writers whose names the world has very wisely forgotten. But, even if we suppose him to have possessed all that is most valuable in the literature of Rome, I say with perfect confidence that, both in respect of intellectual improvement, and in respect of intellectual pleasures, he was far less favorably situated than a man who now, knowing only the English language, has a bookcase filled with the best English works. Our great man of the middle ages could not form any conception of any tragedy approaching Macbeth or Lear, or of any comedy equal to Henry the

Fourth or Twelfth Night.   The best epic poem that he had
read was far inferior to the Paradise Lost; and all the tomes
of his philosophers were not worth a page of the Novum
Organum.

The Novum Organum, it is true, persons who know only
English must read in a translation: and this reminds me of
one great advantage which such persons will derive from
our institution.   They will, in our library, be able to form
some acquaintance with the master minds of remote ages
and foreign countries.   A large part of what is best worth
knowing in ancient literature, and in the literature of France,
Italy, Germany and Spain, has been translated into our own
tongue.   It is scarcely possible that the translation of any
book of the highest class can be equal to the original.   But,
though the finer touches may be lost in the copy, the great
outlines will remain. .An Englishman who never saw the
frescoes in the Vatican may yet, from engravings, form some
notion of the exquisite grace of Raphael, and of the sublimity and energy of Michael Angelo.   And so the genius of
Homer is seen in the poorest version of the Iliad; the genius
of Cervantes is seen in the poorest version of Don Quixote.
Let it not be supposed that I wish to dissuade any person
from studying either the ancient languages or the languages
of modern Europe.   Far from it.   I prize most highly those
keys of knowledge; and I think that no man who has leisure
for study ought to be content until he possesses several of
them.   I always much admired a saying of the Emperor
Charles the Fifth.   "When I learn a new language," he said,
"I feel as if I had got a new soul."   But I would console
those who have not time to make themselves linguists by
assuring them that, by means of their own mother tongue,
they may obtain ready access to vast intellectual treasures,

to treasures such as might have been envied by the greatest linguists of the age of Charles the Fifth, to treasures surpassing those which were possessed by Aldus, by Erasmus, and by Melancthon.

And thus I am brought back to the point from which I started. I have been requested to propose a toast to the Literature of Britain; to that literature, the brightest, the purest, the most durable of all the glories of our country; to that literature, so rich in precious truth and precious fiction; to that literature which boasts of the prince of all poets and of the prince of all philosophers; to that literature which has exercised an influence wider than that of our commerce, and mightier than that of our arms; to that literature which has taught France the principles of liberty, and has furnished Germany with models of art; to that literature which forms a tie closer than the tie of consanguinity between us and the commonwealth of the Valley of the Mississippi; to that literature before the light of which impious and cruel superstitions are fast taking flight on the banks of the Ganges; to that literature which will, in the future ages, instruct and delight the unborn millions who will have turned the Australasian and Caffrarian deserts into cities and gardens. To the Literature of Britain, then! And, wherever British literature spreads, may it be attended by British virtue and by British freedom.

## PEDAGOGY.

*From Sartor Resartus.*

THOMAS CARLYLE.

Hitherto we see young Gneschen, in his indivisible case of yellow serge, borne forward mostly on the arms of kind Nature alone; seated, indeed, and much to his mind, in the terrestrial workshop, but (except his soft hazel eyes, which we doubt not already gleamed with a still intelligence) called upon for little voluntary movement there. Hitherto, accordingly, his aspect is rather generic, that of an incipient Philosopher and Poet in the abstract; perhaps it would puzzle Herr Heuschrecke himself to say wherein the special Doctrine of Clothes is as yet foreshadowed or betokened. For with Gneschen, as with others, the Man may indeed stand pictured in the Boy (at least all the pigments are there); yet only some half of the Man stands in the Child, or young Boy, namely, his Passive endowment, not his Active. The more impatient are we to discover what figure he cuts in this latter capacity; how, when, to use his own words, "he understands the tools a little, and can handle this or that," he will proceed to handle it.

Here, however, may be the place to state that, in much of our Philosopher's history, there is something of an almost Hindoo character: nay perhaps in that so well-fostered and everyway excellent "Passivity" of his, which, with no free development of the antagonist Activity, distinguished his childhood, we may detect the rudiments of much that, in after days, and still in these present days, astonishes the world. For the shallow-sighted, Teufelsdröckh is oftenest a man without Activity of any kind, a No-man; for the deep-sighted, again, a man with Activity almost superabundant, yet so spiritual, close-hidden, enigmatic, that no mortal can foresee its explosions, or even when it has exploded, so much as ascertain its significance. A dangerous, difficult temper for the modern European; above all disadvantageous in the hero of a Biography! Now as heretofore it will behoove the Editor of these pages, were it never so unsuccessfully, to do his endeavors.

Among the earliest tools of any complicacy which a man, especially a man of letters, gets to handle, are his Class-books. On this portion of his History, Teufelsdröckh looks down professedly as indifferent. Reading he "cannot remember ever to have learned;" so perhaps had it by nature. He says generally: " Of the insignificant portion of my Education, which depended on Schools, there need almost no notice be taken. I learned what others learn; and kept it stored by in a corner of my head, seeing as yet no manner of use in it. My Schoolmaster, a downbent, brokenhearted, underfoot martyr, as others of that guild are, did little for me, except discover that he could do little: he, good soul, pronounced me a genius, fit for the learned professions; and that I must be sent to the Gymnasium, and one day to the University. Meanwhile, what printed thing soever I could meet with I read. My very copper pocket-money I laid-out on stall-literature; which, as it accumulated, I with my own hands sewed into volumes. By this means was the young head furnished with a considerable miscellany of things and shadows of things: History in authentic fragments lay mingled with Fabulous chimeras, wherein also was reality; and the whole not as dead stuff, but as living pabulum, tolerably nutritive for a mind as yet so peptic."

That the Entepfuhl Schoolmaster judged well, we now know. Indeed, already in the youthful Gneschen, with all

his outward stillness, there may have been manifest an inward vivacity that promised much; symptoms of a spirit
singularly open, thoughtful, almost poetical.   Thus, to say
nothing of his Suppers on the Orchard-wall, and other phenomena of that earlier period, have many readers of these
pages stumbled, in their twelfth year, on such reflections as
the following?   "It struck me much, as I sat by the Kuhbach, one silent noon-tide, and watched it flowing, gurgling,
to think how this same streamlet had flowed and gurgled,
through all changes of weather and of fortune, from beyond
the earliest date of History.   Yes, probably on the morning
when Joshua forded Jordan; even as at the mid-day when
Cæsar, doubtless with difficulty, swam the Nile, yet kept his
*Commentaries* dry,—this little Kuhbach, assiduous as Tiber,
Eurotas or Siloa, was murmuring on across the wilderness,
as yet unnamed, unseen: here, too, as in the Euphrates
and the Ganges, is a vien or veinlet of the grand World-
circulation of Waters, which with its atmospheric arteries,
has lasted and lasts simply with the World.   Thou fool!
Nature alone is antique, and the oldest art a mushroom;
that idle crag thou sittest on is six-thousand years of age."
In which little thought, as in a little fountain, may there not
lie the beginning of those well-nigh unutterable meditations
on the grandeur and mystery of TIME, and its relation to
ETERNITY which play such a part in this Philosophy of
Clothes?

Over his Gymnasic and Academic years the Professor by
no means lingers so lyrical and joyful as over his childhood.
Green sunny tracts there are still; but intersected by bitter
rivulets of tears, here and there stagnating into sour marshes
of discontent.

"With my first view of the Hinterschlag Gymnasium."

writes he, " my evil days began. Well do I still remember
the red sunny Whitsuntide morning, when, trotting full of
hope by the side of Father Andreas, I entered the main
street of the place, and saw its steeple-clock (then striking
eight) and *Schuldthurm* (Jail), and the aproned or disaproned
Burghers moving-in to breakfast : a little dog, in mad terror,
was rushing past ; for some human imps had tied a tin-kettle
to its tail ; thus did the agonized creature, loud-jingling, ca-
reer through the whole length of the Borough, and become
notable enough. Fit emblem of many a Conquering Hero,
to whom Fate (wedding Fantasy to Sense, as it often elsewhere does) has malignantly appended a tin-kettle of Ambition, to chase him on ; which the faster he runs, urges him
the faster, the more loudly and the more foolishly ! Fit emblem also of much that awaited myself, in that mischievous
Den ; as in the World, whereof it was a portion and epitome !

"Alas, the kind beech rows of Entepfuhl were hidden in
the distance : I was among strangers, harshly, at best indif-
ferently, disposed towards me : the young heart felt, for the
first time, quite orphaned and alone." His school-fellows,
as is usual, persecuted him : "They were Boys." he says.
" mostly rude Boys, and obeyed the impulse of rude Nature,
which bids the deer-herd fall upon any stricken hart, the
duck-flock put to death any broken-winged brother or sister,
and on all hands the strong tyrannize over the weak." He
admits, that though "perhaps in an unusual degree morally
courageous," he succeeded ill in battle, and would fain have
avoided it ; a result, as would appear, owing less to his small
personal stature (for in passionate seasons he was "incredibly
nimble"), than to his " virtuous principles ": "if it was dis-
graceful to be beaten," says he, " it was only a shade less dis-
graceful to have so much as fought ; thus was I drawn two

ways at once, and in this important element of school-history, the war-element, had little but sorrow." On the whole, that same excellent "Passivity," so notable in Teufelsdröckh's childhood, is here visibly enough again getting nourishment. " He wept often ; indeed to such a degree that he was nicknamed *Der Weinende* (the Tearful), which epithet, till towards his thirteenth year, was indeed not quite unmerited.   Only at rare intervals did the young soul burst-forth into fire-eyed rage, and, with a stormfulness (*Ungestüm*) under which the boldest quailed, assert that he too had Rights of Man, or at least of Mankin." In all which, who does not discern a fine flower-tree and cinnamon-tree (of genius) nigh chocked among pumpkins, reed-grass and ignoble shrubs ; and forced if it would live, to struggle upwards only, and not outwards; into a *height* quite sickly and disproportionate to its *breadth ?*

We find, moreover, that his Greek and Latin were " mechanically " taught; Hebrew scarce even mechanically; much else which they called History, Cosmography, Philosophy, and so forth, no better than not at all.   So that, except inasmuch as Nature was still busy ; and he himself " went about, as was of old his wont, among the Craftsmen's workshops, there learning many things ; " and farther lighted on some small store of curious reading, in Hans Wachtel the Cooper's house, where he lodged,—his time, it · would appear, was utterly wasted.   Which facts the Professor has not yet learned to look upon with any contentment.   Indeed throughout the whole of this Bag *Scorpio,* where we now are, and often in the following Bag, he shows himself unusually animated on the matter of Education, and not without some touch of what we might presume to be anger.

" My Teachers," says he, " were hide-bound Pedants, without knowledge of man's nature, or of boy's ; or of aught save their lexicons and quarterly account-books. Innumerable dead Vocables (no dead Language, for they themselves knew no Language) they crammed into us, and called it fostering the growth of mind. How can an inanimate, mechanical Gerund-grinder, the like of whom will, in a subsequent century, be manufactured at Nürnberg out of wood and leather, foster the growth of anything; much more of Mind, which grows, not like a vegetable (by having its roots littered with etymological compost), but like a spirit, by mysterious contact of Spirit ; Thought kindling itself at the fire of living Thought ? How shall *he* give kindling, in whose own inward man there is no live coal, but all is burnt out to a dead grammatical cinder? The Hinterschlag Professors knew syntax enough ; and of the human soul thus much : that it had a faculty called Memory, and could be acted-on through the muscular integument by appliance of birch-rods.

"Alas, so is it everywhere, so will it ever be; till the Hodman is discharged, or reduced to hod-bearing; and an Architect is hired, and on all hands fitly encouraged : till communities and individuals discover, not without surprise, that fashioning the souls of a generation by Knowledge can rank on a level with blowing their bodies to pieces by Gunpowder; that with Generals and Fieldmarshals for killing, there should be world-honored Dignitaries, and were it possible, true God-ordained Priests, for teaching. But as yet, though the Soldier wears openly, and even parades, his butchering-tool, nowhere, far as I have travelled, did the Schoolmaster make show of his instructing-tool: nay, were he to walk abroad with birch girt on thigh, as if he therefrom expected honor, would there not, among the idler class, perhaps a certain levity be excited?"

In the third year of this Gymnasic period, Father Andreas seems to have died: the young Scholar, otherwise so maltreated, saw himself for the first time clad outwardly in sables, and inwardly in quite inexpressible melancholy. "The dark bottomless Abyss, that lies under our feet, had yawned open; the pale kingdoms of Death, with all their innumerable silent nations and generation, stood before him; the inexorable word, NEVER! now first showed its meaning. My Mother wept, and her sorrow got vent; but in my heart there lay a whole lake of tears, pent-up in silent desolation. Nevertheless the unworn Spirit is strong; Life is so healthful that it even finds nourishment in Death: these stern experiences, planted down by Memory in my Imagination, rose there to a whole cypress forest, sad but beautiful; waving with not unmelodious sighs, in dark luxuriance, in the hottest sunshine, through long years of youth:—as in manhood also it does, and will do; for I have now pitched my tent under a Cypress-tree; the Tomb is now my inexpugnable Fortress, ever close by the gate of which I look upon the hostile armaments, and pains and penalties of tyrannous Life placidly enough, and listen to its loudest threatenings with a still smile. O ye loved ones, that already sleep in the noiseless Bed of Rest, whom in life I could only weep for and never help; and ye, who wide-scattered, still toil lonely in the monster-bearing Desert, dyeing the flinty ground with your blood,—yet a little while, and we shall all meet THERE, and our Mother's bosom will screen us all; and Oppression's harness, and Sorrow's fire-whip, and all the Gehenna Bailiffs that patrol and inhabit ever-vexed Time, cannot thenceforth harm us any more!"

Close by which rather beautiful apostrophe, lies a labored
Character of the deceased Andreas Futteral; of his natural
ability, his deserts in life (as Prussian Sergeant); with long
historical inquiries into the genealogy of the Futteral Family, here traced back as far as Henry the Fowler: the whole
of which we pass over, not without astonishment. It only
concerns us to add that now was the time when Mother
Gretchen revealed to her foster-son that he was not at all of
this kindred; or indeed, of any kindred, having come into historical existence in the way already known to us. "Thus was
I doubly orphaned," says he; "bereft not only of Possession,
but even of Remembrance. Sorrow and Wonder, here suddenly united, could not but produce abundant fruit. Such
a disclosure, in such a season, struck its roots through my
whole nature: ever till the years of mature manhood, it
mingled with my whole thoughts, was as the stem whereon
all my day-dreams and night-dreams grew. A certain poetic
elevation, yet also a corresponding civic depression, it naturally imparted: *I was like no other;* in which fixed-idea, lead-
ing sometimes to highest, and oftener to frightfullest results,
may there not be the first spring of tendencies, which in my
life have become remarkable enough? As in birth, so in action, speculation and social position, my fellows are perhaps
not numerous."

In the Bag *Sagittarius*, as we at length discover, Teufelsdröckh has become a University man; thoughhow, when,
or of what quality, will nowhere disclose itself with the
smallest certainty. Few things in the way of confusion and
capricious indistinctness, can now surprise our readers; not
even the total want of dates, almost without parallel in a
Biographical work. So enigmatic, so chaotic we have always found, and must always look to find, these scattered

Leaves. In *Sagittarius*, however, Teufelsdröckh begins to show himself even more than usually Sibylline: fragments of all sorts; scraps of regular Memoir, College-Exercises, Programs, Professional Testimoniums, Milkscores, torn Billets sometimes to appearance of an amatory cast; all blown together as if by merest chance, henceforth bewilder the sane Historian. To combine any picture of these University, and the subsequent, years; much more, to decipher therein any illustrative primordial elements of the Clothes-Philosophy, becomes such a problem as the reader may imagine.

So much we can see; darkly, as through the foliage of some wavering thicket: a youth of no common endowment, who has passed happily through Childhood, less happily yet still vigorously through Boyhood, now at length perfect in "dead vocables," and set down, as he hopes, by the living Fountain, there to superadd Ideas and Capabilities. From such Fountain he draws, diligently, thirstily, yet never or seldom with his whole heart, for the water nowise suits his palate; discouragements, entanglements, aberrations are discoverable or supposable. Nor perhaps are even pecuniary distresses wanting; for "the good Gretchen, who in spite of advices from not disinterested relatives has sent him hither, must after a time withdraw her willing but too feeble hand." Nevertheless in an atmosphere of Poverty and manifold Chagrin, the Humor of that young Soul, what character is in him, first decisively reveals itself; and, like strong sunshine in weeping skies, gives out variety of colors, some of which are prismatic. Thus, with the aid of Time and of what Time brings, has the stripling Diogenes Teufelsdröckh waxed into manly stature; and into so questionable an aspect, that we ask with new eagerness, How he specially came by it, and regret anew that there is no more explicit answer.

Certain of the intelligible and partially significant fragments, which are few in number, shall be extracted from that Limbo of a Paper-bag, and presented with the usual preparation.

As if, in Bag *Scorpio*, Teufelsdröckh had not already expectorated his antipedagogic spleen; as if, from the name *Sagittarius*, he had thought himself called upon to shoot arrows, we here again fall-in with such matter as this: "The University where I was educated still stands vivid enough in my remembrance, and I know its name well; which name, however, I, from tenderness to existing interests and persons, shall in nowise divulge. It is my painful duty to say that, out of England and Spain, ours was the worst of all hitherto discovered Universities. This is indeed a time when right Education is, as nearly as may be, impossible: however, in degrees of wrongness there is no limit: nay, I can conceive a worse system than that of the Nameless itself; as poisoned victual may be worse than absolute hunger.

"It is written, When the blind lead the blind, both shall fall into the ditch: wherefore, in such circumstances, may it not sometimes be safer, if both leader and led simply—sit still? Had you, anywhere in Crim Tartary, walled-in a square enclosure; furnished it with a small, ill-chosen Library; and then turned loose into it eleven-hundred Christian striplings, to tumble about as they listed, from three to seven years: certain persons, under the title of Professors, being stationed at the gates, to declare aloud that it was a University, and exact considerable admission-fees,—you had, not indeed in mechanical structure, yet in spirit and result, some imperfect resemblance of our High Seminary. I say, imperfect; for if our mechanical structure was quite other, so neither was our result altogether the same: unhappily we were not

in Crim Tartary, but in a corrupt European city, full of
smoke and sin; moreover, in the middle of a Public, which,
without far costlier apparatus than that of the Square Enclosure and Declaration aloud, you could not be sure of
gulling.

"Gullible, however, by fit apparatus, all Publics are; and
gulled, with the most surprising profit.  Towards anything
like a *Statistics of Imposture*, indeed, little as yet has been done:
with a strange indifference, our Economists, nigh buried
under Tables for minor Branches of Industry, have altogether overlooked the grand all over-topping Hypocrisy
Branch; as if our whole arts of Puffery, of Quackery, Priest-
craft, Kingcraft, and the innumerable other crafts and mys-
teries of that genius, had not ranked in Productive Industry at all!  Can any one, for example, so much as say,What
moneys, in Literature and Shoeblacking, are realized by actual Instruction and actual jet Polish; what by fictitious-
persuasive Proclamation of such; specifying, in distinct
items, the distributions, circulations, disbursements, incom-
ings of said moneys, with the smallest approach to accuracy?
But to ask, How far, in all the several infinitely-completed departments of social business, in government, education, in
manual, commercial, intellectual fabrication of every sort,
man's Want is supplied by true Ware; how far by the mere
Appearance of true Ware:—in other words, To what extent,
by what methods, with what effects, in various times and
countries, Deception takes the place of wages of Performance:
here truly is an Inquiry big with results for the future
time, but to which hitherto only the vaguest answer can be
given.  If for the present, in our Europe, we estimate the
ratio of Ware to Appearance of Ware so high even as at
One to a Hundred (which, considering the Wages of a Pope,

Russian Autocrat, or English Game-Preserver, is probably not far from the mark),—what almost prodigious saving may there not be anticipated, as the *Statistics of Imposture* advances, and so the manufacturing of Shams (that of Realities rising into clearer and clearer distinction therefrom) gradually declines, and at length becomes all but wholly unnecessary!

"This for the coming golden ages. What I had to remark, for the present brazen one, is, that in several provinces, as in Education, Polity, Religion, where so much is wanted and indispensable, and so little can as yet be furnished, probably Imposture is of sanative, anodyne nature, and man's Gullibility not his worst blessing. Suppose your sinews of war quite broken; I mean your military chest insolvent, forage all but exhausted; and that the whole army is about to mutiny, disband, and cut your and each other's throat,—then were it not well could you, as if by miracle, pay them in any sort of fairy-money, feed them on coagulated water, or mere imagination of meat; whereby, till the real supply came up, they might be kept together and quiet? Such perhaps was the aim of Nature, who does nothing without aim, in furnishing her favorite, Man, with this his so omnipotent or rather omnipatient Talent of being Gulled.

"How beautifully it works, with a little mechanism; nay, almost makes mechanism for itself! These Professors in the Nameless lived with ease, with safety, by a mere Reputation, constructed in past times, and then too with no great effort, by quite another class of persons. Which Reputation, like a strong, brisk-going undershot wheel, sunk into the general current, bade fair, with only a little annual repainting on their part, to hold long together, and of its own

accord assiduously grind for them.  Happy that it was so,
for the Millers!  They themselves needed not to work;
their attempts at working, at what they called Educating,
now when I look back on it, fill me with a certain mute
admiration.

" Besides all this, we boasted ourselves a Rational University; in the highest degree hostile to Mysticism; thus was
the young vacant mind furnished with much talk about
Progress of the Species, Dark Ages, Prejudice, and the like;
so that all were quickly enough blown out into a state of
windy argumentativeness; whereby the better sort had soon
to end in sick, impotent Scepticism; the worser sort explode
(*crepiren*) in finished Self-conceit, and to all spiritual in-
tents become dead.—But this too is a portion of mankind's
lot.  If our era is the Era of Unbelief, why murmur under
it; is there not a better coming, nay come?  As in long-
drawn systole and long-drawn diastole, must the period of
Faith alternate with the period of Denial; must the vernal
growth, the summer luxuriance of all Opinions, Spiritual
Representations and Creations, be followed by, and again
follow, the autumnal decay, the winter dissolution.  For
man lives in Time, has his whole earthly being, endeavor
and destiny shaped for him by Time : only in the transitory
Time-Symbol is the ever-motionless Eternity we stand on
made manifest.  And yet, in such winter-seasons of Denial,
it is for the nobler-minded perhaps a comparative misery
to have been born, and to be awake and work; and for the
duller a felicity, if, like hibernating animals, safe-lodged in
some Salamanca Univerity, or Sybaris City, or other super-
stitious or voluptuous Castle of Indolence, they can slum-
ber-through, in stupid dreams, and only awaken when the
loud-roaring hailstorms have all done their work, and to our

prayers and martyrdoms the new Spring has been vouch-
safed."

That in the environment, here mysteriously enough shad-
owed forth, Teufelsdröckh must have felt ill at ease, cannot
be doubtful. "The hungry young," he says, "looked up to
their spiritual Nurses; and, for food, were bidden eat the
east-wind. What vain jargon of controversial Metaphysic,
Etymology, and mechanical Manipulation falsely named
Science, was current there, I indeed learned, better perhaps
than the most. Among eleven-hundred Christian youths,
there will not be wanting some eleven eager to learn. By
collision with such, a certain warmth, a certain polish was
communicated; by instinct and happy accident, I took less
to rioting (*renommiren*), than to thinking and reading,
which latter also I was free to do. Nay from the chaos of
that Library, I succeeded in fishing-up more books perhaps
than had been known to the very keepers thereof. The
foundations of a Literary Life was hereby laid: I learned,
on my own strength, to read fluently in almost all cultivated languages, on almost all subjects and sciences; farther,
as man is ever the prime object to man, already it was my
favorite employment to read character in speculation, and
from the Writing to construe the Writer. A certain ground-
plan of Human Nature and Life began to fashion itself
in me; wondrous enough, now when I look back on it;
for my whole Universe, physical and spiritual, was as yet a
Machine! However, such a conscious recognized ground-
plan, the truest I had, *was* beginning to be there, and by
additional experiments might be corrected and indefinitely
extended."

Thus from poverty does the strong educe nobler wealth;
thus in the destitution of the wild desert does our young

Ishmael acquire for himself the highest of all possessions, that of Self-help. Nevertheless a desert this was, waste, and howling with savage monsters. Teufelsdröckh gives us long details of his "fever-paroxysms of Doubt;" his Inquiries concerning Miracles, and the Evidences of religious Faith; and how "in the silent night-watches, still darker in his heart than over sky and earth, he cast himself before the All-seeing, and with audible prayers cried vehemently for Light, for deliverance from Death and the Grave. Not till after long years, and unspeakable agonies, did the believing heart surrender; sink into spell-bound sleep, under the nightmare, Unbelief; and, in this hag-ridden dream, mistake God's fair living world for a pallid, vacant Hades and extinct Pandemonium. But through such Purgatory pain," continues he, "it is appointed us to pass; first must the dead Letter of Religion own itself dead, and drop piece meal into dust, if the living Spirit of Religion, freed from this its charnel-house, is to arise on us, newborn of Heaven, and with new healing under its wings."

To which Purgatory pains, seemingly severe enough, if we add a liberal measure of earthly distresses, want of practical guidance, want of sympathy, want of money, want of hope; and all this in the fervid season of youth, so exaggerated in imagining, so boundless in desires, yet here so poor in means,—do we not see a strong incipient spirit oppressed and overloaded from without and from within; the fire of genius struggling-up among fuel-wood of the greenest, and as yet with more of bitter vapor than of clear flame?

From various fragments of Letters and other documentary scraps, it is to be inferred that Teufelsdröckh, isolated, shy, retiring as he was, had not altogether escaped notice: certain established men are aware of his existence; and, if stretching-out no helpful hand, have at least their eyes on him. He appears, though in dreary enough humor, to be addressing himself to the Profession of Law;—whereof, indeed, the world has since seen him a public graduate. But omitting these broken, unsatisfactory thrums of Economical relation, let us present rather the following small thread of Moral relation; and therewith, the reader for himself weaving it in at the right place, conclude our dim arras-picture of these University years.

"Here also it was that I formed acquaintance with Herr Towgood, or, as it is perhaps better written, Herr Toughgut; a young person of quality (*von Adel*), from the interior parts of England. He stood connected, by blood and hospitality, with the Counts von Zähdarm, in this quarter of Germany; to which noble Family I likewise was, by his means, with all friendliness, brought near. Towgood had a fair talent, unspeakably ill-cultivated; with considerable humor of character: and, bating his total ignorance, for he knew nothing except Boxing and a little Grammar, showed less of that aristocratic impassivity, and silent fury, than for most part belongs to Travelers of his nation. To him I owe my first practical knowledge of the English and their ways; perhaps also something of the partiality with which I have ever since regarded that singular people. Towgood was not without an eye, could he have come at any light. Invited doubtless by the presence of the Zähdarm Family, he had traveled hither, in the almost frantic hope of perfecting his studies; he, whose studies had as yet been those of infancy, hither to a University where so much as the notion of perfection, not to say the effort after it, no longer existed! Often we would condole over the hard destiny of the Young in this era: how, after all our toil, we were to be turned-out

G—17

into the world, with beards on our chins indeed, but with
few other attributes of manhood; no existing thing that we
were trained to Act on, nothing that we could so much as
Believe. 'How has our head on the outside a polished
Hat,' would Towgood exclaim, 'and in the inside Vacancy,
or a froth of Vocables and Attorney-Logic! At a small cost
men are educated to make leather into shoes; but at a great
cost, what am I educated to make? By Heaven, Brother!
What I have already eaten and worn, as I came thus far,
would endow a considerable Hospital of Incurables.'—
'Man, indeed,' I would answer, ' has a Digestive Faculty,
which must be kept working, were it even partly by stealth.
But as far our Mis-education, make not bad worse; waste
not the time yet ours, in trampling on thistles because they
have yielded us no figs. *Frisch zu Bruder!* Here are Books,
and we have brains to read them; here is a whole Earth
and a whole Heaven, and we have eyes to look on them:
*Frisch zu!*'

"Often our talk was gay; not without brilliancy, and
even fire. We looked-out on Life, with its strange scaffold-
ing, where all at once harlequins dance, and men are beheaded and quartered: motley, not unterrific was the aspect; but we looked on it like brave youths. For myself,
these were perhaps my most genial hours. Towards this
young warmhearted, strongheaded and wrongheaded Herr
Towgood I was even near experiencing the now obsolete sentiment of Friendship. Yes, foolish Heathen that I was, I
felt that, under certain conditions, I could have loved this
man, and taken him to my bosom, and been his brother
once and always. By degrees, however, I understood the
new time, and its wants. If man's *Soul* is indeed, as in the
Finnish Language, and Utilitarian Philosophy, a kind of

*Stomach,* what else in the true meaning of Spiritual Union but an Eating together? Thus we, instead of Friends, are Dinner-guests; and here as elsewhere have cast away chimeras."

So ends, abruptly as is usual, and enigmatically, this little incipient romance. What henceforth becomes of the brave Herr Towgood, or Toughgut? He has dived-under, in the Autobiographical Chaos, and swims we see not where. Does any reader "in the interior parts of England" know of such a man?

---

## INDIRECTION.

### RICHARD REALF.

Fair are the flowers and the children, but their subtle suggestion is fairer,
Rare is the rose-burst of dawn, but the secret that clasps it is rarer;
Sweet the exultance of song, but the strain that precedes it is sweeter,
And never a poem was writ, but the meaning outmastered the meter.

Never a daisy that grows, but a mystery guideth the growing,
Never a river that flows, but a majesty scepters the flowing;
Never a Shakespeare that soared, but a stronger than he did enfold him,
Nor ever a prophet fore-tell, but a mightier seer had fore-told him.

Back of the canvass that throbs, the painter is hinted and
    hidden,
Into the statute that breathes, the soul of the sculptor is
    bidden;                              .
Under the joys that are felt, lie the infinite issues of feeling,
Crowning the glory revealed, is the glory that crowns the
    revealing.              .

Great are the symbols of being, but that which is symboled
    is greater,
Vast the creation beheld, but vaster the inward Creator;
Back of the sound broods the silence, back of the gift stands
    the giving,
Back of the hand that receives, thrill the sensitive nerves
    of receiving.

Space is as nothing to spirit; the deed is outdone by the
    doing;
The heart of the wooer is warm, but warmer the heart of the
    wooing,
And up from the pits where these shiver, and up from
    heights where those shine,
Twin voices and shadows swim starward, and the essence of
 . life is divine.

## COMUS

JOHN MILTON.

*The first Scene discovers a wild wood.*

. THE ATTENDANT SPIRIT *descends or enters.*

Before the starry threshold of Jove's court
My mansion is, where those immortal shapes
Of bright aërial spirits live inspher'd
In regions mild of calm and serene air;
Above the smoke and stir of this dim spot,
Which men call Earth, and with low-thoughted care
Confin'd, and pester'd in this pinfold here,
Strive to keep up a frail and feverish being;
Unmindful of the crown that Virtue gives,
After this mortal change, to her true servants
Amongst the enthron'd gods on sainted seats.
Yet some there be that by due steps aspire
To lay their just hands on that golden key
That opes the palace of eternity:
To such my errand is, and but for such,
I would not soil these pure ambrosial weeds
With the rank vapours of this sin-worn mould.
        But to my task.   Neptune, besides the sway
Of every salt flood and each ebbing stream,
Took in by lot, 'twixt high and nether Jove,
Imperial rule of all the sea-girt iles,
That like to rich and various gems inlay
The unadorned bosom of the deep;
Which he to grace his tributary gods
By course commits to several government,
And gives them leave to wear their sapphire crowns,
And wield their little tridents; but this ile,
The greatest and the best of all the main,

He quarters to his blue-hair'd deities;
And all this tract that fronts the falling sun,
A noble peer of mickle trust and power
Has in his charge, with temper'd awe to guide
An old and hauty nation, proud in arms:
Where his fair offspring nurst in princely lore,
Are coming to attend their father's state,
And new-entrusted scepter; but their way
Lies through the perplext paths of this drear wood,
The nodding horror of whose shady brows
Threats the forlorn and wandering passenger.
And here their tender age might suffer peril,
But that, by quick command from sovran Jove,
I was dispatcht for their defence and guard;
And listen why; for I will tell ye now
What never yet was heard in tale or song,
From old or modern bard, in hall or bow'r.

   Bacchus, that first from out the purple grape
Crush't the sweet poison of misused wine,
After the Tuscan mariners transform'd,
Coasting the Tyrrhene shore, as the winds listed,
On Circe's iland fell: (who knows not Circe
The daughter of the Sun? whose charmed cup
Whoever tasted, lost his upright shape,
And downward fell into a groveling swine)
This Nymph that gaz'd upon his clust'ring locks,
With ivy berries wreath'd, and his blithe youth,
Had by him. ere he parted thence, a son
Much like his father, but his mother more,
Whom therefore she brought up and Comus nam'd;
Who ripe, and frolic of his full-grown age,
Roving the Celtic and Iberian fields,

At last betakes him to 'this ominous wood;
And in thick shelter of black shades imbowr'd,
Excels his mother at her mighty art,
Offering to every weary travailer
His orient liquor in a crystal glass,
To quench the drouth of Phœbus; which as they taste
(For most do taste through fond intemperate thirst),
Soon as the potion works, their human count'nance,
Th' express resemblance of the gods, is chang'd
Into some brutish form of wolf, or bear,
Or ounce, or tiger, hog, or bearded goat,
All other parts remaining as they were;
And they, so perfect is their misery,
Not once perceive their foul disfigurement,
But boast themselves more comely than before;
And all their friends and native home forget,
To roll with pleasure in a sensual sty.
Therefore when any favour'd of high Jove
Chances to pass through this adventrous glade,
Swift as the sparkle of a glancing star
I shoot from Heav'n, to give him safe convoy:
As now I do: but first I must put off
These my sky-robes spun out of Iris' woof,
And take the weeds and likeness of a swain
That to the service of this house belongs;
Who with his soft pipe, and smooth-dittied song,
Well knows to still the wild winds when they roar,
And hush the waving woods, nor of less faith,
And in this office of his mountain watch
Likeliest, and nearest to the present aid
Of this occasion. But I hear the tread
Of hateful steps; I must be viewless now.

*Comus enters, with a charming-rod in his hand, his glass in the
other; with him a rout of monsters headed like sundry sorts of wild
beasts, but otherwise like men and women, their apparel glistring;
they come in making a riotous and unruly noise, with torches in
their hands.*

COMUS.

The star that bids the shepherd fold,
Now the top of Heav'n doth hold;
And the gilded car of day
His glowing axle doth allay
In the steep Atlantic stream;
And the slope Sun his upward beam
Shoots against the dusky pole;
Pacing toward the other goal
Of his chamber in the East.
Meanwhile welcome joy, and feast,
Midnight shout, and revelry,
Tipsy dance, and jollity.
Braid your locks with rosy twine,
Dropping odours, dropping wine,
Rigour now is gone to bed,
And Advice with scrupulous head,
Strict Age, and Sour Severity,
With their grave saws in slumber lie.
We that are of purer fire
Imitate the starry quire,
Who in their nightly watchful spheres
Lead in swift round the months and years.
The sounds, and seas with all their finny drove
Now to the moon in wavering morrice move;
And on the tawny sands and shelves,

Trip the pert fairies and the dapper elves.
By dimpled brook, and fountain brim,
The wood-nymphs deckt with daisies trim,
Their merry wakes and pastimes keep :
What hath night to do with sleep?
Night hath better sweets to prove,
Venus now wakes, and wak'ns Love.
Come, let us our rites begin,
'Tis only daylight that makes sin,
Which these dun shades will ne'er report.
Hail Goddess of nocturnal sport,
Dark veil'd Cotytto, t' whom the secret flame
Of midnight torches burns; mysterious dame
That ne'er art call'd, but when the dragon womb
Of Stygian Darkness spets her thickest gloom,
And makes one blot of all the air ;
Stay thy cloudy ebon chair,
Wherein thou rid'st with Hecat', and befriend
Us thy vow'd priests ; till utmost end
Of all thy dues be done, and none left out ;
Ere the blabbing eastern scout,
The nice Morn on th' Indian steep,
From her cabin'd loophole peep,
And to the tell-tale Sun descry
Our conceal'd solemnity.
Come, knit hands, and beat the ground,
In a light fantastic round.

### THE MEASURE.

Break off, break off, I feel the different pace
Of some chaste footing near about this ground.
Run to your shrouds, within these brakes and trees ;

Our number may affright: some virgin sure
(For so I can distinguish by mine art)
Benighted in these woods.   Now to my charms,
And to my wily trains; I shall ere long
Be well stock't with as fair a herd as graz'd
About my mother Circe.   Thus I hurl
My dazzling spells into the spungy air,
Of power to cheat the eye with blear illusion,
And give it false presentments; lest the place
And my quaint habits breed astonishment,
And put the damsel to suspicious flight,
Which must not be, for that's against my course:
I under fair pretense of friendly ends,
And well-plac't words of glozing courtesy,
Baited with reasons not unplausible,
Wind me into the easy-hearted man,
And hug him into snares.   When once her eye
Hath met the virtue of this magic dust
I shall appear some harmless villager
Whom thrift keeps up about his country gear.
But here she comes; I fairly step aside
And hearken, if I may, her business here.

*The* LADY *enters.*

*Lady.*   This way the noise was, if mine ear be true,
My best guide now; methought it was the sound
Of riot, and ill-manag'd merriment;
Such as the jocund flute, or gamesome pipe
Stirs up among the loose unletter'd hinds,
When for their teeming flocks, and granges full,
In wanton dance they praise the bounteous Pan,
And thank the gods amiss.   I should be loth

To meet the rudeness, and swill'd insolence
Of such late wassailers; yet O where else
Shall I inform my unacquainted feet
In the blind mazes of this tangl'd wood?
My brothers when they saw me wearied out
With this long way, resolving here to lodge
Under the spreading favour of these pines,
Stept, as they sed, to the next thicket side
To bring me berries, or such cooling fruit
As the kind hospitable woods provide.
They left me then, when the gray-hooded Ev'n,
Like a sad votarist in palmer's weed,
Rose from the hindmost wheels of Phœbus' wain.
But where they are, and why they came not back,
Is now the labour of my thoughts; 't is likeliest
They had engag'd their wandring steps too far,
And envious Darkness, ere they could return,
Had stole them from me; else, O thievish Night,
Why shouldst thou, but for some felonious end,
In thy dark lantern thus close up the stars,
That Nature hung in Heav'n and fill'd their lamps
With everlasting oil, to give due light
To the misled and lonely travailer?
This is the place, as well as I may guess,
Whence even now the tumult of loud mirth
Was rife, and perfect in my list'ning ear,
Yet nought but single darkness do I find.
What might this be? A thousand fantasies
Begin to throng into my memory
Of calling shapes, and beck'ning shadows dire,
And airy tongues, that syllable men's names
On sands, and shores, and desert wildernesses.

These thoughts may startle well, but not astound
The virtuous mind, that ever walks attended
By a strong siding champion, Conscience.—
O welcome pure-ey'd Faith, white-handed Hope.
Thou hovering angel girt with golden wings,
And thou unblemish't form of Chastity!
I see ye visibly, and now believe
That he, the Supreme good, t' whom all things ill
Are but as slavish officers of vengeance,
Would send a glistring guardian, if need were,
To keep my life and honour unassail'd.
Was I deceiv'd, or did a sable cloud
Turn forth her silver lining on the night?
I did not err, there does a sable cloud
Turn forth her silver lining on the night,
And casts a gleam over this tufted grove.
I can not hallow to my brothers, but
Such noise as I can make to be heard farthest
I'll venture, for my new enliv'nd spirits
Prompt me; and they perhaps are not far off.

SONG.

Sweet Echo, sweetest Nymph, that liv'st unseen
          Within thy airy shell
          By slow Meander's margent green;
And in the violet embroider'd vale,
          Where the love-lorn nightingale
Nightly to thee her sad song mourneth well
Canst thou not tell me of a gentle pair
          That likest thy Narcissus are?
          O if thou have
          Hid them in some flowry cave,

Tell me but where,
Sweet queen of parly, daughter of the sphere;
So may'st thou be translated to the skies,
And give resounding grace to all heav'ns harmonies.
   *Comus.* Can any mortal mixture of earth's mould
Breathe such divine enchanting ravishment?
Sure something holy lodges in that breast,
And with these raptures moves the vocal air
To testify his hidd'n residence;
How sweetly did they float upon the wings
Of silence, through the empty-vaulted night
At every fall smoothing the raven down
Of Darkness till it smil'd: I have oft heard
My mother Circe with the Sirens three,
Amidst the flowry-kirtl'd Naiades
Culling their potent herbs and baleful drugs;
Who, as they sung, would take the prison'd soul
And lap it in Elysium; Scylla wept,
And chid her barking waves into attention;
And fell Charybdis murmur'd soft applause:
Yet they in pleasing slumber lull'd the sense,
And in sweet madness robb'd it of itself;
But such a sacred and home-felt delight,
Such sober certainty of waking bliss,
I never heard till now.   I'll speak to her,
And she shall be my queen.
Hail foreign wonder,
Whom certain these rough shades did never breed:
Unless the goddess that in rural shrine
Dwell'st here with Pan, or
Sylvan, by blest song
Forbidding every bleak unkindly fog

To touch the prosperous growth of this tall wood.

*Lady.*   Nay, gentle shepherd, ill is lost that praise
That is addrest to unattending ears;
Not any boast of skill, but extreme shift
How to regain my sever'd company,
Compell'd me to awake the courteous Echo
To give me answer from her mossy couch.

  *Comus.*   What chance, good lady, hath bereft you thus?
  *Lady.*   Dim darkness, and this leafy labyrinth.
  *Comus.*   Could that divide you from near-ushering guides?
  *Lady.*   They left me weary on a grassy turf.
  *Comus.*   By falsehood, or discourtesy, or why?
  *Lady.*   To seek i' th' valley some cool, friendly spring.
  *Comus.*   And left your fair side all unguarded, lady?
  *Lady.*   They were but twain, and purpos'd quick return.
  *Comus.*   Perhaps forestalling night prevented them.
  *Lady.*   How easy my misfortune is to hit!
  *Comus.*   Imports their loss, beside the present need?
  *Lady.*   No less than if I should my brothers lose.
  *Comus.*   Were they of manly prime, or youthful bloom?
  *Lady.*   As smooth as Hebe's their unrazor'd lips.
  *Comus.*   Two such I saw, what time the labour'd ox
In his loose traces from the furrow came,
And the swink't hedger at his supper sate;
I saw them under a green mantling vine
That crawls along the side of yon small hill,
Plucking ripe clusters from the tender shoots,
Their port was more than human, as they stood;
I took it for a faëry vision
Of some gay creatures of the element
That in the colours of the rainbow live,
And play i' th' plighted clouds.

I was awe-strook,
And, as I past, I worshipt; if those you seek,
It were a journey like the path to heav'n,
To help you find them.

    *Lady.*                  Gentle villager,
What readiest way would bring me to that place?

    *Comus.*  Due west it rises from this shrubby point.

    *Lady.*  To find out that, good shepherd, I suppose,
In such a scant allowance of star-light,
Would overtask the best land-pilot's art,
Without the sure guess of well-practic'd feet.

    *Comus.*  I know each lane, and every alley green,
Dingle, or bushy dell of this wild wood,
And every bosky bourn from side to side,
My daily walks and ancient neighbourhood:
And if your stray attendance be yet lodg'd,
Or shroud within these limits, I shall know
Ere morrow wake, or the low-roosted lark
From her thatch't pallet rouse; if otherwise,
I can conduct you, lady, to a low
But loyal cottage, where you may be safe
Till further quest.

    *Lady.*            Shepherd, I take thy word,
And trust thy honest offer'd courtesy,
Which oft is sooner found in lowly sheds
With smoky rafters, than in tapstry halls
In courts of princes, where it first was nam'd,
And yet is most pretended: in a place
Less warranted than this, or less secure,
I can not be, that I should fear to change it.
Eye me, blest Providence, and square my trial

To my proportion'd strength.
Shepherd lead on.

[*Exeunt.*

*Enter the* Two Brothers.

   *Elder Bro.*  Unmuffle, ye faint stars; and thou fair Moon
That wont'st to love the travailer's benison,
Stoop thy pale visage through an amber cloud,
And disinherit Chaos, that reigns here
In double night of darkness, and of shades;
Or if your influence be quite damm'd up
With black usurping mists, some gentle taper,
Though a rush-candle from the wicker hole
Of some clay habitation, visit us
With thy long levell'd rule of streaming light,
And thou shalt be our star of Arcady,
Or Tyrian Cynosure.

   *Second Brother.*          Or if our eyes
Be barr'd that happiness, might we but hear
The folded flocks penn'd in their wattled cotes,
Or sound of pastoral reed with oaten stops,
Or whistle from the lodge, or village cock
Count the night watches to his feathery dames,
'T would be some solace yet, some little cheering
In this close dungeon of innumerous boughs.
But O that hapless virgin our lost sister,
Where may she wander now, whither betake her
From the chill due, among rude burs and thistles?
Perhaps some cold bank is her bolster now,
Or 'gainst the rugged bark of some broad elm
Leans her unpillow'd head, fraught with sad fears.
What if in wild amazement, and affright,

Or, while we speak, within the direful grasp
Of savage hunger, or of savage heat?

*Elder Brother.* Peace brother, be not over-exquisite
To cast the fashion of uncertain evils;
For grant they be so, while they rest unknown,
What need a man forestall his date of grief,
And run to meet what he would most avoid?
Or if they be but false alarms of fear,
How bitter is such self-delusion?
I do not think my sister so to seek,
Or so unprincipl'd in virtue's book,
And the sweet peace that goodness bosoms ever,
As that the single want of light and noise
(not being in danger, as I trust she is not),
Could stir the constant mood of her calm thoughts,
And put them into misbecoming plight.
Virtue could see to do what virtue would
By her own radiant light, though sun and moon
Were in the flat sea sunk.
And Wisdom's self
Oft seeks to sweet retired solitude;
Where with her best nurse, Contemplation,
She plumes her feathers, and lets grow her wings,
That in the various bustle of resort
Were all to-ruffl'd and sometimes impair'd.
He that has light within his own clear breast,
May sit i' th' centre, and enjoy bright day;
But he that hides a dark soul and foul thoughts,
Benighted walks under the mid-day sun;
Himself is his own dungeon.

*Second Brother.* 'T is most true
That musing Meditation most affects

G—18

The pensive secrecy of desert cell,
Far from the cheerful haunt of men, and herds,
And sits as safe as in a senate-house;
For who would rob a hermit of his weeds,
His few books, or his beads, or maple dish,
Or do his gray hairs any violence?
But Beauty, like the fair Hesperian tree
Laden with blooming gold, had need the guard
Of dragon watch with unenchanted eye,
To save her blossoms, and defend her fruit
From the rash hand of bold Incontinence.
You may as well spread out the unsunn'd heaps
Of misers' treasure by an outlaw's den,
And tell me it is safe, as bid me hope
Danger will wink on Opportunity,
And let a single helpless maiden pass
Uninjur'd in this wild surrounding waste.
Of night, or loneliness it recks me not;
I fear the dread events that dog them both.
Lest some ill greeting touch attempt the person
Of our unowned sister.
    *Elder Brother.*       I do not, brother,
Infer, as if I thought my sister's state
Secure without all doubt, or controversy:
Yet where an equal poise of hope and fear
Does arbitrate th' event, my nature is
That I incline to hope, rather than fear,
And gladly banish squint suspicion.   ·
My sister is not so defenseless left
As you imagine; she has a hidden strength
Which you remember not.
    *Second Brother.*       What hidden strength,

Unless the strength of Heav'n, if you mean that?
   *Elder Brother.*   I mean that too, but yet a hidden strength
Which, if Heav'n gave it, may be term'd her own;
'T is chastity, my brother, chastity!
She that has that, is clad in complete steel,
And like a quiver'd nymph with arrows keen
May trace huge forests and unharbour'd heaths,
Infamous hills and sandy perilous wilds;
Where through the sacred rays of chastity
No savage, fierce, bandite, or mountaineer
Will dare to soil her virgin purity;
Yea there, where very desolation dwells
By grots, and caverns shagg'd with horrid shades,
She may pass on with unblench't majesty;
Be it not done in pride, or in presumption.
Some say, no evil thing that walks by night
In fog or fire, by lake or moorish fen,
Blue, meager hag, or stubborn, unlaid ghost
That breaks his magic chains at curfeu time,
No goblin, or swart faëry of the mine,
Hath hurtful power o'er true virginity.
Do ye believe me yet, or shall I call
Antiquity from the old schools of Greece
To testify the arms of chastity?
Hence had the huntress Dian her dread bow,
Fair, silver-shafted queen, for ever chaste,
Wherewith she tam'd the brinded lioness
And spotted mountain pard, but set at naught
The frivolous bolt of Cupid: gods and men
Fear'd her stern frown, and she was queen o' th' woods.
What was that snaky-headed Gorgon shield
That wise Minerva wore, unconqur'd virgin,

Wherewith she freez'd her foes to congeal'd stone?
But rigid looks of chaste austerity,
And noble grace that dash't brute violence
With sudden adoration, and blank awe.
So dear to Heav'n is saintly chastity,
That when a soul is found sincerely so
A thousand liveried angels lackey her,
Driving far off each thing of sin and guilt;
And in clear dream, and solemn vision,
Tell her of things that no gross ear can hear,
Till oft converse with heav'nly habitants
Begin to cast a beam on th' outward shape,
The unpolluted temple of the mind,
And turns it by degrees to the soul's essence.
Till all be made immortal: but when lust,
By unchaste looks, loose gestures, and foul talk,
But most by lewd and lavish act of sin,
Lets in defilement to the inward parts,
The soul grows clotted by contagion,
Imbodies, and imbrutes, till she quite lose
The divine property of her first being.
Such are those thick and gloomy shadows damp
Oft seen in charnel vaults and sepulchres
Lingering, and sitting by a new-made grave;
As loth to leave the body that it lov'd,
And link't itself by carnal sensuality
To a degenerate and degraded state.

   *Second Brother.*   How charming is divine philosophy!
Not harsh, and crabbed as dull fools suppose,
But musical as is Apollo's lute,
And a perpetual feast of nectar'd sweets,
Where no crude surfeit reigns.

*Elder Brother.* List, list, I hear
Some far off hallow break the silent air.
   *Second Brother.* Methought so too; what should it be?
   *Elder Brother.* For certain
Either some one like us night-founder'd here,
Or else some neighbour woodman, or, at worst,
Some roving robber calling to his fellows.
   *Second Brother.* Heav'n keep my sister! Again, again, and
near;
Best draw, and stand upon our guard.
   *Elder Brother.* I'll hallow;
If he be friendly he comes well; if not,
Defence is a good cause, and Heav'n be for us.

   *Enter the* ATTENDANT SPIRIT, *habited like a shepherd.*

That hallow I should know, what are you? speak;
Come not too near, you fall on iron stakes else.
   *Spirit.* What voice is that? my young lord? speak again.
   *Second Brother.* O brother, 'tis my father's shepherd, sure.
   *Elder Brother.* Thyrsis? Whose artful strains have oft
delay'd
The huddling brook to hear his madrigal,
And sweeten'd every muskrose of the dale;
How cam'st thou here, good swain? hath any ram
Slip't from the fold, or young kid lost his dam,
Or straggling wether the pen't flock forsook?
How could'st thou find this dark sequester'd nook?
   *Spirit.* O my lov'd master's heir, and his next joy,
I came not here on such a trivial toy
As a stray'd ewe, or to pursue the stealth
Of pilfering wolf; not all the fleecy wealth
That doth enrich these downs, is worth a thought

To this my errand, and the care it brought.
But O my virgin lady, where is she?
How chance she is not in your company?
   *Elder Brother.*   To tell thee sadly, shepherd, without blame
Or our neglect, we lost her as we came.
   *Spirit.*  Ay me unhappy! then my fears are true.
   *Elder Brother.*  What fears, good Thyrsis?  Prithee briefly
shew.
   *Spirit.*  I'll tell ye; 'tis not vain or fabulous,
(Though so esteem'd by shallow ignorance),
What the sage poets taught by th' heav'nly Muse,
Storied of old in high immortal verse,
Of dire chimeras and enchanted iles,
And rifted rocks whose entrance leads to hell;
For such there be, but unbelief is blind. ·
Within the navel of this hideous wood,
Immur'd in cypress shades a sorcerer dwells,
Of Bacchus and of Circe born, great Comus,
Deep skill'd in all his mother's witcheries;
And here to every thirsty wanderer,
By sly enticement gives his baneful cup,
With many murmurs mixt; whose pleasing poison
The visage quite transforms of him that drinks,
And the inglorious likeness of a beast
Fixes instead, unmolding reason's mintage,
Character'd in the face; this have I learn't
Tending my flocks hard by i' th' hilly crofts
That brow this bottom glade; whence night by night
He and his monstrous rout are heard to howl
Like stabl'd wolves, or tigers at their prey,
Doing abhorred rites to Hecate
In their obscured haunts of inmost bow'rs.

Yet have they many baits and guileful spells
To inveigle and invite th' unwary sense
Of them that pass unweeting by the way.
This evening late, by then the chewing flocks
Had ta'en their supper on the savoury herb
Of knot-grass dew-besprent, and were in fold,
I sate me down to watch upon a bank
With ivy canopied, and interwove
With flaunting honeysuckle; and began,
Wrapt in a pleasing fit of melancholy,
To meditate my rural minstrelsy
Till Fancy had her fill; but ere a close,
The wonted roar was up amidst the woods,
And fill'd the air with barbarous dissonance;
At which I ceas't, and listen'd them a while,
Till an unusual stop of sudden silence
Gave respite to the drowsy frightened steeds
That draw the litter of close-curtain'd sleep.
At last a soft and solemn-breathing sound
Rose like a steam of rich distill'd perfumes,
And stole upon the air, that even silence
Was took ere she was ware, and wish't she might
Deny her nature, and be never more
Still to be so displac't. I was all ear,
And took in strains that might create a soul
Under the ribs of Death; but O ere long
Too well I did perceive it was the voice
Of my most honour'd Lady, your dear sister.
Amaz'd I stood harrow'd with grief and fear:
And "O poor hapless nightingale," thought I,
"How sweet thou sing'st, how near the deadly snare!"
Then down the lawns I ran with headlong haste.

Through paths and turnings oft'n trod by day,
Till guided by mine ear I found the place
Where that damn'd wisard hid in sly disguise
(For so by certains signs I knew) had met
Already, ere my best speed could prevent,
The aidless, innocent lady, his wish't prey:
Who gently ask't if he had seen such two,
Supposing him some neighbour villager,
Longer I durst not stay, but soon I guess't
Ye were the two she mean't; with that I sprung
Into swift flight till I had found you here.
But further know I not.
    *Second Brother.*        O night and shades,
How are ye join'd with hell in triple knot
Against th' unarmed weakness of one virgin.
Alone, and helpless! Is this the confidence
You gave me brother?
    *Elder Brother.*        Yes, and keep it still;
Lean on it safely, not a period
Shall be unsaid for me: against the threats
Of malice or of sorcery, or that power
Which erring men call Chance, this I hold firm;
Virtue may be assail'd but never hurt,
Surpris'd by unjust force, but not enthrall'd;
Yea, even that which Mischief meant most harm,
Shall in the happy trial prove most glory.
But evil on itself shall back recoil.
And mix no more with goodness, when at last
Gather'd like scum, and settl'd to itself.
It shall be in eternal, restless change.
Self-fed, and self-consumed; if this fail,
The pillar'd firmament is rottenness,

And earth's base built on stubble.
But come, let's on.
Against th' opposing will and arm of Heav'n
May never this just sword be lifted up;
But for that damn'd magician, let him be girt
With all the grisly legions that troop
Under the sooty flag of Acheron.
Harpies and hydras, or all the monstrous forms
'Twixt Africa and Ind, I'll find him out,
And force him to return his purchase back.
Or drag him by the curls to a foul death,
Curs'd as his life.

    *Spirit.*          Alas! good ventrous youth,
I love thy courage yet, and bold emprise,
But here thy sword can do thee little stead;
Far other arms and other weapons must
Be those that quell the might of hellish charms:
He with his bare wand can unthread thy joints,
And crumble all thy sinews.

    *Elder Brother.*        Why prithee, shepherd,
How durst thou then thyself approach so near
As to make this relation?

    *Spirit.*        Care and utmost shifts
How to secure the lady from surprisal,
Brought to my mind a certain shepherd lad
Of small regard to see to, yet well skill'd
In every virtuous plant and healing herb
That spreads her verdant leaf to th' morning ray:
He lov'd me well, and oft would beg me sing,
Which when I did, he on the tender grass
Would sit, and hearken even to ecstacy;
And in requital ope his leathern scrip.

And show me simples of a thousand names,
Telling their strange and vigorous faculties:
Amongst the rest a small, unsightly root,
But of divine effect, he cull'd me out;
The leaf was darkish, and had prickles on it,
But in another country, as he said,
Bore a bright golden flow'r, but not in this soil:
Unknown, and like esteem'd, and the dull swain
Treads on it daily with his clouted shoon;
And yet more med'cinal is it than that moly
That Hermes once to wise Ulysses gave;
He call'd it haemony, and gave it me,
And bade me keep it as of sovran use
'Gainst all enchantments, mildew blast, or damp,
Or gastly furies' apparition;
I purs't it up, but little reck'ning made,
Till now that this extremity compell'd,
But now I find it true; for by this means
I knew the foul enchanter though disguis'd,
Enter'd the very lime-twigs of his spells,
And yet came off: if you have this about you
(As I will give you when we go), you may
Boldly assault the necromancer's hall;
Where if he be, with dauntless hardihood
And brandish't blade, rush on him, break his glass,
And shed the luscious liquor on the ground,
But seize his wand; though he and his curst crew
Fierce sign of battle make, and menace high,
Or like the sons of Vulcan vomit smoke,
Yet will they soon retire, if he but shrink.

*Elder Brother.*   Thyrsis lead on apace, I'll follow thee;
And some good angel bear a shield before us.

*The scene changes to a stately palace, set out with all manner of deliciousness; soft music, tables spread with all dainties.* COMUS *appears with his rabble, and the* LADY *set in an enchanted chair, to whom he offers his glass, which she puts by, and goes about to rise.*

*Comus.* Nay lady, sit; if I but wave this wand,
Your nerves are all chain'd up in alabaster,
And you a statue; or as Daphne was
Rootbound, that fled Apollo.

*Lady.* Fool, do not boast;
Thou canst not touch the freedom of my mind
With all thy charms, although this corporal rind
Thou hast immanel'd, while
Heav'n sees good.

*Comus.* Why are you vext, lady? Why do you frown?
Here dwell no frowns, nor anger; from these gates
Sorrow flies far. See, here be all the pleasures
That fancy can beget on youthful thoughts,
When the fresh blood grows lively, and returns
Brisk as the April buds in primrose season.
And first behold this cordial julep here,
That flames and dances in his crystal bounds,
With spirits of balm and fragrant syrops mixt.
Not that Nepenthes, which the wife of Thone
In Egypt gave to Jove-born Helena,
Is of such power to stir up joy as this,
To life so friendly, or so cool to thirst.
Why should you be so cruel to yourself,
And to those dainty limbs which nature lent
For gentle usage and soft delicacy?
But you invert the cov'nants of her trust,
And harshly deal like an ill borrower

With that which you receiv'd on other terms;
Scorning the unexempt condition
By which all mortal frailty must subsist,
Refreshment after toil, ease after pain;
That have been tir'd all day without repast,
And timely rest have wanted; but, fair virgin,
This will restore all soon.
    *Lady.*        'T will not, false traitor;
'T will not restore the trust and honesty
That thou hast banish't from thy tongue with lies.
Was this the cottage and the safe abode
Thou told'st me of? What grim aspects are these,
These ugly-headed monsters? Mercy guard me!
Hence with thy brew'd enchantments, foul deceiver;
Hast thou betray'd my credulous innocence
With visor'd falsehood, and base forgery,
And wouldst thou seek again to trap me here
With lickerish baits fit to ensnare a brute?
Were it a draught for Juno when she banquets,
I would not taste thy treasonous offer; none
But such as are good men can give good things.
And that which is not good, is not delicious
To a well-govern'd and wise appetite.
    *Comus.* O foolishness of men! that lend their ears
To those budge doctors of the Stoic fur,
And fetch their precepts from the Cynic tub,
Praising the lean and sallow Abstinence.
Wherefore did nature pour her bounties forth
With such a full and unwithdrawing hand,
Covering the earth with odours, fruits, and flocks,
Thronging the seas with spawn innumerable,
But all to please, and sate the curious taste?

And set to work millions of spinning worms,
That in their green shops weave the smooth-hair'd silk
To deck her sons; and that no corner might
Be vacant of her plenty, in her own loins
She hutch't th' all-worshipt ore, and precious gems
To store her children with; if all the world
Should in a pet of temperance feed on pulse,
Drink the clear stream, and nothing wear but frieze,
Th' All-giver would be unthank't, would be unprais'd,
Not half his riches known, and yet despis'd;
And we should serve him as a grudging master,
As a penurious niggard of his wealth;
And live like nature's bastards, not her sons,
Who would be quite surcharg'd with her own weight,
And strangl'd with her waste fertility,
Th' earth cumber'd, and the wing'd air dark't with plumes;
The herds would over-multitude their lords,
The sea o'erfraught would swell, and th' unsought diamonds
Would so emblaze the forehead of the deep,
And so bestud with stars, that they below
Would grow inur'd to light, and come at last
To gaze upon the sun with shameless brows.
List, lady; be not coy, and be not cozen'd
With that same vaunted name, Virginity;
Beauty is Nature's coin, must not be hoarded,
But must be current; and the good thereof
Consists in mutual and partak'n bliss,
Unsavoury in th' enjoyment of itself:
If you let slip time, like a neglected rose
It withers on the stalk with languish'd head.
Beauty is Nature's brag, and must be shown
In courts, at feasts and high solemnities,

Where most may wonder at the workmanship;
It is for homely features to keep home,
They had their name thence; coarse complexions
And cheeks of sorry grain will serve to ply
The sampler, and to tease the huswife's wool.
What need a vermeil-tinctur'd lip for that,
Love-darting eyes, or tresses like the morn?
There was another meaning in these gifts;
Think what, and be advis'd; you are but young yet.

    *Lady.*   I had not thought to have unlock't my lips
In this unhallow'd air, but that this juggler
Would think to charm my judgment, as mine eyes,
Obtruding false rules prankt in reason's garb.
I hate when Vice can bolt her arguments,
And virtue has no tongue to check her pride:
Imposter, do not charge most innocent Nature,
As if she would her children should be riotous
With her abundance; she, good cateress,
Means her provision only to the good,
That live according to her sober laws
And holy dictate of spare Temperance:
If every just man that now pines with want
Had but a moderate and beseeming share
Of that which lewdly-pamper'd Luxury
Now heaps upon some few with vast excess,
Nature's full blessings would be well dispens't
In unsuperfluous even proportion,
And she no whit encumber'd with her store;
And then the Giver would be better thank't,
His praise due paid; for swinish Gluttony
Ne'er looks to Heav'n amids't his gorgeous feast,
But with besotted base ingratitude

Crams, and blasphemes his feeder. Shall I go on?
Or have I said enough? To him that dares
Arm his profane tongue with contemptuous words
Against the sun-clad power of Chastity,
Fain would I something say, yet to what end?
Thou hast nor ear, nor soul to apprehend
The sublime notion, and high mystery
That must be utter'd to unfold the sage
And serious doctrine of Virginity;
And thou art worthy that thou should'st not know
More happiness than this thy present lot.
Enjoy your dear wit, and gay rhetoric
That hath so well been taught her dazzling fence,
Thou art not fit to hear thyself convinc't:
Yet should I try, the uncontrolled worth
Of this pure cause would kindle my rapt spirits
To such a flame of sacred vehemence,
That dumb things would be moved to sympathize,
And the brute Earth would lend her nerves, and shake
Till all thy magic structures rear'd so high
Were shatter'd into heaps o'er thy false head.
   *Comus.* She fables not, I feel that I do fear
Her words set off by some superior power;
And though not mortal, yet a cold, shudd'ring dew
Dips me all o'er; as when the wrath of Jove
Speaks thunder and the Chains of Erebus
To some of Saturn's crew. I must dissemble,
And try her yet more strongly. Come, no more;
This is mere moral babble, and direct
Against the canon laws of our foundation;
I must not suffer this; yet 'tis but the lees
And settlings of a melancholy blood;

But this will cure all straight; one sip of this
Will bathe the drooping spirits in delight
Beyond the bliss of dreams.   Be wise, and taste.

*The* BROTHERS *rush in with swords drawn, wrest his glass out
of his hand, and break it against the ground ; his rout make sign
of resistance, but are all driven in.* The ATTENDANT SPIRIT
comes in.

*Spirit.*  What, have you let the false enchanter scape?
O ye mistook; ye should have snatcht his wand
And bound him fast; without his rod revers't,
And backward mutters of dissevering power,
We cannot free the lady that sits here
In stony fetters fix't, and motionless;
Yet stay, be not disturb'd; now I bethink me,
Some other means I have which may be us'd,
Which once of Meliboeus old I learn't,
The soothest shepherd that e'er pip't on plains.
There is a gentle nymph not far from hence,
That with moist curb sways the smooth Severn stream,
Sabrina is her name, a virgin pure,
Whilom she was the daughter of Locrine,
That had the scepter from his father Brute.
She, guiltless damsel, flying the mad pursuit
Of her enraged stepdame, Guendolen,
Commended her fair innocence to the flood
That stay'd her flight with his cross-flowing course.
The water-nymphs that in the bottom play'd,
Held up their pearled wrists and took her in,
Bearing her straight to aged Nereus' hall;
Who, piteous of her woes, rear'd her lank head,
And gave her to his daughters to imbathe

In nectar'd lavers strew'd with asphodel,
And through the porch and inlet of each sense
Dropt in ambrosial oils; till she reviv'd,
And underwent a quick immortal change,
Made goddess of the river; still she retains
Her maid'n gentleness, and oft at eve
Visits the herds along the twilight meadows, ·
Helping all urchin blasts, and ill-luck signs
That the shrew meddling elf delights to make,
Which she with pretious vial'd liquors heals.
For which the shepherds at their festivals
Carol her goodness loud in rustic lays,
And throw sweet garland wreaths into her stream
Of pansies, pinks, and gaudy daffodils.
And, as the old swain said, she can unlock
The clasping charm, and thaw the numbing spell,
If she be right invok't in warbled song;
Fair maid'nhood she loves, and will be swift
To aid a virgin, such as was herself,
In hard-besetting need; this will I try,
And add the power of some adjuring verse.

SONG.

Sabrina fair,
  Listen where thou art sitting
Under the glassy, cool, translucent wave;
  In twisted braids of lillies knitting
The loose train of thy amber-dropping hair;
   Listen for dear honour's sake,
   Goddess of the silver lake,
   Listen and save.

Listen and appear to us

In name of great Oceanus.
By the earth-shaking Neptune's mace,
And Tethys' grave majestic pace,
By hoary Neureus' wrinkled look,
And the Carpathian wizard's hook,
By scaly Triton's winding shell,
And old sooth-saying Glaucus' spell.
By Leucothea's lovely hands.
And her son that rules the strands,
By Thetis' tinsel-slipper'd feet,
And the songs of Sirens sweet,
By dead Parthenope's dear tomb,
And fair Ligea's golden comb,
Wherewith she sits on diamond rocks,
Sleeking her soft alluring locks.
By all the nymphs that nightly dance
Upon thy streams with wily glance.
Rise, rise, and heave thy rosy head
From thy coral-pav'n bed,
And bridle in thy headlong wave,
Till thou our summons answer'd have.
        Listen and save.


SABRINA *rises, attended by* WATER-NYMPHS, *and sings.*


By the rushy-fringed bank,
Where grows the willow and the osier dank,
        My sliding chariot stays;
Thick set with agate, and the azurn sheen
Of turkis blue, and em'rald green
        That in the channel strays;
Whilst from off the water's fleet,

Thus I set my printless feet
O'er the cowslip's velvet head,
    That bends not as I tread;
Gentle swain, at thy request
    I am here.
  *Spirit.*  Goddess dear,
We implore thy powerful hand
To undo the charmed band
Of true virgin here distrest,
Through the force, and through the wile
Of unbles't enchanter vile.
  *Sabrina.*  Shepherd, 'tis my office best
To help ensnared chastity;
Brightest lady, look on me;
Thus I sprinkle on thy breast
Drops that from my fountain pure
I have kept of pretious cure,
Thrice upon thy finger's tip,
Thrice upon thy rubied lip;
Next this marble venom'd seat
Smear'd with gums of glutinous heat
I touch with chaste palms moist and cold;
Now the spell hath lost his hold;
And I must haste ere morning hour
To wait in Amphitrite's bow'r.

SABRINA *descends, and the* LADY *rises out of her seat.*

  *Spirit.*  Virgin, daughter of Locrine,
Sprung of old Anchises' line,
May thy brimmed waves for this
Their full tribute never miss
From a thousand petty rills,

That tumble-down the snowy hills;
Summer drouth, or singed air
Never scorch thy tresses fair;
Nor wet October's torrent flood
Thy molten crystal fill with mud;
May thy billows roll ashore
The beryl, and the golden ore;
May thy lofty head be crown'd
With many a tower and terrace round,
And here and there thy banks upon
With groves of myrrh and cinnamon.

     Come lady, while heaven lends us grace
Let us fly this cursed place,
Lest the sorcerer us entice
With some other new device.
Not a waste, or needless sound
Till we come to holier ground;
I shall be your faithful guide
Through this gloomy covert wide;
And not many furlongs thence
Is your father's residence,
Where this night are met in state
Many a friend to gratulate
His wish't presence; and beside,
All the swains that there abide,
With jigs, and rural dance resort;
We shall catch them at their sport,
And our sudden coming there    .
Will double all their mirth and cheer;
Come let us haste, the stars grow high,
But night sits monarch yet in the mid sky.

*The scene changes, presenting Ludlow town and the President's*

*castle ; then come in Country Dancers ; after them the* ATTENDANT
SPIRIT, *with the two* BROTHERS *and the* LADY.

*Spirit.*   Back Shepherds, back, anough your play,
Till next sunshine holiday;
Here be without duck or nod
Other trippings to be trod
Of lighter toes; and such court guise
As Mercury did first devise
With the mincing Dryades
On the lawns and on the leas.

*This second Song presents them to their Father and Mother.*

Noble lord, and lady bright,
I have brought ye new delight;
Here behold so goodly grown
Three fair branches of your own;
Heav'n hath timely tri'd their youth,
Their faith, their patience, and their truth;
And sent them here through hard assays
With a crown of deathless praise,
To triumph in victorious dance
O'er sensual Folly and Intemperance.

*The dances ended, the* SPIRIT *epiloguizes.*

*Spirit.*   To the ocean now I fly,
And those happy climes that lie
Where day never shuts his eye,
Up in the broad fields of the sky:

There I suck the liquid air
All amidst the gardens fair
Of Hesperus, and his daughters three
That sing about the golden tree :
Along the crisped shades and bowers
Revels the spruce and jocund Spring;
The Graces, and the rosy-bosom'd Hours,
Thither all there bounties bring,
That there eternal summer dwells;
And west winds, with musky wing
About the cedarn alleys fling
Nard, and Cassia's balmy smells.
Iris there with humid bow
Waters the odorous banks that blow
Flowers of more mingled hue
Than her purfl'd scarf can shew,
And drenches with Elysian dew
(List mortals, if your ears be true)
Beds of hyacinth and roses,
Where young Adonis oft reposes,
Waxing well of his deep wound
In slumber soft; and on the ground
Sadly sits th' Assyrian queen:
But far above in spangled sheen
Celestial Cupid her fam'd son advanc't,
Holds his dear Psyche sweet entranc't,
After her wand'ring labours long;
Till free consent the gods among
Make her his eternal bride;
And from her fair unspotted side
Two blissful twins are to be born,
Youth and Joy; so Jove hath sworn.

But now my task is smoothly done, •
I can fly or I can run
Quickly to the green earth's end,
Where the bow'd welkin slow doth bend;
And from thence can soar as soon
To the corners of the moon.
Mortals that would follow me,
Love Virtue; she alone is free:
She can teach ye how to climb
Higher than the sphery chime;
Or if Virtue feeble were,
Heav'n itself would stoop to her.

---

## EXTRACT FROM SHAKESPEARE'S MERCHANT OF VENICE.

*Portia.* The quality of mercy is not strain'd,
It droppeth as the gentle rain from heaven
Upon the place beneath; it is twice blest;
It blesseth him that gives and him that takes:
'Tis mightiest in the mightiest: it becomes
The throned monarch better than his crown;
His sceptre shows the force of temporal power,
The attribute to awe and majesty,
Wherein doth sit the dread and fear of kings:
But mercy is above this sceptred sway;
It is enthroned in the hearts of kings,
It is an attribute to God himself:
And earthly power doth then show likest God's
When mercy seasons justice. Therefore, Jew,
Though justice be thy plea, consider this,
That, in the course of justice, none of us

Should see salvation: we do pray for mercy;
And that same prayer dóth teach us all to render
The deeds ot mercy.   I have spoke thus much
To mitigate the justice of thy plea;
Which if thou follow, this strict court of Venice
Must needs give sentence 'gainst the merchant there.

-----

### EXTRACT FROM JULIUS CÆSAR.

*Brutus.*  Be patient till the last.—Romans, countrymen,
and lovers!  Hear me for my cause, and be silent, that you
may hear.  Believe me for mine honor, and have respect to
mine honor, that you may believe.  Censure me in your
wisdom, and awake your senses, that you may the better
judge.

If there be any in this assembly, any dear friend of Cæsar's,
to him I say, that Brutus' love to Cæsar was no less than his.
If, then, that friend demand why Brutus rose against Cæsar,
this is my answer:  Not that I lov'd Cæsar less, but that I
lov'd Rome more.  Had you rather Cæsar were living and
die all slaves, than that Cæsar were dead, to live all freemen?

As Cæsar lov'd me, I weep for him; as he was fortunate,
I rejoice at it; as he was valiant, I honor him: but, as he
was ambitious, I slew him.  There is tears for his love; joy
for his fortune; honor for his valor; and death for his ambition!

Who is here so base that would be a bondman?  If any,
speak! for him have I offended.  Who is here so rude that
would not be a Roman?  If any, speak! for him have I
offended.  Who is here so vile that will not love his country?  If any, speak! for him have I offended.  I pause for
a reply.—

*All.* None, Brutus, none.

*Brutus.* Then none have I offended. I have done no more to Cæsar than you shall do to Brutus. The question of his death is enrolled in the Capitol; his glory not extenuated, wherein he was worthy, nor his offences enforced, for which he suffered death.

*Enter Antony and others, with Cæsar's body.*

Here comes his body, mourned by Mark Antony: who, though he had no hand in his death, shall receive the benefit of his dying; a place in the commonwealth; as which of of you shall not?

With this I depart,—that, as I slew my best lover for the good of Rome, I have the same dagger for myself, when it shall please my country to need my death.

*Antony.* Friends, Romans, countrymen, lend me your ears: I come to bury Cæsar, not to praise him.
The evil that men do lives after them;
The good is oft interred with their bones.
So let it be with Cæsar.
The noble Brutus
Hath told you Cæsar was ambitious:
If it were so, it were a grievous fault,
And grievously hath Cæsar answer'd it.
Here, under leave of Brutus and the rest,—
For Brutus is an honorable man;
So are they all, all honorable men,—
Come I to speak in Cæsar's funeral.
He was my friend, faithful and just to me:
But Brutus says he was ambitious;
And Brutus is an honorable man.
He hath brought many captives home to Rome.

Whose ransoms did the general coffers fill:
Did this in Cæsar seem ambitious?
When that the poor have cried, Cæsar hath wept:
Ambition should be made of sterner stuff.
Yet Brutus says he was ambitious;
And Brutus is an honorable man.
You all did see that on the Lupercal
I thrice presented him a kingly crown,
Which he did thrice refuse: was this ambition?
Yet Brutus says he was ambitious;
And, sure, he is an honorable man.
I speak not to disprove what Brutus spoke,
But here I am to speak what I do know.
You all did love him once, not without cause:
What cause withholds you, then, to mourn for him?
O judgment! thou art fled to brutish beasts,
And men have lost their reason.   Bear with me;
My heart is in the coffin there with Cæsar,
And I must pause till it come back to me.

    *First Citizen.*  Methinks there is much reason in his sayings.
    *Second Citizen.*  If thou consider rightly of the matter,
Cæsar has had great wrong.
    *Third Citizen.*  Has he, masters?
I fear there will be a worse come in his place.
    *Fourth Citizen.*  Mark'd ye his words?
He would not take the crown;
Therefore 't is certain he was not ambitious.
    *First Citizen.*  If it be found so, some will dear abide it.
    *Second Citizen.*  Poor soul! his eyes are red as fire with
weeping.
    *Third Citizen.*   There's not a nobler man in Rome than
Antony.

*Fourth Citizen.* Now mark him: he begins again to speak.

*Antony.* But yesterday the word of Cæsar might
Have stood against the world; now lies he there,
And none so poor to do him reverence.
O masters! if I were dispos'd to stir·
Your hearts and minds to mutiny and rage,
I should do Brutus wrong, and Cassius wrong,
Who, you all know, are honorable men.
I will not do them wrong; I rather choose
To wrong the dead, to wrong myself and you,
Than I will wrong such honorable men.
But here's a parchment with the seal of Cæsar;
I found it in his closet, 't is his will:
Let but the commons hear this testament,—
Which, pardon me, I do not mean to read,—
And they would go and kiss dead Cæsar's wounds
And dip their napkins in his sacred blood;
Yea, beg a hair of him for memory,
And, dying, mention it within their wills,
Bequeathing it as a rich legacy.
Unto their issue.

*Fourth Citizen.* We'll hear the will: read it, Mark Antony.

*All.* The will, the will! we will hear Cæsar's will.

*Antony.* Have patience, gentle friends, I must not read it:
It is not meet you know how Cæsar lov'd you.
You are not wood, you are not stones, but men;
And, being men, hearing the will of Cæsar,
It will inflame you, it will make you mad:
'T is good you know not that you are his heirs;
For, if you should, oh, what would come of it!

*Fourth Citizen.* Read the will! we'll hear it, Antony!
You shall read us the will! Cæsar's will!

*Antony.*   Will you be patient? will you stay awhile?
I have o'ershot myself to tell you of it :
I fear I wrong the honorable men
Whose daggers have stabb'd Cæsar.   I do fear it.
    *Fourth Citizen.*   They were traitors! honorable men!
    *All.*   The will! the testament!
    *Second Citizen.*   They were villians, murderers! the will!
read the will!
    *Antony.*   You will compel me, then, to read the will?
Then make a ring about the corpse of Cæsar,
And let me show you him that made the will.
Shall I descend, and will you give me leave?
    *Several Citizens.*   Come down.
    *Second Citizen.*   Descend.
    *Third Citizen.*   You shall have leave.
[*Antony comes down*].
    *Fourth Citizen.*   A ring; stand round.
    *First Citizen.*   Stand from the hearse, stand from the body.
    *Second Citizen.*   Room for Antony! most noble Antony!
    *Antony.*   Nay, press not so upon me; stand far off.
    *Several Citizens.*   Stand back! room! bear back!
    *Antony.*   If you have tears, prepare to shed them now.
You all do know this mantle: I remember
The first time ever Cæsar put it on;
'Twas on a summer's evening, in his tent,
That day he overcame the Nervii.
Look, in this place ran Cassius' dagger through!
See what a rent the envious Casca made:
Through this the well-beloved Brutus stabb'd;
And as he pluck'd his cursed steel away,
Mark how the blood of Cæser follow'd it,
As rushing out of doors, to be resolv'd

If Brutus so unkindly knock'd, or no;
For Brutus, as you know, was Cæsar's angel.
Judge, O you gods, how dearly Cæser lov'd him!
This was the most unkindest cut of all;
For when the noble Cæsar saw him stab,
Ingratitude, more strong than traitors arms,
Quite vanquish'd him: then burst his mighty heart.
And, in his mantel muffling up his face,
Even at the base of Pompey's statue,
Which all the while ran blood, great Cæsar fell.
O, what a fall was there, my countrymen!
Then I, and you, and all of us fell down,
Whilst bloody treason flourish'd over us!
Oh, now you weep! and, I perceive, you feel
The dint of pity: these are gracious drops.
Kind souls, what! weep you when you but behold
Our Cæsar's vesture wounded? Look you here,
Here is himself, marr'd, as you see, with traitors.

*First Citizen.* O piteous spectacle!

*Second Citizen.* O noble Cæsar!

*Third Citizen.* O woful day!

*Fourth Citizen.* O traitors, villains!

*First Citizen.* O most bloody sight!

*Second Citizen.* We will be reveng'd.

Revenge! About! Seek! Burn! Fire! Kill! Slay! Let not
a traitor live!

*Antony.* Stay, countryman.

*First Citizen.* Peace there! hear the noble Antony.

*Second Citizen.* We'll hear him, we'll follow him, we'll die
with him!

*Antony.* Good friends, sweet friends, let me not stir you up
To such a sudden flood of mutiny.

They that have done this deed are honorable:
What private griefs they have, alas, I know not,
That made them do it; they are wise and honorable,
And will, no doubt, with reasons answer you.
I come not, friends, to steal away your hearts:
I am no orator, but Brutus is;
But, as you know me all, a plain blunt man,
That love my friend; and that they know full well
That gave me public leave to speak of him:
For I have neither wit, nor words, nor worth,
Action, nor utterance, nor the power of speech,
To stir men's blood: I only speak right on;
I tell you that which you yourself do know;
Show you sweet Cæsar's wounds, poor, poor dumb mouths!
And bid them speak for me: but, were I Brutus,
And Brutus Antony, there were an Antony
Would ruffle up your spirits and put a tongue
In every wound of Cæsar, that should move
The stones of Rome to rise and mutiny.
    *All.* We'll mutiny.
    *First Citizen.* We'll burn the house of Brutus.
    *Third Citizen.* Away, then! come, seek the conspirators.
    *Antony.* Yet hear me, countrymen; yet hear me speak.
    *All.* Peace, ho! Hear Antony! Most noble Antony!
    *Antony.* Why, friends, you go to do you know not what.
Wherein hath Cæsar thus deserv'd your loves?
Alas, you know not! I must tell you, then:
You have forgot the will I told you of.
    *All.* Most true. The will! Let's stay and hear the will.
    *Antony.* Here is the will, and under Cæsar's seal.
To every Roman citizen he gives,
To every several man, seventy-five drachmas.

*Second Citizen.* Most noble Cæsar!
We'll revenge his death.
 *Third Citizen.* O royal Cæsar!
 *Antony.* Hear me with patience.
 *All.* Peace, ho!
 *Antony.* Moreover, he hath left you all his walks,
His private arbors and new-planted orchards,
On this side Tiber. He hath left them you,
And to your heirs forever, common pleasures,
To walk abroad, and recreate yourselves.
Here was a Cæsar! when comes such another?
 *First Citizen.* Never, never! Come, away, away!
We'll burn his body in the holy place,
And with the brands fire the traitors' houses.
Take up the body.
 *Second Citizen.* Go fetch fire.
 *Third Citizen.* Pluck down benches.
 *Fourth Citizen.* Pluck down forms, windows, anything.

      *[Exeunt Citizens with the body.]*

 *Antony.* Now let it work. Mischief, thou art afoot,
Take thou what course thou wilt!

---

## EXTRACT FROM BURKE'S SPEECH ON CONCILIA-
## TION WITH AMERICA.

I am sensible, Sir, that all which I have asserted in my
detail, is admitted in the gross; but that quite a different
conclusion is drawn from it. America, Gentlemen say, is a
noble object. It is an object well worth fighting for. Certainly it is, if fighting a people be the best way of gaining
them. Gentlemen in this respect will be led to their choice

of means by their complexions and their habits. Those who understand the military art, will of course have some predilection for it.

Those who wield the thunder of the state, may have more confidence in the efficacy of arms. But I confess, possibly for want of this knowledge, my opinion is much more in favour of prudent management, than of force; considering force not as an odious, but a feeble instrument, for preserving a people so numerous, so active, so growing, so spirited as this, in a profitable and subordinate connexion with us.

First, Sir, permit me to observe, that the use of force alone is but *temporary*. It may subdue for a moment; but it does not remove the necessity of subduing again : and a nation is not governed, which is perpetually to be conquered.

My next objection is its *uncertainty*. Terror is not always the effect of force; and an armament is not a victory. If you do not succeed, you are without resource; for conciliation failing, force remains; but, force failing, no further hope of reconciliation is left. Power and authority are sometimes bought by kindness; but they can never be begged as alms by an impoverished and defeated violence.

A further objection to force is, that you *impair the object* by your very endeavours to preserve it. The thing you fought for is not the thing which you recover; but depreciated, sunk, wasted, and consumed in the contest. Nothing less will content me, than *whole America*. I do not choose to consume its strength along with our own; because in all parts it is the British strength that I consume. I do not choose to be caught by a foreign enemy at the end of this exhausting conflict; and still less in the midst of it. I may escape; but I can make no insurance against such an event. Let me add, that I do not choose wholly to break the American spirit; because it is the spirit that has made the country.

Lastly, we have no sort of *experience* in favor of force as an instrument in the rule of our colonies. Their growth and their utility has been owing to methods altogether different. Our ancient indulgence has been said to be pursued to a fault. It may be so. But we know, if feeling is evidence, that our fault was more tolerable than our attempt to mend it; and our sin far more salutary than our penitence.

\* \* \* \* \* \* \* \*

In this character of the Americans, a love of Freedom is the predominating feature which marks and distinguishes the whole: and as an ardent is always a jealous affection, your colonies become suspicious, restive, and untractable, whenever they see the least attempt to wrest from them by force, or shuffle from them by chicane, what they think the only advantage worth living for. This fierce spirit of Liberty is stronger in the English Colonies probably than in any other people of the earth ; and this from a great variety of powerful causes ; which, to understand the true temper of their minds, and the direction which this spirit takes, it will not be amiss to lay open somewhat more largely.

First, the people of the Colonies are descendants of Englishmen. England, Sir, is a nation, which still I hope respects, and formerly adored, her freedom. The Colonists emigrated from you when this part of your character was most predominate ; and they took this bias and direction the moment they parted from your hands. They are, therefore, not only devoted to Liberty, but to Liberty according to English ideas, and on English principles. Abstract Liberty, like other mere abstactions, is not to be found. Liberty inheres in some sensible object ; and every nation has formed to itself some favorite point, which by way of eminence becomes the

G—20

criterion of their happiness.   It happened, you know, Sir,
that the great contests for freedom in this country were from
the earliest times chiefly upon the question of Taxing.
Most of the contests in the ancient commonwealths turned
primarily on the right of election of magistrates ; or on the
balance among the several orders of the State.   The question of money was not with them so immediate.   But in
England it was otherwise.   On this point of Taxes the
ablest pens, and most eloquent tongues have been exercised ;
the greatest spirits have acted and suffered.   In order to
give the fullest satisfaction concerning the importance of
this point, it was not only necessary for those who in argument defended the excellence of the English Constitution, to
insist on this privilege of granting money as a dry point of
fact, and to prove, that the right had been acknowledged in
ancient parchments, and blind usages, to reside in a certain
body called an House of Commons.

They went much farther ; they attempted to prove, and
they succeeded, that in theory it ought to be so, from the
particular nature of an House of Commons, as an immediate
representative of the people ; whether the old · records had
delivered this oracle or not.   They took infinite pains to in-
culcate, as a fundamental principle, that in all monarchies
the people must in effect themselves, mediately or immediately possess the power of granting their own money, or
no shadow of liberty can subsist.   The Colonies draw from
you, as with their life-blood, these ideas and principles.
Their love of liberty, as with you, fixed and attached on
this specific point of taxing.   Liberty might be safe, or might
be endangered, in twenty other particulars, without their
being much pleased or alarmed.   Here they felt its pulse ;
and as they found that beat, they thought themselves

sick or sound. I do not say whether they were right or
wrong in applying your general arguments to their own
case. It is not easy indeed to make a monopoly of theorems
and corollaries. The fact is, that they did thus apply those
general arguments; and your mode of governing them,
whether through lenity or indolence, through wisdom or
mistake, confirmed them in the imagination, that they, as
well as you, had an interest in these common principles.

They were further confirmed in this pleasing error by the
form of their provincial legislative assemblies. Their governments are popular in a high degree; some are merely popular; in all, the popular representative is the most weighty;
and this share of the people in their ordinary government
never fails to inspire them with lofty sentiments, and with
a strong aversion for whatever tends to deprive them of their
chief importance.

If anything were wanting to this necessary operation of
the form of government, religion would have given it a complete effect. Religion, always a principle of energy, in this
new people is no way worn out or impaired; and their mode
of professing it is also one main cause of this free spirit.
The people are protestants; and of that kind which is the
most adverse to all implicit submission of mind and opinion. This is a persuasion not only favorable to liberty, but
built upon it. I do not think, Sir, that the reason of this
averseness in the dissenting churches, from all that looks
like absolute government, is so much to be sought in their
religious tenets, as in their history. Every one knows that
the Roman Catholic religion is at least coeval with most of
the governments where it prevails; that it has generally gone
hand in hand with them, and received great favor and every
kind of support from authority.. The Church of England

too was formed from her cradle under the nursing care of
regular government.   But the dissenting interests have
sprung up in direct opposition to all the ordinary powers of
the world ; and could justify that opposition only on a strong
claim to natural liberty.   Their very existence depended on
the powerful and unremitted assertion of that claim.   All
protestanism, even the most cold and passive, is a sort of
dissent.   But the religion most prevalent in our Northern
Colonies is a refinement on the principal of resistance; it is
the dissidence of dissent, and the protestanism of the pro-
testant religion.   This religion, under a variety of denom-
inations agreeing in nothing but in the communion of the
spirit of liberty, is predominant in most of the northern
provinces; where the Church of England, notwithstanding
its legal rights, is in reality no more than a sort of private
sect, not composing most probably the tenth of the people.
The Colonists left England when this spirit was high, and
in the emigrants was the highest of all; and even that stream
of foreigners, which has been constantly flowing into these
Colonies, has, for the greatest part, been composed of dissent-
ers from the establishments of their several countries, and
have brought with them a temper and character far from
alien to that of the people with whom they mixed.

Sir, I can perceive by their manner, that some Gentlemen
object to the latitude of this description ; because in the
Southern Colonies the Church of England forms a large body,
and has a regular establishment.   It is certainly true.   There
is, however, a circumstance attending these Colonies, which,
in my opinion, fully counterbalances this difference, ·and
makes the spirit of liberty still more high and haughty than
in those to the Northward.   It is, that in Virginia and the
Carolinas they have a vast multitude of slaves.   Where this

is the case in any part of the world, those who are free, are
by far the most proud and jealous of their freedom.   Freedom is to them not only an enjoyment, but a kind of rank
and privilege.   Not seeing there, that freedom, as in countries where it is a common blessing, and as broad and general as the air, may be united with much abject toil, with
great misery, with all the exterior of servitude, liberty looks,
amongst them, like something that is more noble and liberal.
I do not mean, Sir, to commend the superior morality of
this sentiment, which has at least as much pride as virtue
in it; but I cannot alter the nature of man.   The fact is so:
and these people of the Southern Colonies are much more
strongly, and with an higher and more stubborn spirit, attached to liberty, than those to the Northward.   Such were
all the ancient commonwealths; such were our Gothick ancestors; such in our days were the Poles; and such will be
all masters of slaves, who are not slaves themselves.   In
such a people, the haughtiness of domination combines
with the spirit of freedom, fortifies it, and renders it invin-
cible.

Permit me, Sir, to add. another circumstance in our Colonies, which contributes no mean part towards the growth
and effect of this untractable spirit.   I mean their education.
In no country perhaps in the world is the law so general a
study.   The profession itself is numerous and powerful;
and in most provinces it takes the lead.   The greater number of the Deputies sent to the Congress were Lawyers.   But all
who read, (and most do read), endeavor to obtain some smattering in that science.   I have been told by an eminent Book-
seller, that in no branch of his business, after tracts of popular devotion, were so many books as those on the Law ex-
ported to the plantations.

The Colonists have now fallen into the way of printing them for their own use. I hear that they have sold nearly as many of Blackstone's Commentaries in America as in England. General Gage marks out this disposition very particularly in a letter on your table. He states, that all the people in his government are lawyers, or smatterers in law; and that in Boston they have been enabled, by successful chicane, wholly to evade many parts of one of your capital penal constitutions. The smartness of debate will say, that this knowledge ought to teach them more clearly the rights of legislature, their obligations to obedience, and penalties of rebellion. All this is mighty well. But my Honorable and Learned Friend on the floor, who condescends to mark what I say for animadversion, will disdain that ground. He has heard, as well as I, that when great honours and great emoluments do not win over this knowledge to the service of the state, it is a formidable adversary to government. If the spirit be not tamed and broken by these happy methods, it is stubborn and litigious. *Abeunt studia in mores.* This study renders men acute, inquisitive, dexterous, prompt in attack, ready in defence, full of resources. In other countries, the people, more simple, and of a less mercurial cast, judge of an ill principle in government only by an actual grievance; here they anticipate the evil, and judge of the pressure of the grievance by the badness of the principle. They augur misgovernment at a distance; and snuff the approach of tyranny in every tainted breeze.

The last cause of this disobedient spirit in the Colonies is hardly less powerful than the rest, as it is not merely moral, but laid deep in the natural constitution of things. Three thousand miles of ocean lie between you and them. No contrivance can prevent the effect of this distance in weakening government. Seas roll, and months pass, between the order and the execution; and the want of a speedy explanation of a single point is enough to defeat a whole system. You have, indeed, winged ministers of vengeance, who carry your bolts in their pounces to the remotest verge of the sea. But there a power steps in, that limits the arrogance of raging passions and furious elements, and says, *So far shalt thou go, and no farther.* Who are you, that you should fret and rage, and bite the chains of Nature? Nothing worse happens to you than does to all nations who have extensive Empire; and it happens in all the forms into which Empire can be thrown. In large bodies, the circulation of power must be less vigorous at the extremities. Nature has said it. The Turk cannot govern Egypt, and Arabia, and Curdistan, as he governs Thrace; nor has he the same dominion in Crimea and Algiers, which he has at Brusa and Smyrna. Despotism itself is obliged to truck and huckster. The Sultan gets such obedience as he can. He governs with a loose rein, that he may govern at all; and the whole of the force and vigour of his authority in his centre is derived from a prudent relaxation in all his borders. Spain, in her provinces, is, perhaps, not so well obeyed as you are in yours. She complies too; she submits; she watches times. This is the immutable condition, the eternal law of extensive and detached Empire.

Then, Sir, from these six capital sources; of Descent; of Form of Government; of Religion in the Northern Provinces; of Manners in the Southern; of Education; of the Remoteness of Situation from the First Mover of Government; from all these causes a fierce Spirit of Liberty has grown up. It has grown with the growth of the people in your Colonies, and increased with the increase of their wealth; a Spirit, that unhappily meeting with an exercise of Power in England, which, however lawful, is not reconcilable to any ideas of Liberty, much less with theirs, has kindled this flame that is ready to consume us.

# INDEX.

*The references are to pages.*

www.ingramcontent.com/pod-product-compliance
Lightning Source LLC
Chambersburg PA
CBHW021220270326
41929CB00010B/1201